Jack Benny's Lost Radio Broadcasts

Volume Two: August 1 – October 26, 1932

Jack Benny's Lost Radio Broadcasts

Volume Two: August 1 – October 26, 1932

by Jack Benny and Harry Conn

Edited and with an introduction by Kathryn Fuller-Seeley

BearManor Media

2021

The Jack Benny Program Radio Scripts, 1932–1936, Volume 2
by Jack Benny and Harry Conn

Introduction © 2021 Kathryn Fuller-Seeley

All rights reserved.

No portion of this publication may be reproduced, stored, and/or copied electronically (except for academic use as a source), nor transmitted in any form or by any means without the prior written permission of the publisher and/or author.

Published in the United States of America by:

BearManor Media
1317 Edgewater Dr #110
Orlando FL 32804
bearmanormedia.com

Printed in the United States.

Typesetting and layout by John Teehan

Back cover illustration: Jack Benny, George Olsen and Ethel Shutta, ca. 1932
Front cover illustration: Young and Rubicam advertisement, *Fortune*, June 1935

ISBN—978-1-62933-844-6

Table of Contents

Introduction 1
Chapter Episode Synopses 9

August 1, 1932 11
August 3, 1932 21
August 8, 1932 33
August 10, 1932 43
August 15, 1932 55
August 17, 1932 67
August 22, 1932 77
August 24, 1932 89
August 29, 1932 101
August 31, 1932 113

September 5, 1932 123
September 7, 1932 133
September 12, 1932 145

September 14, 1932 155

September 19, 1932 167

September 21, 1932 179

September 28, 1932 191

October 3, 1932 201

October 5, 1932 211

October 10, 1932 221

October 12, 1932 231

October 17, 1932 241

October 19, 1932 255

October 24, 1932 267

October 26, 1932 279

Introduction

IN THIS SECOND INSTALLMENT of Jack Benny's Canada Dry radio program, covering 26 episodes/ 13 weeks from August 1 through October 26, 1932, Mary Livingstone became a regular member of the show's cast, and the Olsen-Shutta-band-Jack-Mary-announcer group coalesced into a sharp-witted comedy troupe, under the tutelage of Jack Benny and Harry Conn. During these weeks of continued experimentation, Conn and Benny augmented their mix of lightly satirical commentary on early 1930s urban pop culture by creating several more explicitly political skits, less outrageous but still announcer-fueled obnoxious Canada Dry ads, the development of the Mary-Jack romance, and the first parodies of current Hollywood blockbusters and time-worn Victorian melodramas. The surprise twist at the end of this second volume is that Canada Dry decided to end the current set up and move Benny's comedy to a new network, with the comedy augmented by two additional writers (Sid Silvers and Dave Freedman) whom Benny, Conn and Livingstone did not want at all! I must APOLOGIZE that, in a pandemic-influenced oversight, I neglected to capture images from the September 26, 1932 episode of the Benny program. When we can travel to archives again, I will race to the UCLA archives and secure it for inclusion (I hope!) in Volume 3 of the "Jack Benny's Lost Radio Broadcast" collection. I also invite you to learn more about Benny's broadcasting career in my book *Jack Benny and the Golden Age of American Radio Comedy* (University of California Press, 2017) and through the excellent research, fellowship and fun created by members of the International Jack Benny Fan Club (www.jackbenny.org and on Facebook).

BRIEF RECAP OF VOLUME 1 OF *JACK BENNY'S LOST RADIO BROADCASTS* (Canada Dry Program May 2-July 27, 1932) (BearManor Media, 2020)

The Canada Dry radio program, featuring Jack Benny, George Olsen and Ethel Shutta (pronounced shu-TAY), debuted on Monday May 2, 1932 at 9:30 pm Eastern time on the NBC Blue network. Broadcast twice a week (Mondays and Wednesdays) the program was produced in a small-glass-walled studio that NBC had erected in the former Roof Garden of the New Amsterdam Theatre in New York City. The new show was advertised as "30 minutes of music and quips" featuring Olsen's band and vocals by Ziegfeld Follies alumna Shutta. Their music would be interspersed with brief monologue segments performed by 38-year-old Jack Benny, a Midwestern-voiced, genially-self-deprecating vaudeville veteran known around New York as "that sleekly bored joker" and a "Broadway Romeo."

The earliest episodes were heavy on monologues drawn from Benny's masters-of-ceremonies chatter, and were enlivened by some very droll commercials for the sponsor's product. Quickly exhausting his library of vaudeville material, Benny soon hired vaudeville writer Harry Conn to provide fresh material for each show. The two worked out a concept for the Canada Dry program that melded Benny's well-practiced but seeming-easy repartee with other members of a vaudeville show cast on stage, with elements that seemed innovative to commercial radio in 1932. Jack joked with the announcer *du jour* and pulled him to the microphone to read lines and become a participant. Olsen and his musicians also became speaking cast members. The program began to resemble a sketchy version of a workplace situation comedy, with outrageously satirical commercials and product plugs scattered throughout the episode. The sponsor was appalled at the manhandling of the precious product's reputation, but good reviews and piles of letters from delighted listeners convinced the show's advertising agency, N.W. Ayer & Sons, to let Benny and Conn continue.

Over the Canada Dry program's first thirteen weeks/ 26 episodes, the increasingly cohesive troupe moved away from the liveness of the studio microphone to go on make-believe journeys to a soda fountain, the zoo, and prize fights at Madison Square Gardens. Benny and Conn wrote skits that satirized sporting events, 4th of July fireworks, interview programs and the write-in-contests that then-currently plagued the airwaves.

Benny and Conn devised a mixture of comic monologues, repartee, pun tossing, and fictional adventures between the musical numbers, avoiding rigid formulas. Some of their experimental ideas were solidly successful, while some were problematic and abandoned as unworkable. Others ended perhaps at the behest of their sponsor. The outrageous Canada Dry middle commercials are a highlight of the earliest portion of Benny's radio career (see the Kentucky factory experiment on May 25 and the foot race between a talking glass of Canada Dry and a bottle of ketchup on May 30). Benny would continue to innovate new techniques of advertising humor with Jell-O and Lucky Strike cigarette commercials in the years to come.

In late June 1932, Jack began to talk about hiring an assistant to handle all the mail the program was receiving in response to the outrageous Canada Dry contests. In the final script of volume one, the July 27, 1932 script for the radio program, (last of the first 13 weeks), Jack's real wife Sadye Benny joined the program as a young woman named "Mary Livingstone," a fan of the program from the small town of Plainfield, New Jersey. As you will see in our second volume, Mary assumed the role of Jack's lackadaisical part-time secretary on the radio show, and soon would become a central character.

INTRODUCTION TO VOLUME 2 – (Canada Dry program August 1 to October 26, 1932)

These Canada Dry scripts from August through October 1932 show Jack Benny and scriptwriter Harry Conn continuing to craft a personality-based radio variety program, drawing on Benny's vaudeville style and exploring new constructions of comedy characters and situations. Experimenting as the program progressed from week to week, Benny and Conn developed quirky-yet-likeable identities for the major performers - orchestra leader, vocalist, and band members, although the constantly changing announcer put a limit on how much they could involve him. The cast bounced jokes, reactions and bad puns off each other. The newest addition, young fan Mary Livingstone from Plainfield New Jersey, began to fit in with the established group.

Among the new and noteworthy elements we will find in this 13-week/ 26-episode chapter of the Jack Benny radio saga are:

- "Nickel Back on the Bottle" becomes a nationally popular catch phrase

- Mary's first Labor Day poem is declaimed on September 5

- Jack's in-show monologues continue to showcase crazy events that can't be seen by radio audiences, such as Japanese tumbling acrobats, a flea circus, a rodeo, and athletic events at the Summer Olympics being held out in Los Angeles

- Jack's alter-ego "Jake" makes perhaps his only appearance on October 5

- The show's first parody of a popular film, "Grand Hotel" on October 10 is a huge success

- Prince the mathematically-adept dog appears on October 12; he will make a return appearance in December 1950's "Dreer Poosen" radio episode. Jack's Lucky Strike-era writers were happy to delve into these earliest scripts for inspiration, many years later

- Jack and Mary profess their love for on October 17 and 19 (more on this below)

- In a rare political comedy sketch, Jack provides running commentary on a prize fight between "Battling Herbert Hoover and Fighting Franklin Roosevelt" on October 19

- Mary takes the lead in a parody of a creaky Victorian melodrama, "Bertha the Sewing Machine Girl," and Jack and Mary say farewell to George and Ethel and the orchestra. Jack, Mary and Harry are headed to New Orleans, where they will meet a new radio network, new cast, new writers, and new broadcast days (that jealous NBC will not allow them to identify on the air)

After several months of twice-a-week programs, Benny and Conn began to garner critical notice for their experimentations with advertising and comedy situations. *Variety* reported in August, 1932, "Jack Benny was in good form on last week's program, having evolved sundry effective gags for plugging Canada Dry. In line with the recent trend toward a humorous plug for the sponsor, he is sugar-coating and making palatable what is usually a boresome interlude in the best of programs." In October, it commented, "Jack Benny is improving on his Canada Dry humor. Benny has built up a unique style of comedy, especially with those puns which, however, are not injudiciously primed for strong returns."

However, just when Benny and Conn thought they had achieved a solid, successful mixture of comedy and music, with distinct characters, situations and parody sketches, their program was completely upended. In October, 1932 Canada Dry and its ad agency abruptly declared its displeasure with many aspects of the program. NW Ayer & Sons found what it considered to be a more propitious broadcasting time over at the rival commercial network, CBS, where a larger number of stations (27) were available to carry the half hour program, on Thursdays at 8:15p.m. and Sundays at 10:00p.m. Benny's bandleader George Olsen, his orchestra and Ethel Shutta were all under contract to NBC, however, and couldn't move with them. Pouting at the departure of a program they had nurtured from the beginning, NBC would not allow Canada Dry to have Jack Benny to even mention on-air the new network and broadcasting times that awaited the program in November, 1932.

Even more outrageous, in the opinions of Jack Benny, Harry Conn and Mary Livingstone, sponsor Canada Dry decided that they did not like the comedy routines, either. *Variety* reported the ham-handed efforts of the ginger ale manufacturer to re-structure the show:

> At the insistence of the advertiser the staff of authors for Jack Benny's material on the Canada Dry session has been augmented to three. Original gagman on the show was Harry W. Conn. When the show went CBS, Sid Silvers was not only added to the cast as foil for Benny but given a writing assignment. While the program was being broadcast from New Orleans the account complained that the script was in need of strengthening, with David Freedman, collaborator (Cantor) on the Chase & Sanborn stanza, now filling a similar niche for Canada Dry.

In the forthcoming third volume of *Jack Benny's Lost Radio Broadcasts*, we will learn what changes Silvers and Freedman brought to the program, and how Benny, Conn and Livingstone fought tooth and nail to regain their autonomy.

"What are you Laughing at, Mary?" Sadye Marks and the creation of Mary Livingstone's comic voice

Mary Livingstone's boisterous laughter and forthright puncturing of Jack Benny's vanity were the cornerstones of one of the most unusual characters in American radio comedy. Chief "stooge" (or comic foil for the main character) of the Benny radio program from 1932 until Rochester's eventual assumption of that position in the 1940s, Mary occupied the rare radio role of an attractive, unmarried female who had full equality with the fellows in Benny's gang. Mary was the first character on the Benny radio program who did not have a defined duty on the show (neither bandleader, singer, nor announcer.) Serving vaguely as Jack's secretary, she haphazardly performed a few tasks, impertinently disobeyed his requests, prattled like a mild version of Gracie Allen, and read letters from her hapless family back in Plainfield, New Jersey. Mary mainly functioned as Jack's sometimes cynical, sometimes silly, heckling friend.

In the mid-1920s, Jack Benny varied the format of his vaudeville performances between acting as a master of ceremonies for a big show at prominent theaters like the Palace in New York City, working a solo routine, and doing a skit paired with a young female assistant performing a "Dumb Dora" role, as a dimwitted but pretty young woman who exchanged light banter with him.

Benny had used other assistants in the past, but in 1927 (one story suggests to save money) he asked his new wife, Sadye Marks Benny, if she might try it. Even though she had never worked as a performer before, Sadye joined Jack as his on-stage "stooge," or comic foil, and although she was a reluctant and nervous performer, managers reported that audiences were pleased with the results. Benny family lore maintains that Jack re-hired the original actress when they played Los Angeles, but after several performances the theater manager stated that the reviews weren't as good as when Sadye was on stage, so the girl was sacked and Sadye got the job permanently.

Adopting the stage name "Marie Marsh," Sadye performed together with Jack in occasional vaudeville bookings between 1927 and 1931. They also appeared together in a 1928 Vitaphone talkie short, Bright *Moments*. Even though Sadye's stage appearances were successful, she did not request equal billing in the act, unlike their friends Burns and Allen, or Block and Sully. When Benny took roles in films, or on Broadway in *Earl Carroll's Vanities* in 1931, Sadye apparently was content to remain behind the scenes. When Benny decided to appear on radio, his original contract with Canada Dry was for a solo act. The coincidence of

Mary's introduction beginning with the renewal of Benny's next 13-week contract indicates to me that Benny intentionally added her to the program cast.

Sadye Marks always downplayed the early moments of her radio career. Throughout her life, Sadye adamantly maintained that her entrance onto the Canada Dry Program was unintentional, and that it was just as unplanned and happenstance that she might become a radio actress as it had been when she'd become a vaudeville performer. Sadye's determination to cast herself as a reluctant star and self-effacing spouse is unusual in an American show business star culture that fostered and promoted stories of unique talents, Cinderella stories, large egos and preordained destinies. Over the years, Sadye's story of her entrance into the Benny program toggled back and forth between her late incorporation into the show in order to pad out a short script, or as a last minute substitute due to Benny's inability to find a suitable actress to play a small part. Either way, the Mary Livingstone role is set out as a one-time occurrence. As a 1935 newspaper profile of the Bennys' radio origins recounted:

> One night Jack's script ran short. He had to fill in for a couple of minutes and an idea flashed through his mind. He waved to George Olsen to start a number, walked over to where Mary was sitting and brought her over to the microphone with him. He signaled to the engineer to fade the music out and started an impromptu bit of dialog with her. They succeeded in ending the broadcast without any "dead air." Within two weeks Jack had received so many requests that Mary be made a regular part of the show that there was nothing to do but get Harry Conn, his writer, to bring her into scripts regularly. In spite of herself, Mary Livingstone became a radio star.

In a 1965 interview, Mary retrospectively claimed:

> One day they had a bit on the show for a girl from Plainfield, New Jersey, who was supposed to come on and read a silly poem. They auditioned a lot of girls and by the afternoon they still hadn't found one to satisfy them. The director asked me if I would try. So that night I read the poem on the show and the next thing I knew so many letters came in they wanted me to do another one, which I did. Before I knew it, I was on steady as Mary Livingstone, the girl from Plainfield."

Such self-generated stories explain that it was Sadye's delightful laughter (induced by her nervousness, Sadye suggested) that provoked the welcome, if unexpected, audience response. This unanticipated success purportedly kept Sadye on the show in a onetime role that transformed into a major character on the show.

For many years the July 27, 1932 script was considered lost, as there is no copy of it in Benny's scripts at UCLA. Jack and Mary were sentimental about their performing past. Perhaps they stored this July 27th script separately from the other documents in Benny's script collection, to share with friends and reporters. Eventually they misplaced their only copy. With no other written evidence of the script (and its status as a live radio broadcast for which no recordings survive), critics and historians have tended to accept the Bennys' version of Mary's origin story. A copy of the script has been located, however, on microfilm in the NBC Masterfile script collection at the Library of Congress, and we include it in this volume. From it, we can examine how the particular narrative elements introduced into the show on this one episode would have long-lasting consequences.

As opposed to the version of the story the Bennys crafted to explain Sadye's unintentional radio debut, the original script shows that the Mary character was involved throughout the program, not just in a few lines tagged on at the end. Conn seemed to have created a fleshed-out Mary Livingstone character in one episode, as Mary exhibited aspects of her character's personality and biographical details in this one broadcast that would remain remarkably stable over the years, such as her hometown, the importance of her mother, her jumping into conversations, her scatterbrained dialogue, and her flirtatious, contentious relationship with Jack. Above all, in the first show, Sadye brought Mary Livingstone that attention-getting laugh.

The Mary Livingstone character was central to the following episode, broadcast August 1st. Mary was not there in person, however. Ethel read out a letter Mary had sent to Jack, who had been fidgeting that the young fan had not reappeared. Mary returned in person on August 3rd, laughing and announcing that everything she encountered was "swell." Sadye was then absent for two weeks, (one source suggests she was ill), but she returned on the August 17 program, when Jack hired Mary to be his personal secretary. Subsequently, Mary appeared in every episode. Looking at the scripts in the Benny collection broadcast during August, September and October, 1932, we can see that Sadye Marks began to adopt "Mary Livingstone" as both her professional stage name and her personal name. Sadye might have continued to use her vaudeville moniker "Marian Marsh," but several actresses now in New York and Hollywood had similar-sounding names. By mid-October 1932, Benny radio scripts, which had previously cued her as "Sadye" began calling her "Mary" as well.

In September, Benny and Conn introduced a romantic subplot into the shows. Jack ceased joking about his "girlfriend in Newark" and began to flirt with Mary, and the growing romance became a major element of the narrative. There were complications and misunderstandings as Mary asked Ethel for romantic advice, members of the band flirted with Mary, and she overheard Jack flirting with Ethel. In the October 17 and 19 episodes, Mary and Jack impetuously professed their love for one another.

This experiment by Benny and Conn was one of the narrative avenues that they quickly abandoned. The imposition of too heavy a romantic story line would seriously hamper the informal, joking atmosphere they had been building, so they abruptly ended it. Mary Livingstone remained Jack's boisterous, incompetent secretary - she forgot to put paper in the typewriter, asked Jack for definitions of words she did not understand, and hampered his efforts to get correspondence completed. Mary also returned to flirting with the other members of George Olsen's band and allowed them to escort her home, while Jack stood by and quietly fumed in frustration. There was much more humor to be mined from unresolved affection than in true love. Milt Josefsberg, one of Benny's later writers, noted that Mary's ill-defined role on the radio program "was a complete contradiction of the most basic rule in creating comedy programs. For a running character to sustain as a regular member of a successful series, she, or he, must have a clearly-defined function in relationship to the star." Breaking the standard comedy narrative rules with incorporation of this unruly, unattached woman was another of the Benny show's many innovations.

Endnotes

1. "Little Bits from the Air," *Variety*, August 23, 1932, 42.

2. "Little Bits from the Air," *Variety* Oct 18 1932, 42.

3. James Cannon, untitled, undated newspaper clipping, Benny Scrapbook 1932-1933, Jack Benny Papers, American Heritage Center, University of Wyoming, Box 90

4. "Inside Stuff – Radio" *Variety* November 29, 1932, 36.

5. Mary Livingstone Benny, Hilliard Marks, and Marcia Borie. *Jack Benny*. Doubleday, 1978, p. 50, 54.

6. Mary Benny, "Mary Benny Tells why she quit show biz," *Chicago Tribune*, June 19, 1965, p A1.

7. Fred Wilson, "She couldn't help being a radio star," *Boston Globe* June 30, 1935, p13.

8. "Mary Benny Tells why she quit show biz."

9. Canada Dry program, August 1 1932 episode.

10. Jack Benny with Charles Martel," Never Try to Be Funny," *Tower Radio*, September 1934, p21.

11. Canada Dry program, August 17 1932 episode.

12. Canada Dry program, Oct 17, 1932 episode.

13. Canada Dry program, Sept 19, 1932 episode.

14. Milt Josefsberg, *The Jack Benny Show* (New York: Crown, 1977) pp 68-69.

Jack Benny Resources

Benny, Jack and Joan Benny, *Sunday Nights at Seven: The Jack Benny Story* (Warner Books, 1990)

Benny, Jack and Harry Conn, *Jack Benny's Lost Radio Broadcasts, Volume One: May 2 – July 27, 1932*. Edited and with an introduction by Kathryn Fuller-Seeley (BearManor Media, 2020)

Fuller-Seeley, Kathryn, *Jack Benny and the Golden Age of American Radio Comedy* (University of California Press, 2017)

International Jack Benny Fan Club (www.jackbenny.org and on Facebook)

Old Time Radio Researchers Group (https://otrrpedia.net/hotrod.html) Jack Benny radio shows digitized to enjoy for free, as well as through www.archive.org and other websites

Acknowledgements

I would like to express my great appreciation to Joan Benny, her family and the Jack Benny Estate for permission to publish these radio scripts. I owe Laura Leibowitz many thanks (and many indulgent future celebratory dinners) for her incredible support of my Benny projects and for her tremendous work leading the IJBFC. All the members of the International Jack Benny Fan Club (in facebook discussions, online chats and Benny conventions) have proven to be kind, generous and wonderful people who continue to celebrate Benny's comedy, and to provide happy fellowship. Garth Johnson has an amazing ability to find photos and articles, and Don M. Yowp as well. Barbara Thunell is allowing us to explore the wonders of her lifetime Benny scrapbook collection. Darrel Lantz (buckbenny otr), John Henderson, Terry Philips and Vincent Longo are the Saturday morning podcast "gang" who are always teaching me new things about Jack Benny, comedy and 20th century history. Ben Ohmart is such a generous and supportive publisher, and John Teehan is a terrific production editor. The William P. Hobby Centennial fellowship through the University of Texas at Austin has also played a large role in making this series possible. Thanks to you all!

August 1, 1932

Novelty Night with Japanese acrobats (who exclaim "Hup! Hup! Hup!" while performing their act) and trained dog Prince, who can count. (Prince will appear again on the January 8, 1950 "Dreer Poosen" radio episode, which demonstrates how Benny's later radio writers mined comedy gold from these early scripts). Mary Livingstone does not appear on this episode of the program (last week was her first appearance), but Jack wonders where she is. Mary sends a note to Jack that Ethel reads on-air.

STATION WJZ   PROGRAM   CANADA DRY GINGER ALE, INC.

      AND   DATE   MONDAY, AUGUST 1, 1932

    BLUE NETWORK   TIME   9:30 – 10:00 P.M. (E.D.T.)

SIGNATURE – JOLLY GOOD COMPANY

1. MARIETTA   ORCHESTRA & PAUL SMALL

2. MY LITTLE DREAMBOAT   ORCHESTER & ETHEL SHUTTA

3. CIRCUS DAYS   ORCHESTRA & FRAN FREY

4. HOLDING MY HONEY'S HAND   ORCHESTRA & ETHEL SHUTTA

5. SENTIMENTAL GENTLEMAN   ORCHESTRA & DICK "HOTCHA"
    GARDNER

ANNOUNCER: Ladies and Gentlemen, Another half-hour of entertainment about Canada Dry, the Champagne of Ginger Ales, now available by the glass at soda fountains, as well as in bottles for the home. You'll find the new large size bottle very economical and particularly convenient for home use.

George Olsen, Ethel Shutta, and Jack Benny, the Canada Dry Humorist, again perform for your enjoyment.

George Olsen opens the program with "Marietta", Paul Small singing.

1.   MARIETTA   ORCHESTRA & PAUL SMALL

ANNOUNCER: O.K., Jack – take the mike.

JACK: Hello, more people than you can get into a rumble sent… This is Jack Benny and his Canada Dry wit----

ANNOUNCER: Wit what?

JACK: wit ice cream…. Ah, that came without notice. Well, well, how time flies. It's already the <u>first of August</u>. Imagine… only one hundred and fifty-six more days to do your Christmas shopping…. And two and a half years to 1935. It doesn't seem possible.

Oh well, that's life and there's no use worrying; about it. The more you worry, the older you look…. and older you look, the more you worry. And that's the way it goes. Just think… it was 1861 when we had the Civil War, and It seems like yesterday to me …. How tune flies. Here I just started talking to you <u>thirty seconds</u> ago, and it seems like <u>ten minutes to you</u>…. What am I talking about, Jimmy?

ANNOUNCER: I don't know, Jack … something about time flying.

JACK: This is Jack Benny soliloquizing folks.

ANNOUNCER: What does "soliloquizing" mean, Jack?

JACK: How time flies… yes sir.

ANNOUNCER:	Jack you've wasted <u>three minutes</u> already.
JACK:	Three minutes! How time flies.
ANNOUNCER:	And <u>now</u> is the time, ladies and gentlemen, to drink Canada Dry Ginger Ale, made to order by the glass at all fountains. Everybody's drinking it, and it's very simple to get…. Just walk up to the fountain, ask for a glass of Canada Dry Ginger Ale, made-to-order, and the clerk <u>quickly</u> puts the right amount of syrup in the glass…adds charged water <u>in a jiffy</u>… and in a few seconds, you have a cooling and refreshing drink.
JACK:	How time flies with Canada Dry. How before going into our next number, I want to announce that our new series of programs starts tonight. And, as I told you last Wednesday, it will be known as <u>Novelty Night.</u> You know we always keep our promise, and tonight we're going to give it away. We have brought to you this evening such <u>impossible</u> things that even <u>we</u> are afraid of the results. However, the <u>show</u> must go on. For the first novelty on our program, Ethel Shutta will sing "Little Dream Boat" in the same <u>novel</u> manner she has been singing for years. It will be played by George Olsen and his <u>unusual</u> orchestra. Of course, tonight being Novelty Night, they will all finish together. Oh, Ethel….
ETHEL:	Yes Jack.
JACK:	Ethel, you'll have to put a little something extra into this.
ETHEL:	All right, Jack.
JACK:	Of course, you know what a <u>novelty</u> is, don't you?
ETHEL:	Sure…It's a <u>book</u>.
JACK:	Ethel, just forget our conversation.

2. MY LITTLE DREAM BOAT   ORCHESTRA AND ETHEL SHUTTA

JACK:	A novelty is a book… Go, Ethel.
	And now, ladies and gentlemen, we are going to spike the rumor that all you can got on the air are songs, talk and music. So just all back, folks, relax…. close your eyes and <u>visualize</u>. We have more talent up here tonight than you could shake a stick at…. <u>and probably will</u>.
	Now first to appear on our Novelty Program this evening is a great troupe of hand-balancers from Japan… who have just arrived from <u>Tokyo</u> where they finished making several <u>tokey</u>-pictures for the Fox-akowa Studios…. They have brought with them these two famous Japanese golfers… <u>Mashi Shotto</u> and <u>Socka Balli</u>. These marvels from the Orient are <u>first</u> class <u>hand</u>-balancers… not <u>second-hand</u>, mind you.
	And one of their great feats before leaving Japan was to <u>balance the budget</u> while spinning a hoop on each arm.

So, I now take great pleasure in introducing to you the famous Disha Washa Japs.

(CHORD – FOLLOWED BY APPLAUSE)

(SOUND EFFECT: FOOTSTEPS RUNNING)

PAUL AND FRAN: Hup – hup – hup.

FRAN: (GERMAN DIALECT) Mak schnell, Ludvig…mak schnell.

JACK: Clever, these Japanese… they speak several languages. Say, do you boys speak Japanese?

PAUL: Vy not?

JACK: All right, boys….do your first stunt.

PAUL AND FRAN: Hup – hup – hup -- -- hup – hup;

(APPLAUSE)

JACK: There they stand… <u>six high</u> … what a pyramid! …let me describe to you, Ladies and gentlemen…

The strong man <u>Yaki</u> is on the ground… with his hands in the air, holding up Matse Yama………. on Matse's hands is Seven-Year Itchee Yama…. on his hands is Tsuras, and Tsuras has a <u>wife and four children</u> on <u>his</u> hands… What a pyramid …don't fall, boys…. All right, you can come down now.

FRAN AND PAUL: Hup – hup – hup – hup.

(SOUND EFFECT: HEAVY JUMPING)

(CHORD)

JACK: Now show your muscles, boys… <u>What muscles</u> on this little feller… Oh, that's Paul…Stay out of this, Paul. And now for the next stunt.

FRAN AND PAUL: Hup – hup – hup – hup.   (APPLAUSE)

JACK: This time George Olsen-uma is on the ground, holding up Ethel Shutta-kowa…. Say, George and Ethel, will you please stand back? I can't tell one balancer from the other.

FRAN AND PAUL: Hup - hup hup hup.

JACK: Now Togi is standing on the ground… while Tsuras is balancing himself, nose to nose, with Togi… with his feet in the air. Standing on Tsuras's feet is <u>Tackey</u>…. and don't forget to tackey home some Canada Dry Ginger Ale made-to-order at the fountain.

FRAN AND PAUL: Hup – hup – hup.

JACK: Oh yes… the pyramid… Now standing on Tackey's head are Matsa Yuma and his brother, Sensa…. while on top of them are Pokey and Hokey-Jokey with the sheriff on Pokey's neck…. What a formation! All right, boys…. come on down.

FRAN AND PAUL:	Hup – hup – hup – hup.
	(CHORD)
JACK:	And now for the next and last stunt – Thank Heaven, George ---- you don't have to do this one if you don't want to, boys.
FRAN AND PAUL:	Hup – hup –hup.
JACK:	All right, go ahead.
FRAN AND PAUL:	Hup – hup – hup-hup – hup.
	(APPLAUSE)
JACK:	Ah, folks, what sight… On the ground is <u>nobody</u>… who is holding up Yoki, six feet in the air… on Yoki's head is Hotchee Mura Gardner… who seems to be in everything… I don't know how he got there…
	Hotchee, who seems to be stronger than Hatchie the rest, is holding up Hootchee, Kootchee and Sextette from Luchee… And now Luchee will throw six glasses of Canada Dry from Hootchee to Kootchee…<u>no mura, no lessa</u>…. and sold by the glassa. All right, boys, let's go.
PAUL AND FRAN:	Hup – hup – hup – hup.
	(DRUM ROLL – SOUND EFFECT: TERRIFIC
	GLASS CRASH, FOLLOWED BY THUD)
JACK:	Well. that's too bad…. Luchee threw the glasses from Hootchee to Kootchee… but Kootchee <u>no catchee</u>. And now the lone survivor of this troupe will say something to you.
PAUL (WITH JEWISH ACCENT):	Mr. Benny, ven do us Japs get paid?
JACK:	Later, fellows …. <u>SCRAM</u>.
	And now George Olsen….
PAUL (WHISPERS):	You see, Mox, I told you he wouldn't pay ys.
FRAN:	Vait, you big swindler—you, some day you'll need Chinese here.
JACK:	And now George Olsen and his Sapanese Jandman----I mean, Japanese Sandmen will repeat that novelty number, "Circus Days", while I change a dollar and pay off the boys.
	ORCHESTRA AND FRAN FREY
2.	CIRCUS DAYS

JACK:	George, that last number is right in keeping with our next novelty. And now, ladies and gentlemen, we bring to you two of the world's greatest trained dogs… who come here direct from the Panama <u>Kennel</u>…. One is New York police dog… the other is a <u>Boston</u> bull… Come here, boys…. I mean, dogs. Say something.
BARKER (MIMICING BOTH DOGS --- ONE HIGHER—PITCHED VOICE):	Woof - woof – woof – woof -.
JACK:	First, we'll take the police dog who is very good at mathematics. Come here, Prince…. Roll over…that's it…Sit up…Attaboy.
BARKER:	Woof – woof.
JACK:	Now Prince, I'm going to ask you a few questions. If you had two lollipops and I gave you another, how many would you have?
BARKER:	Woof – woof – woof.
JACK:	That's right – three…. How many days are there in a week?
BARKER:	Woof – woof – woof.
JACK:	Right again -- three…. Friday, Saturday and Sunday… the other four are very dull and we won't bother to count them. Now, Prince, think hard. How much are two and two?
BARKER:	FOUR. I mean, woof – woof – woof – woof.
JACK:	Be more careful there, Prince…. Now one more question. Will someone in the audience kindly call out a number.
BALDWIN:	TWO.
JACK:	Did you hear that, Prince? What number did the gentlemen call?
BARKER:	Woof – woof.
JACK:	That's right.
BARKER:	Woof – woof – woof.
JACK:	That's enough, Prince.
BARKER:	Woof – woof – woof.
JACK:	Take him out, Fran.
BARKER:	Woof – woof (INTO DISTANCE)
JACK:	Just a little enthused…. And now, ladies, and gentlemen, I bring you MIKE, the famous talking dog…who will now talk over the mike. Are you ready?
BARKER (IN DIFFERENT VOICE):	Woof – woof.
JACK:	I see I'm going to have trouble with you, too…. All right now, Mike, I want to ask you a few questions. Answer clearly and pronounce each syllable.

BARKER:	Woof – woof.
JACK:	Mike, what do they call the top of a house?
BARKER:	Aroof – aroof – aroof.
JACK:	That's right – a roof…. Now, Mike, tell us what did you have for breakfast this morning?
BARKER:	Waffle – waffle – waffle.
JACK:	That's right – three waffles…waffles and what?
BARKER:	(MAKES WHINING SOUND)
JACK:	Waffles and syrup… that's marvelous. Now, Mike, tell us who is governor of New York State.
BARKER:	Grrr—roosevelt…grrr—roosevelt.
JACK:	Mike you don't have get them all good. You can miss once in a while. And now, Mike, when I play and hit a ball out of bounds, where does it go?
BARKER:	Ruff – ruff – ruff.
JACK:	In the rough --- you're telling me. And now, folks, the most marvelous achievement of any dumb animal… Mike is going to sing his favorite song… "Paradise".
JACK:	All right, Mike, I'll start it – (SINGS) "And when I hold your hand" ….
BARKER:	(WHINING) Mm –um –um – a mm.
JACK:	"then you'll understand"
BARKER:	Mm – um – um – a –mum.
JACK:	Ah, what a crooner! that's fine, Mike. You can go now. Here's a piece of liver, what do you say?
BARKER (SPEAKING VOICE):	What no onions?
	(SOUND EFFECT: SLAP)
	BARKER (STARTS WHINING AND KEEPS IT UP, TRAILING OFF INTO THE DISTANCE)
ANNOUNCER:	This program has gone to the dogs … thru the courtesy of Canada Dry Ginger Ale, made-to-order by the glass. Everybody's drinking it. And now Ethel Shutta will sing, "Holding My Honey's Hand," played by George Olsen and his Jazz Hounds.

4. HOLDING MY HONEY'S HAND   ORCHESTRA & ETHEL SHUTTA

JACK:	Say, Ethel, I just happened to think of something. Do you renumber that little girl from Plainfield who came up to see me last Wednesday?
ETHEL:	You mean Mary Livingston?
JACK:	Yes, she promised to come back here tonight.
Ethel:	Oh, she's got you worried – eh?
JACK:	Aw, no, Ethel…. but I was wondering why she didn't come back, that's all. Oh, well – starts whistling… Oh, doorman, was there anyone looking for me tonight?
BALDWIN:	<u>NO</u>!
JACK:	(CONTINUES TO WHISTLE)
ETHEL:	What's the matter, Jack?
JACK:	Oh, nothing, Ethel.
Ethel:	Say, there's a letter over there for you. It's marked Plainfield…might be from Mary.
JACK:	Yeah?
ETHEL:	I'll get it for you.
JACK:	Oh, don't bother with it, Ethel. <u>What does it say</u>? … I mean…
ETHEL:	Shall I read it for you?
JACK:	Yes, if you want to…. it's up to you.
ETHEL:	Now, Jack, I think you kind-a like her.
JACK:	Aw, don't be silly…And, besides…I have a sweetheart living in Newark…You remember Helen, my sweetheart in Newark.
ETHEL:	Yes….by the way, whatever happened to her?
JACK:	Oh, we correspond right along. I wrote her a letter last April and I expect an answer any day now…. She's probably busy… you know. The last time I saw her she had a birthday party. I didn't know what to buy her for a present. I was going to get one of those 16-cylinder cars.
ETHEL:	You were?
JACK:	Yeah… but it takes so long before they deliver them. So, I bought her some <u>handkerchiefs</u>…. Anyway, I'm thru with girls, Ethel.
ETHEL:	Then you don't want me to read this letter from Mary?
JACK:	Yeah…see what it says. What can we lose?
ETHEL:	Wait until I open it.
	(SOUND EFFECT: CRUMPLING OF PAPER)

JACK (IMPATIENTLY): Hurry up.

ETHEL: All right, here it is.

"DEAR JACK:

YOU PROBABLY DON'T RENUMBER ME, BUT I'M THE GIRL WHO CAME UP TO THE STUDIO WEDNESDAY NIGHT. REMEMBER ME…. MARY? I'M SORRY I CAN'T BE WITH YOU TONIGHT, BUT YOU SEE I HAVE BEEN VERY BUSY HELPING MOTHER WITH THE DISHES AS SHE HAS A SORE THUMB FROM <u>TRYING TO TUNE YOU OUT ON OUR RADIO</u>……

AND, BESIDES THAT, OUR CAT HAD KITTENS TODAY. I WILL SEND YOU ONE WHEN THEY ARE RIPE.

THANKS VERY MUCH FOR THE PICTURE YOU SENT ME. I HAVE PICTURES OF ALL THE MOVIE STARS…GABLE, MONTGOMERY, CHEVALIER AND ALL OF THEM…YOUR PICTURE LOOKS SO SWEET. I GOT IT RIGHT BETWEEN FRANKENSTEIN AND JIMMY DURANTE……

August 3, 1932

Jack as an auctioneer disposes of some trinkets and then sells some glasses of Canada Dry, which draws an appreciative crowd. The Olympic Games, being held across the country in Los Angeles, are described on the air. Jack interviews a "health" expert who coughs a lot. Mary appears on the program again (accompanied by a friend named Dot) and flirts with Jack. Trained fleas do their act as Jack calls play-by-play.

STATION WJZ	PROGRAM	CANADA DRY GINGER ALE, INC.
AND	DATE	WEDNESDAY, AUGUST 3, 1932
BLUE NETWORK	TIME	9:30 – 10:00P.M. (E.D.T.)

SIGNATURE – JOLLY GOOD COMPANY

1. OLD MAN OF THE MOUNTAIN — ORCHESTRA & DICK GARDNER

2. LOST IN YOUR ARMS — ORCHESTRA & PAUL SMALL

3. TENDER CHILD — ORCHESTRA & ETHEL SHUTTA & FRAN FREY

4. I'LL NEVER BE THE SAME — ORCHESTRA & ETHEL SHUTTA

5. ALL THE WORLD IS WAITING FOR THE SUNRISE — ORCHESTRA

SIGNATURE – ROCKABYE MOON

ANNOUNCER: Ladies and gentlemen. Another half-hour of entertainment about Canada Dry, the champagne of ginger ales, now available by the glass at soda fountains, as well as in bottles for the home. You'll find the new large size bottle very economical and particularly convenient for home use. George Olsen, Ethel Shutta, and Jack Benny, the Canada Dry humorist, again perform for your enjoyment. George Olsen opens the program with "Old Man of the Mountain," "Hotcha" Gardner singing.

1. OLD MAN OF THE MOUNTAIN   ORCHESTRA & GARDNER

ANNOUNCER: And now, folks, I give you Jack Benny, the auctioneer. (MUMBLING OF MEN AND WOMEN HEARD UNDER FOLLOWING)

JACK: Hello, male, female and fan mail customers… This is auctioneer Jack Benny… kindly step up a little closer…. Inside, folks, … don't stand in the doorway…. you are under no obligations whatsoever… (PLEADING TONE) please step in… don't be afraid… that's it… Now close the door, Mr. Kvetch…yes, lock it. AND NOW, LADIES AND GENTLEMEN, I have here a watch…an eighty-five jewel watch…count 'em….ten, twenty, forty, sixty…eighty— five jewels….this watch has the genuine <u>Swiss</u>-on-rye <u>movement</u>…open face and above board…This little watch not only tells time, but tells the future….wakes you up in the morning… takes out the dog and minds the baby… <u>What</u> am I offered for it? …. Do I hear anything…. Who'll say fifty thousand dollars?...... Who'll say <u>fifty</u> dollars? All right, them who'll say <u>fifty cents</u>? Who'll take it for nothing? …So you won't talk, eh?.... All right, we'll pass up this number. Hand me article no. 2.

Well, <u>here's</u> something that night interest you…. I have here in my hand a genuine, slightly-used razor blade…. guaranteed not to cut your chin…. or your beard…. This blade is made of one hundred percent India Rubber, a shipment of which just arrived from <u>Calcutta.</u> What am I offered for this little <u>cutta</u>?.... Who'll say a <u>quarter</u>? …. Who'll say a nickel?...Who'll say anything?.... All right, we'll pass <u>this</u> up.

Boy, hand me that combination… Number 3…Step up, ladies and gentlemen, and get a good look at this number…. It is a combination set for a man and his sweetheart…a man's <u>walking stick</u>… and a lady's <u>lipstick</u>…something for man and woman…. what am I offered for this sap-head cane and non-swallow lipstick?…. Well, we might as well pass this up, too…. Whew! what a market…. Now give me that glass.

And now, folks, I have a glass of CANADA DRY GINGER ALE…. genuine, made to order and sold at all fountains…It comes in <u>two</u> sizes …. who'll make….

(GENERAL NOISE)

PAUL:	Give me one.
DOROTHY ROSS:	I'll take the large one…here's my dime.
BALDWIN:	Two small ones.
ETHEL:	Five over here.
FRAN:	WHO'RE YOU SHOVIN'?
SADYE:	I was here first – give me that one.
PAUL:	Give me a small one…hey, that's my nickel.
FRAN:	GET OFF MY FOOT!
ANNOUNCER:	Quiet, please… what's the trouble, Jack?
JACK:	I don't mind selling things, Jimmy, but I hate to have the shirt torn from my back…. What am I offered for my shirt? Where's my hat? This is Jack Benny appearing here…<u>almost</u> in the flesh.
SADYE (ENTERS SCENE):	Gee, I think we're late… looks like they had a fight here…. This is the studio I told you about, Dot…there's the orchestra… and there are the actors and actresses.
DOROTHY:	Yeah…which one is Jack Benny?
SADYE:	The fellow standing on the soap-box without the shirt.
DOROTHY:	Oh, he's not handsome.
SADYE:	No, that's the microphone… I mean the fellow that's standing next to it.
DOROTHY:	What do you see in him?
SADYE:	I don't know…he has that…er… he.. so…er, well he…he… So, I think he's swell.
DOROTHY:	I thought you said knew him?
SADYE:	I met him here last Wednesday night…Hey… Jack!…. I guess he doesn't see me… Gosh, Dot, he says the <u>cutest</u> things… Last Wednesday he said when you drink Canada Dry in Scotland, where does the Glasgow?
DOROTHY:	I don't see anything funny about that.

SADYE:	I know, Dot…but, oh, the way he said it.
ANNOUNCER:	Ladies, will you kindly take a seat?
JACK:	The next number will "Lost in Your Arms" …. George Olsen and his orchestra will play… Paul Small will sing… and I will get another shirt.
SADYE:	Gee, I think that's clever.

2. LOST IN YOUR ARMS   ORCHESTRA & PAUL SMALL

JACK:	This is Jack Benny again…with a new shirt… new hat… and new skin. And now, ladies and gentlemen, we have brought to you again one of our unusual surprises which we have on every program…. We bring these to you regardless of the expense to our guests. And tonight, I have pleasure of introducing a man … no, not Herbert Hoover… not George Bernard Shaw… not Albert Einstein… not the great Mussolini… not Gene Sarazen… not Arthur Brisbane… not --
ANNOUNCER:	For Heaven's sake…who?
JACK:	A man whom you all know…a man whom you all respect… a man whom you all like…a man who would go the limit for you…
ANNOUNCER:	WHAT A MAN! …Who is he?
JACK:	Let me tell you something about this man… let me give you the inside story of his life…let me tell you his record… and give him full credit for what he has done… let me tell you the sacrifices he has made… let me tell you the noble----
ANNOUNCER:	For Heaven's sake, tell us his name … will you?
JACK:	I now take great pleasure in introducing that great health expert and muscle builder … the man whose advice has saved thousands of lives… a student of physiology and anatomy…a graduate of Iowa U…. an LL.B… a Ph.D…. and a L-O-U-S-E.
ANNOUNCER:	Well, for Heaven's sake… who is he?
JACK:	JACK BENNY…will now introduce to you a man who needs no introduction… that great body and health builder… PROFESSOR J. QUAGMIRE TORSO
	(APPLAUSE)
JACK:	Where is he?
ANNOUNCER:	I think the Professor left…he couldn't wait.
JACK:	There he is … by the door. Grab him quick, Jimmy.
ANNOUNCER:	Professor… Oh, Professor…
JACK:	Carry him over, Jimmy…… Professor, take the mike.

PROFESSOR (MILTON HERMAN): (STARTS TO COUGH)

JACK: A little nervous…eh, prof?

PROFESSOR: Yes.

JACK: The professor will now give you a few hints on health… a little lecture on the care building up of your body.

PROFESSOR: (COUGHS) Ladies and gentlemen… (COUGHS)

JACK: I see.

PROFESSOR: It affords me great pleasure to be to convey to this vast audience my secrets on health (COUGHS)… How in keeping physically fit, the first thing to think of is PLENTY OF EXERCISE…which should be taken immediately on (COUGHS)…….

JACK: on arising.

PROFESSOR: Yes… I also advise good wholesome food…plenty of fresh air… sunshine… and… and…(COUGHS)…proper rest. What it has done for me, it can surely do for you. (COUGHS)

JACK: Heaven forbid!

PROFESSOR: I am very happy to be here tonight (COUGHS)---

JACK: With that cough, he should be happy to be any place… OH, PROFESSOR, do you advocate long walks in the country?

PROFESSOR: Yes. I take three or four a day

JACK: Can you give us a sample of one right now?

PROFESSOR: (COUGHS)… (then MOANS) oh!...oh!...

JACK: What's the matter… what's the matter?

PROFESSOR: Oh, my back!

JACK: Be careful… just lean over the microphone.

PROFESSOR: Thank you.

And now I'm going to tell you how to avoid coughs and colds (COUGHS) …. iron in your blood will tone up your system (COUGHS WORSE)… it will build up your body… I have gained a hundred pounds in forty-seven years….

JACK: How old are now, Professor?

PROFESSOR: Forty-eight. (STARTS VIOLENT COUGH)

JACK: I doubt if you will reach forty-nine.

PROFESSOR: (COUGHS MORE VIOLENTLY)

JACK:	Come on, Jimmy…help him out…. IS THERE A DOCTOR IN THE STUDIO? (PROFESSOR'S COUGH HEARD IN THE DISTANCE)
JACK:	The next cough…er, number, ladies and gentlemen, is "Tender Child," sung by Ethel Shutta and Fran Frey (COUGHS)….and played by George Olsen (COUGHS) and his (COUGHS)-----

3. TENDER CHILD   ORCHESTRA AND ETHEL SHUTTA AND FRAN FREY

ANNOUNCER:	That was "Tender Child", sung by Ethel Shutta and Fran Frey… this is Jimmy Wallington announcing. How many of you folks realize that when you a step up to the fountain and order a glass of Canada Dry Ginger Ale made-to-order---
JACK:	Say, Jimmy, what are you trying to do?
ANNOUNCER:	I'm boosting Canada Dry Ginger Ale.
JACK:	On this program?...Why, Jimmy!
ANNOUNCER:	This is the Canada Dry program… isn't it?
JACK:	I don't know… nobody ever said anything to me about it. Say Jimmy, I was thinking how many people are sacrificing the Olympic Games just to be able to listen in to our program tonight.
ANNOUNCER:	Oh, I don't know.
JACK:	Yes, Jimmy, it's true…there are lot of people who would like to listen to our program and hear the Olympic Games, and I don't see why we can't kill two birds with one stone.
ANNOUNCER:	That's an idea, Jack. There's a radio in the corner. We can tune in Los Angeles and bring in part of the Olympic Games on our program.
JACK:	All right, Jimmy, let's do it. I think we owe it to our public. So stand by, ladies and gentlemen, for just a moment, and we will bring the Olympic Games right here to you, making it a double-header for the same price. What other program gives you two for one? …. All right, Jimmy, tune in the Olympic Stadium. (SOUND EFFECT: STATIC NOISES AND WHISTLE. CHEERING AND APPLAUDING)
FRAN:	Canada Dry Ale. Get your glass of Canada Dry.
PAUL:	Drink Canada Dry Ginger Ale made-to-order by the glass.
BALDWIN:	Everybody's drinking Canada Dry Ginger Ale, and you'll like it.
BOB:	You can't enjoy the Olympic Games without a glass of Canada Dry Ginger Ale.

(SILENCE FOR A MOMENT)

JACK: Wasn't that marvelous, Jimmy?... Just to think, <u>one turn</u> of the dial and you've got the Olympic Games... <u>Did you see</u> that 100-yard dash?...

JACK: Wasn't that great? Ah, boy! what a world we live in.

SADYE: Hello, Jack.

JACK: Oh, Mary...hello, Mary...how are you?

SADYE: Oh, Jack, I didn't think you would remember me.... Did you get my letter Monday?

JACK: Sure, I did, Mary...but I was terribly disappointed you didn't show up.

SADYE: Oh, were you, Jack?

JACK: Huh-huh...you know, Mary, it's awfully nice of you to come over to New York just to hear this program.

SADYE: Well, I really came over to do some shopping. Look...I just bought these trousers for my father. I always come to New York when there's a sale.

JACK: Oh, you did!...how much did pay for them?

SADYE: Ninety-eight cents...they were marked down from <u>four bits</u>.

JACK: Yes, they're very nice.

SADYE: Jack, is that George Olsen there?

JACK: Yes, I'll have you meet him ...George, this is Mary Livingston.

GEORGE: How do you do, Miss Livingston?...I'm glad to meet you.

SADYE: Hello, Mr. Olsen...you know I wrote you a letter a long time ago, and you never even answered it.

GEORGE: Maybe I never got it.

SADYE: Oh, I guess that's the reason it come back to me .... So <u>you're</u> George Olsen. Funny... you don't <u>look</u> cheap.

GEORGE: Oh!..... <u>Jack's</u> been talking to you. Well, ask him about that seven dollars <u>he owes me</u>.

JACK: All right, Mary...now I want you to meet Ethel Shutta...Ethel, this is Mary Livingston.

ETHEL: I'm very glad to know you, Mary...I've heard a lot about you.

SADYE: You know, Miss Shutta, you're a big hit in our town...We all like your singing and those funny jokes you do with Mr. Benny... Don't you think he's swell?

ETHEL: Yes, he's nice...if you like nice men.

SADYE: Miss Shutta, can I talk to you about something? You see, I bought these trousers for father and---

ETHEL:	Come over here, dear, and can talk. I think we're interfering with the program.
SADYE:	You see, I was going with a feller in Plainfield…and when I first heard Jack talk----
	(VOICE FADES OUT)
GEORGE:	Hey, where's everybody around here?...Ethel, where's Jimmy Wallington and Jack?
ETHEL:	Oh, they went down to the fountain for a drink.
GEORGE:	Oh, so Jimmy and Jack have gone for a drink, eh?... Well, there's bound to be a <u>deadlock</u>, so I'd better announce the next number. It is called "I Guess I'll Have to Change My Plans" …. You're singing it. Ethel

4. I GUESS I'LL HAVE TO CHANGE MY PLANS   ORCHESTRA & ETHEL SHUTTA

JACK:	Thanks, Jimmy…some time I'll buy you a drink. Ladies and gentlemen, we regret to say that we still have some novelties left over from Monday night. We tried to get rid of them. But they stowed away in some of the instruments and sheets of music. You have, no doubt, heard a buzzing sound around the studio all evening and probably thought it was static. But such was <u>not</u> the case. That <u>buzz</u> was the South American troupe of Trained Fleas…each and every one a thoroughbred and a blue-ribbon winner. They came to you <u>direct</u> from the trained dogs who entertained you on Monday night. I would suggest that you tune in a little louder as you might miss some of the clever remarks from these little fleas. As you know, a <u>flea is a flea</u>.
	Now let me introduce to you John… Joe…Sam…and Alexender Flea…and a large supporting cast of musicians, strong men, dancers and stooges… say something boys.
	(SOUND EFFECT: BUZZING SOUND)
JACK :	Now the first trick will be performed by John Flea…who tips the scales $1/8^{th}$ of a gram…and stands $1/64^{th}$ of an inch high in his stocking feet…Now just imagine… this little flea will pull a ten-ton truck, loaded with iron rails…across the studio….. John is now hitched up to the truck and <u>there he goes</u>.
	(SOUND EFFECT: AUTO HORN – FOLLOWED BY RUMBLING OF WHEELS. (ROUND OF APPLAUSE) (GALLOPING SOUND)
JACK:	The little devil ran away with the truck…you can't trust these fleas…And now the next trick
PAUL SMALL:	OUCH! OUCH! (SLAP SOUND)
JACK:	(LAUGHS) That was little Sam Flea…who just bit Paul Small. Listen, Sam, don't do any tricks before I tell you to.
	And now little Alexander Flea..who has studied music for the past eight years in the Conservatory of Music at <u>Flea</u>-adelphia – I mean, Philadelphia…will entertain you

	with a saxophone solo. Folks, you'll have to listen very attentively as the lung power of a flea is not quite as husky as that of Hotch Gardner…All right, Alex…OW! Alex, don't bite the leg that's feeding you…. There, be a good little feller and play.
	Do you want a chord?
	(PIANO CHORD – SAXOPHONE SCALES PLAYED LIGHTLY)
	(APPLAUSE)
JACK:	Very good. Alex….and now Joe Flea will offer something very unique…a soft shoe buck-and-wing.
	(TO LIVE MUSIC ACCOMPAITENT – TAP DANCE DONE WITH FINGERS O LEATHER)
	(ROUND OF APPLAUSE)
	Now folks, these fleas could entertain you indefinitely, but they must leave us now as they have another engagement. They are anxious to catch up with the two trained dogs who are appearing this week in Boston. These fleas will fly to Boston as they have not made reservations on the <u>buzz</u>…. or, on the bus.
	Open the window, Kvetch, and let these artistes out.
	(SOUND EFFECT: SEVERAL PEOPLE SLAPPING THEMSELVES REPEATEDLY)
	Say, Paul, will you reach down my neck and get this artist out of here…while George Olsen and his not-so-irritating artists play, "The World is Waiting for the Sunrise." All right George.

5. THE WORLD IS WAITING FOR THE SUNRISE   ORCHESTRA

JACK:	You have just heard the last number of the 28th program on the third of August. Those were all genuine artists we had here this evening… the best that counterfeit money could buy. And, as they say in South America do you <u>Bolivia</u>-me…hmm?
SADYE:	Oh, Mr. Benny…er, Jack.
JACK:	Oh, Mary…I thought you'd gone.
SADYE:	Jack, I thought you were swell tonight.
JACK:	Thanks.
SADYE:	Well, I'm going home now…good-night, Mr. Olsen… good-night, Miss Shutta. I'm taking your advice…good-night, Jack. I have to make the 10:40 bus.
JACK:	Wait, Mary… I'll take you over there.
MARY:	Oh, Jack that will be swell.

JACK: Another victory for Canada Dry.

SIGNATURE – ROCKABYE MOON

ANNOUNCER: Whenever you stop at a soda fountain for a refreshing drink or a sandwich, ask for a Canada dry ice-cream soda or a glass of Canada Dry – Remember it is now available made to order by the glass, as well as in bottles. And remember too, that Canada Dry now comes in large size bottles which are particularly economical for the home. Next Monday night at this same time Jack Benny, Ethel Shutta and George Olsen will again entertain you. This is the National Broadcasting Company.

August 8, 1932

This episode features an outrageous Canada Dry commercial set in Borneo, where cannibals enthusiastically consume the drink, some missionaries and the soda pop sales representative. Mary tells a "naughty" story that Jack used to perform in vaudeville with a female accomplice, conversing with Jack about a man and two girls in the sleeping berths of a train.

STATION WJZ   PROGRAM CANADA DRY GINGER ALE INC.
       AND   DATE MONDAY, AUGUST 8TH 1932.
BLUE NETWORK   TIME 9:30 10:00 P.M.
SIGNATURE – JOLLY G OOD COMPAN Y

OPENING ANNOUNCEMENT
1. THE TARTAR'S DARTER (FREY)
DIALOGUE
2. ANOTHER NIGHT ALONE (SMALL)
DIALOGUE
3. I LOVE YOU, DEAR (SHUTTA AND GARDNER)
DIALOGUE
4. ALL-AMERICAN GIRL (SMALL)
DIALOGUE
5. SO TO BED (SHUTTA AND SMALL)
DIALOGUE
ROCKABYE MOON
CLOSING ANNOUNCEMENT

STATION WJZ   PROGRAM CANADA DRY GINGER ALE INC.
AND   DATE MONDAY, AUGUST 8TH 1932.
BLUE NETWORK   TIME 9:30 10:00 P.M.
SIGNATURE – JOLLY GOOD COMPANY

ANNOUNCER: Ladies and gentlemen. Another half of entertainment about Canada Dry, the Champagne of ginger ales, now available by the glass of soda fountain, as well as in bottles for the home. You'll find the new large size bottle very economical and particularly convenient for home use. George Olsen, Ethel Shutta, and Jack Benny, the Canada Dry Humorist, again perform for your enjoyment. George Olsen opens the program with Paul Small singing "THE TARTAR'S DARTER."

ANNOUNCER: And now, Jack Benny.

JACK: Say Hicks, do you think this is a waste of time? I mean, does anybody listen in to our program?

ANNOUNCER: Don't be foolish…. certainly not.

JACK: Well, hello, <u>nobody</u>… this is Jack Benny…What, <u>again</u>?…. I heard that…. we're all here tonight, happy and say…with a great big show, and no advance in prices…with a cast of one <u>hundred</u> <u>and</u> <u>fifty</u> people, including stars of international reputation and a chorus of <u>sixty</u> of the most beautiful girls in the world…. WHAT A CAST…. say something, girls.

ETHEL: Got a cigarette?

JACK: Sixty beautiful girls!....and we have <u>comedians</u>.

FRAN: George, why is Clark Gable the greatest film star Hollywood?

GEORGE OLSEN: I don't know, Fran…why is Clark Gable the greatest film star in Hollywood?

FRAN: Because he is <u>two</u> <u>ears</u> ahead of the times.

(ORCHESTRA: <u>CHORD</u>)

JACK: Yes, sir, we have comedians…. are you in stitches, folks? And we have <u>great</u> singers.

(BAD HARMONY by Fran, Paul and Hotcha Gardner)

Well, we <u>had</u> great singers… you're fired, boys! Anyway, the members of our company are all looking fine…on their toes and rarin' to go.

GEORGE: I have a terrible headache, Jack.

JACK: I see….and smiling Ethel Shutta. How do you feel this evening, Ethel?

ETHEL:	I feel awful, Jack…I don't know what it is.
JACK:	All right, Ethel…. Fran, you're looking good.
FRAN:	This tooth is killing me, and….
JACK:	Well, here's hoping… Paul, is there anything wrong with you?
PAUL:	I didn't sleep wink last night, and I have severe pain in my back.
JACK:	These aches and pains come to you thru the courtesy of International Form-Fitting Sausage Company…. the skin you love to touch.
ANNOUNCER:	Canada Dry Ginger Ale, made-to-order by the glass, can now be bought at all fountains. And everybody's drinking it.
JACK:	Ethel, they've heard <u>that</u> before. Well, it looks as the we will have to do our program very quickly tonight before our cast passes out. So now George Olsen and his Ginger-Alians will play, "Another Night Aline," sung by Paul Small… Paul, I'm sorry you're not feeling good tonight.
PAUL:	No, I'll be all right.
JACK:	If you want to, I'll sing the next number for you.
PAUL:	Oh, Jack, I'm not <u>that</u> sick.
JACK:	Good old Paul…. <u>always kidding</u>.

2. ANOTHER NIGHT ALONE   PAU L SMALL AND ORCHESTRA

JACK:	And now, ladies and gentlemen, before going any further with our program, we will have to get some of these pests we have here, known as <u>Guest</u> <u>Stars</u>. The first pest…. I mean, guest…. is a fellow who just <u>limped</u> in from the Limping <u>Games</u> in Los Angeles…. a Los Angeles policeman second…and two detectives third and fourth…so you see we get all our celebrities <u>first</u> <u>run</u>…from victory direct to this studio.
	Now the Marathon Race originated and was first run <u>in Greece</u> …and you all know how tough it is to run in <u>Greece</u>…I have before me some Greek literature, which I got at Populous' Corner Food Shoppe…..which tells the history of the Greek Marathon. It seems that there was a young Greek fighter called SOCrates who run from the city of Marathon to Athens to open a restaurant…..and since then the Greeks have run to Cincinnati, Chicago, St. Louis and all points west….which shows that they have better runners than we have, and their strawberry pie isn't bad either.
	And now may I present our <u>Past</u> <u>Star</u> who will tell us how he runs these twenty—six-mile marathons and wins these heart-breaking races…. may I present Mr. er.. Mr.…what's your name, sir?
HARRY CONN:	Paul.

JACK:	Paul – what?
HARRY:	Revere.
JACK:	And you're a runner. Hmm. Well, tell us how you win these races.
HARRY:	Well, I start right out on a fast run for about three blocks… then I turn a corner when nobody run see me… and then I stand on the curb and every time a car passes, I point my thumb to the right.
JACK:	I see…. go ahead.
HARRY:	Then I jump on the first car that stops and ride as far as it goes.
JACK:	What's that got to do with <u>running</u>?
HARRY:	Well, I stand on the <u>running</u> board of the car.
JACK:	Uh-huh…. did you ever try standing <u>in front</u> of a car that is running forty miles an hour?
HARRY:	No, Mr. Benny.
JACK:	Well, try it sometime…it will not only do you good, but help us out. Now go back with the marathon…how do you usually feel after the first fifteen miles?
HARRY:	That all depends on what kind of a car I ride in. If I have to sit in a rumble seat, that tires me out. Of course if I ride in a truck and sit on top of the vegetables, I feel much better.
JACK:	I imagine you must be pretty tired at the finish of a twenty-six-mile Marathon.
HARRY:	Yes, but then I always go to a drug store----
JACK:	I know…and order a glass of Canada Dry Ginger Ale.
HARRY:	<u>No</u>! …I get some bandages for my feet.
JACK:	All right, here's a nice red apple for you. Find yourself a one-way street and do another marathon. Make it <u>sixty miles</u> this time. And now George Olsen will play, "I Love You, Dear", sung by Ethel Shutta and Hotcha Gardner.

3. I LOVE YOU DEAR   ORCHESTRA, SHUTTA & GARDNER

JACK:	During the past month, we held another test of our product known as--- er ---as---- er-----
ANNOUNCER:	Canada Dry Ginger Ale made—to—order by the glass.
JACK:	Oh yes, I remember…. with the right amount of syrup and good in ice cream sodas…. thanks, Hicks.

This time our test took place in the wilds of Borneo…. not East Borneo, not West Borneo or Upper Borneo…or any Borneo that you know. This test was held in New Borneo…which was just Born—eo and not quite a year old—ee….

Its the place where they made that thrilling animal picture called, "Bring 'Em Back Alive…….er, "Bring 'Em Back a Buck" or something like that…… Anyway, it's the place where the Metro-Goldwyn lion was born—ee (ad lib)

As you, all know, the inhabitants of this strange country are very, very wild and live right out in the middle of er…of er….say, George, what do yes call it when silver coins rattle in your pocket?

GEORGE OLSEN: Jingles.

JACK: That's it…. they live right out in the middle of the jungles…. our African representative, Mr. Joe Hannesburg…made this trip to Borneo. When he arrived at the spot where the test was to be conducted, he found the cannibals having a light lunch of roast missionary….and two hunters a la mode. Mr. Hannesburg spoke to the leader of this wild tribe…. Mr. Oscar Wilde…who, by the way, is a large stockholder and owns several shares of American Geo-wild. Well, right after luncheon, he gave each and every one of these wild men a large glass of made—to—order Canada Dry Ginger Ale…. and to the children, he gave a small glass. They immediately drank this precious beverage….they also ate the glasses….and, finally, ate our representative. Unsolicited, we received this letter today from Mr. Wilde. He says:

"WE HAVE TRIED YOUR CANADA DRY GINGER ALE AND IT IS NOT ONLY GOOD IN ICE CREAM SODAS, AS YOU SAY…. BUT IS ALSO GOOD WITH MISSIONARIES….. HUNTERS….AND REPRESENTATIVES."

Another victory for Canada Dry.

Oh yes…. "P.S. WOULD LIKE TO HAVE YOU AND OLSEN HERE FOR OUR NEXT DINNER."

Don't kid yourself, Wilde…. Olsen is tougher than you think he is.

And now George Olsen and his head hunters will play, "All American Girl", sung by Paul Small.

4. ALL AMERICAN GIRL   ORCHESTRA & SMALL

JACK: That was Paul Small singing, "All American Girl". The next number will be a brand new----

SADYE: Hello, Jack Benny.

JACK: Hello, Mary…. I didn't know you were here…. How did you get home the other night?

SADYE: O, all right.

JACK:	Come here and say "hello", Mary…Ladies and gentlemen, I want you to meet little Mary Livingston from Plainfield…who has been coming up here to visit us. [ed. note: this script spells "Livingston" without an "e"]
SADYE:	Hello, people.
JACK:	Hey, Mary did you tell me you live with your folks in Plainfield? With your mother and father?
SADYE:	Yes…and my father is a big doctor in Plainfield.
JACK:	A big doctor there….is that so?
SADYE :	Yes, and he's very expensive, too. He charges <u>twenty-five dollars</u> a visit.
JACK:	Twenty-five dollars…. that's a lot of money for a doctor in Plainfield, isn't it?
SADYE:	Yes, and that's only when you go to see him…. when he comes to see you, he charges <u>fifty</u> dollars.
JACK:	A visit?
SADYE:	Yes.
JACK:	What does it cost to pass him on the street?
SADYE:	Say, is that <u>Small Paul</u> standing over there?
JACK:	Yes, would you like meet him?
SADYE:	Yes, I think he's swell.
JACK:	You think <u>everybody</u> is swell, don't you Mary?
SADYE:	No…. just you and <u>Small Paul.</u>
JACK:	You mean Paul Small…. Paul, come here…. I want you to meet Mary Livingston.
PAUL:	Glad to know you, Miss Livingston.
SADYE:	Same here…. I like your singing very much. We listen in from Plainfield all the time. I like the way you sing, "Lullaby of the Leaves". I've heard you sing it <u>fifty</u> times.
PAUL (embarrassed):	Thanks.
SADYE:	Say, your face is awfully familiar.
PAUL:	Yeah…. seems like I know you, too.
JACK:	Say, Paul, beat it, will you? Mary, can you help us out with something on this program? You know, you been coming up here three or four times already.
SADYE:	Wait, I can crochet the nicest sweater you ever saw.
JACK:	No…. can you sing or do something to entertain?
SADYE:	I don't sing…. but I could tell a story.

JACK:	You could tell a story…. something your folks would approve of?
SADYE:	Yes, they think I'm very clever.
JACK:	All right, tell a story…. Now you're sure it's all right.
SADYE:	Oh yes.
JACK:	Go ahead. And, by the way, is there any place in the story where you can mention Canada Dry Ginger Ale, made-to-order by the glass? After all, our sponsors are paying for your time.
SADYE:	Mention what?
JACK:	Canada Dry Ginger Ale.
SADYE:	Oh, I'll try.
JACK:	All right, go on with the story.
SADYE:	WELL, this story starts on a train going New York to Montreal. About fifty miles out of New York, an old man boarded the train, and this old man carried two large grips and <u>a parasite.</u> WELL, he got on the train with these two large grips and the <u>parasite,</u> and asked the conductor where he could find his berth.
JACK:	Pardon me just a moment, Mary… Mary, you say this gentleman carried…. what?
SADYE:	He carried two large grips and a parasite.
JACK:	I thought I heard that…. You say this gentleman carried a <u>parasite?</u>
SADYE:	Yes, a parasite… you know, <u>an umbrella.</u>
JACK:	I know, an <u>umbrella</u>! So, the old man carried a parasite….and a parasite is an umbrella. Where did you get that?
SADYE:	Oh, out of the cross-word puzzles.
JACK:	Out of the cross-word puzzles…. oh, you <u>still</u> do those…. the puzzles, I mean.
SADYE:	Yes, I like them. I do them every day.
JACK:	I see. And you had one with the word "parasite" and filled it in with "umbrella."
SADYE:	Uh-huh.
JACK:	I imagine it doesn't take you long to work out those puzzles.
SADYE:	Oh, I wish you wouldn't interrupt me, Jack.
JACK:	I'm sorry, Mary.
SADYE:	WELL, ANYWAY…. this old man was a very fine-looking fellow, and he had a long white beard. Well, he found his berth…. got into his pyjamas….and then undressed himself. And as he was lying there…..

JACK:	He got into his pyjamas and <u>then</u> undressed himself…. this fellow was quite adept. This isn't the same old fellow who slept with his beard <u>over</u> the quilts.
SADYE:	No.
JACK:	Oh, I heard a story like that….
SADYE:	ANYWAY….as he was lying there….
JACK (whispers):	Don't forget the Canada Dry Ginger Ale made-to-order by the glass.
SADYE (whispers):	Oh yes, that comes in later…. WELL, as he was lying there, he was reading a book….. something in it about <u>reincarnation</u>….. because the old man believed in reincarnation. Well, he was just about to fall asleep…..
JACK:	You say the old man believed in <u>reincarnation</u>?
SADYE:	<u>He loved flowers.</u>
JACK:	Maybe I'm wrong…. You say he loved flowers…… by that you mean, a reincarnation is a flower.
SADYE:	Yes.
JACK:	And a parasite is an umbrella.
SADYE:	Uh-huh.
JACK:	Whoever rocked your cradle, certainly over-did it. (Whispers to her) Don't forget to mention Canada Dry Ginger Ale made-to-order by the glass.
SADYE (angrily):	Yes…. I'll get to that later, Jack.
SADYE AND JACK (together):	WELL, ANYWAY….
SADYE (alone):	He was just about to fall asleep, when he heard two girls in an upper berth <u>below</u> him.
JACK:	MISS LIVINGSTON.
SADYE AND JACK (together):	WELL, ANYWAY….
SADYE (continuing – alone):	These two girls were holding a conversation that ran something like this…. One girl said to the other, it's so uncomfortable up here…but what can we do. The old man, overhearing the girls talking, took his Grip, put it on the floor… stepped on it…. reached up to the upper berth, opened the curtain…. <u>And what do you think?</u>
JACK:	I don't know…. WHAT?
SADYE:	The girls were drinking CANADA DRY GINGER ALE MADE TO ORDER
JACK:	I suspected that…. Mary, come up here again, but don't tell any more stories.
SADYE:	All right.
JACK:	George, will you introduce the next number?

GEORGE			(Introduces "AND SO TO BED")

5. AND SO TO BED			ORCHESTRA and SHUTTA

SIGNATURE—Rockabye Moon

(DURING ETHEL'S VOCAL OF ROCKABYE MOON---

JACK:		That was the last number of the 29th program on the 8th of August, And So to Bed…. see you all Wednesday night. Good-night, please. Mary, can I take you home tonight?

SADYE:		Thanks, Jack, that would be swell.

[Ed. note: this last page is torn, and the closing announcement is missing.]

August 10, 1932

Jack starts a contest on the show for listeners to guess the names of celebrities. An obnoxious reporter asks everyone questions. The cast makes jokes about a current MGM film release "Strange Interlude," which starred Norma Shearer and Clark Gable. Jack will frequently name-check MGM stars like Gable and Garbo, as he is under contract to the studio. Mary does not appear on this episode of the program, although Jack asks about her whereabouts.

STATION WJZ   PROGRAM CANADA DRY GINGER ALE INC.
        AND   DATE WEDNESDAY, AUGUST 10, 1932
BLUE NETWORK   TIME 9:30 – 10:00 P.M.
SIGNATURE – JOLLY GOOD COMPANY

OPENING ANNOUNCEMENT
1. STRANGE INTERLUDE
DIALOGUE
2. WE'RE DANCING TOGETHER AGAIN   SMALL
DIALOGUE
3. LET'S K-NOCK K-NEEES   SHUTTA & FREY
DIALOGUE
4. AS LONG AS I LIVE   SHUTTA
DIALOGUE
5. OL MAN OF THE MOUNTAIN   GARDNER
DIALOGUE
SIGNATURE – ROCKABYE MOON
CLOSING ANNOUNCEMENT

STATION WJZ   PROGRAM CANADA DRY GINGER ALE INC
        AND   DATE WEDNESDAY, AUGUST 10, 1932
BLUE NETWORK   TIME 9:30 – 10:00 P.M.
SIGNATURE – JOLLY GOOD COMPANY

ANNOUNCER: Ladies and gentlemen. Another half-hour of entertainment about Canada Dry, the champagne of ginger ales, now available by the glass at soda fountains, as well as in bottles for the home. You'll find the new large size bottle very economical and particularly convenient for home use. George Olsen, Ethel Shutta and Jack Benny, the Canada Dry Humorist, again perform for your enjoyment.

George Olsen opens the program with "STRANGE INTERLUDE."

1. STRANGE INTERLUDE   ORCHESTRA

ANNOUNCER: Here he is folks, Jack Benny!

JACK: Hello, folks of the wave length of the people of the radio network audience. This is Jack kilocycle, coming to you thru 760 Bennys. Are you tuned out, hmmmm?... There will be three Guest Stars shot here tonight....and when you hear the three little <u>crimes,</u> it will be exactly the middle of August.

(SOUND EFFECT: THREE SHOTS)

Did you set your watches, hmmm?....Well, tonight, ladies and gentlemen, I am very happy to say that we have no guest stars....no interruptions...no confusion.....just our own happy little family.

HARRY CONN (BREEZILY): Pardon me, are <u>you</u> Jack Benny?

JACK: Yes

HARRY: The <u>real</u> Jack Benny? ...."B" as in Bunk... "E" as in Junk..."E" as in "Punk"....

JACK: Yes, this JACK BENNY…what do you want?

HARRY: Glad to Know you….my name's Lloyd Ribbons…. I'm a newspaper reporter. I'm seeking for some <u>dope</u> on this program.

JACK: Must be Paul Small…. There he is, over there.

HARRY:	No, no.... I mean the dope, the news, the lowdown. Our readers want to know something about George Olsen, Ethel Shutta and yourself. Now, Mr. Benny, you're known as the <u>Slav</u> comedian – aren't you?
JACK:	<u>suave</u> – not Slav.
HARRY:	Mr. Benny, I'd like to get a few interesting news items about you. Tell me, where were you born?
JACK:	Waukegan, Illinois.
HARRY:	Waukegan, eh? …. Well, give me three reasons why.
JACK:	Well, in the first place, I always liked Waukegan… in the second place, it wasn't my fault….and in the third place, what do you mean, <u>three reasons?</u>
HARRY:	Now I'm a very busy man, Mr. Benny. I'm going to ask you a few questions. Just answer "yes" or "no". Have you any sisters or brothers?
JACK:	Yes.
HARRY :	What do they do for a living?
JACK:	No.
HARRY:	I see…. Now, Mr. Benny, what is the <u>secret</u> of your success?
JACK:	WHAT?
HARRY:	What is the <u>secret</u> of your success?
JACK:	Oh, it's a <u>secret</u>, eh?
HARRY:	Just one more question, then I'm thru. I've been listening to all your programs, and I'd like to know <u>what it is</u> your sponsors are trying to sell?
JACK:	Well, I thought we made that clear. They're selling Canada Dry Ginger Ale, made-to-order by the glass.
HARRY :	Oh, is <u>that</u> what it is? No wonder soda clerks thought I was crazy. I've been asking for Fran Freys….well thanks, Mr. Benny. All this will appear in tomorrow's paper.
JACK :	What paper?
HARRY :	Wall paper.
JACK :	I got it….well, I'm glad there are no interruptions tonight…..And now George Olsen and his orchestra will----
HARRY :	Is <u>that</u> George Olsen?
JACK :	Yes.
HARRY :	Of Olsen and Johnson?
JACK :	No…..of Wheeler and Woolsey.

HARRY:	Well, that's just who I want….Now, Mr. Olsen----
JACK:	Wait until he plays the next number, and you can talk to him later. And now George Olsen, of Laurel and Hardy, will play, "We're Dancing Together Again". It will be sung by Paul Small, of Amos 'n' Andy.

3.WE'RE DANCING TOGETHER AGAIN   ORCHESTRA & SHALL

JACK:	You have just heard Paul Small sing, "We're Dancing Together Again," played by George Olsen and his----
HARRY:	Can I talk to George Olson Now?.....Thanks. …..oh, Mr. Olse----
JACK(aside):	Well, he <u>asked</u>, anyway.
GEORGE:	Yes, that's me.
HARRY:	Lloyd Ribbons in my name. I'm the crack reporter on our paper, and I'd like to ask you a few questions.
GEORGE:	A reporter, eh?..... Do you know Walter Winchell?
HARRY:	No, what's his name?
JACK:	Ed Sullivan.
HARRY:	Well, Mr. Olsen, how old are you?
GEORGE:	I'm going on twenty-eight.
HARRY:	Going on twenty-eight, eh?
JACK:	That's been going on for some time, ladies and gentlemen… This is Jack Benny talking.
HARRY:	Quiet …. now where were your born?
GEORGE:	PORTLAND!
HARRY:	Portland, Oregon….or Portland, Maine?
JACK:	Portland Cement….that was cement for a laugh, folks.
GEORGE:	Jack….please!
HARRY:	Now, Mr. Olsen, what do you do for pastime….what's your hobby?
GEORGE:	Horses.
JACK:	<u>Hobby</u> horses….great sport.
HARRY:	NO, I mean what do you do for recreation?

George:	Oh, I read a lot.
HARRY:	Is that so? What is your favorite book?
JACK:	The first National Bank…and <u>what</u> a volume he's got.
GEORGE:	Ssh! Jack, <u>please</u>….well, I like Shakespeare, Homer and…
HARRY:	How do you like <u>Bacon</u>?
JACK:	<u>Crisp</u> --- this is Strange Interlude Benny talking.
HARRY:	Thank <u>you.</u>
JACK:	<u>Thank Heaven!</u>…….Now Ethel Shutta will sing----
HARRY (quickly):	Is <u>that</u> Ethel Shutta ever there?
JACK:	No.
HARRY:	Oh, Miss Shutta.
ETHEL:	Yes?
JACK:	Ethel, this is Lloyd Ribbon, a newspaper reporter. He represents the Mourning Become-Electra.
ETHEL:	How do you do?
HARRY:	Glad to meet you, Miss Shutta.
JACK:	Ethel, take him away somewhere and talk, so that I can introduce the next number.
HARRY:	This is only going to take a <u>second</u>. Mr. Benny…..Now, Miss Shutta, a lot of people have been writing us, inquiring about you….how you look….your habits….your desires, and so on.
ETHEL:	Well, what would you like to know?
HARRY:	Are you married or single?
ETHEL:	I'm married to George Olsen.
JACK:	Give him three good reasons why, Ethel.
ETHEL:	Well, I….er… er…I….Now, Jack, this is my interview, not yours.
JACK:	I'm just trying to help you, that's all.
ETHEL:	Well, I know more about myself than you do.
HARRY:	Never mind—I'll just put down "<u>single</u>".
ETHEL:	But I'm <u>not</u> single – I'm married to George Olsen.
ANNOUNCER:	Even during an interview, Canada Dry Ginger Ale is sold by the glass at all fountains, and everybody's drinking it.

HARRY:	<u>Who</u> is that?
JACK:	Why, that's George Hicks, our announcer.
HARRY (quickly):	Where was he born?.....Never mind, I'll get him later....Now Miss Shutta, just one more second, tell me the story of your life.
JACK:	<u>So long,</u> folks……I'll be back in three weeks.
ETHEL:	Well, my life has been a very sad and interesting one….I was born in Springfield----
HARRY:	Ohio, Missouri, Massachusetts or Illinois?
ETHEL:	No, <u>Springfield</u>.
HARRY:	Well, I'll just put down OHIO, it's shorter….Now go ahead.
ETHEL:	Of course I don't remember much about the first three or four years of my life. But when I was five years old, I had a birthday party and I sang my <u>first</u> song..
	(sings) Shine on, Shine on, Harvest Moon up in the sky, I ain't had no lovin' since----
JACK & ETHEL (together):	January, February----
JACK (alone):	Canada Dry.
ETHEL (resuming):	Everybody loved the way I sang that song, and the next day I took up dancing and studied very hard until I reached the age of eighteen and arrived on Broadway. Then came the struggle…..
HARRY:	<u>Struggle</u>….that's S-T-R-U-G-G-L-E. isn't it?
ETHEL:	Yes…..and I struggled….and struggled….and struggled…and struggled
JACK:	Ethel, stop struggling….we have got to get on with the program.
ETHEL:	Finally, after two years of hardship and privation, <u>opportunity</u> knocked at my door--- and……
JACK:	Were you listening, Ethel?
ETHEL:	I got my first chance on Broadway in a musical comedy success called "<u>Louis, the 14th</u>."
JACK:	And this in <u>August, the 10th</u>….<u>how time files.</u>
ETHEL:	THEN CAME THE DAWN-----
JACK:	That was George Olsen----
ETHEL:	Yes, I met George, and it was a case of love at first sight.
HARRY:	That's very interesting, Miss Shutta. Continue.

ETHEL: And then George and I-----

JACK & ETHEL (together):   ….struggled and struggled and struggled and struggled….

(DURING THIS SOUND EFFECT: Phone rings.)

JACK: Oh, pardon me…hello!...yes, Mr. Ribbons?....Hey, reporter! It's for you.

HARRY: Pardon me, Miss Shutta, it must be the office….hello, hello…yes, I'm here with the Canada Dry program….yes, I gotcha…you want me to drop these guys and interview Russ Columbo? Sure, it's a pleasure, good-bye.

(SOUND EFFECT: Click of receiver)

So long folks, I have to rush away…. see you some other time.

ETHEL: Well, what do you think of that?

JACK: Ethel, remind me to hate that guy…….Can you imagine a rat like that, wasting our time?....Anyway, Ethel, your story was very interesting.

ETHEL: I think that was the meanest thing I ever heard of.

JACK: Aw, don't worry about it, Ethel….And now, ladies and gentlemen, Ethel Shutta and Fran Frey will sing, "Let's K-nock K-nees". It will be played by George Olsen and his boys, who will struggle…and struggle…and struggle….thru this number.

3. LET'S K-NOCK K-NEES   ORCHESTRA & SHUTTA & FREY

JACK: This is Jack Benny again, without a reporter…Now I would like to read a letter that come to us this morning from a lady in Mackeesport, MacPennsylvania… She writes:

"DEAR BY-THE-GLASS AT ALL FOUNTAINS:

I CAN DRINK YOUR CANADA DRY GINGER ALE WITH OR WITHOUT ICE CREAM, BUT I CANNOT DRINK IT WITHOUT PRIZES. WHY DON'T YOUR PROGRAM GIVE SOMETHING AWAY?....I HAVE FURNISHED A HOME COMPLETE WITH PRIZES GIVEN OUT BY DIFFERENT PROGRAMS.

WE HAVE A BEAUTIFUL RUG WHICH WAS THIRD PRIZE ON THE FINK'S MULES PROGRAM. THE PICTURES ON OUR WALLS ARE SECOND PRIZES WHICH WE WON THROUGH A HARD STRUGGLE---- oh, you're going to start that, too! ON THE NEVERBEND CARPET TACK HOUR…AND WE HAVE FIVE LOVELY LITTLE CHILDREN…WHICH WAS OUR OWN IDEA.

NOW WHY HAVE YOU STOPPED CONTESTS AND DISCONTINUED GIVING OUT VALUABLE PRIZES?

HOPING TO HEAR FROM YOU BY RETURN HITCH-HIKE, I AM

YOURS TRULY

MRS. FRANCIS A. <u>TIZZ</u>

  PS. NEVER MIND.

  Well, all right, Mrs. Tizz…we have received thousands of other letters in the same tone, and a battleship doesn't have to run into us to tell us what's what. So, immediately after the next number, we are going to give you --- not a contest, mind you – but a game to play, and our prizes will be just as good as you would get from a contest.

  <u>Meanwhile</u>, while I am preparing the rules of this game, Ethel Shutta will sing and George Olsen will play, "As Long As I Live"….I was afraid of that.

4. AS LONG AS I LIVE   ORCHESTRA & SHUTTA

JACK: And now, folks, here comes the thing you have waiting for – the big opportunity to win our valuable prizes.   (LOUD FANFARE)

  All right, boy, bring our prizes in.

(SOUND EFFECT: LOUD GLASS CRASH)

  There goes the third prize…. well, we'll have to have that fixed…Bring the second prize in, boys…….

(SOUND EFFECT: HEAVY WATER SPLASH)

  That's our second prize….the <u>Hudson River</u>….Boys, keep the river away from my door….All right, boys, bring in our first prize.

(SOUND EFFECT: HEAVY FOOT STEPS)

  That's Jumbo….our India elephant…say something to the folks, Jumbo.

(SOUND EFFECT: HEAVY ELEPHANT SHORT)

  And now, ladies and gentlemen, we are going to give you a new kind of test tonight…not a contest, mind you…..a cross-word puzzle or a limerick…. but a real battle of wits for our customers. All you need for this brain-teaser, folks, is a sheet of paper, a pencil, a Public Library and <u>six years</u> of your spare time…. ARE YOU READY?....We will give you just <u>five seconds</u> to close your stores…. clear up your business, feed the cat…and enter this test. Now here's the idea of this game. We will give you a <u>hint</u> as to the identity of certain great celebrities….either historical, literary, political or theatrical…..<u>that is</u>, all we will give you is a description and tell you the <u>first</u> name, and you must guess who they are and fill in the <u>entire</u> name. So put your thinking caps on…and here goes!

  <u>Celebrity Number One</u>… this man was a great American poet. His first name was Henry….middle initial "W," which I think stands for Wadsworth…. and his last

name…now <u>that</u> is what you have to fill in. Write it out clearly, but don't make it so <u>long</u> that a <u>fellow</u> can't read it….Get it?...... Now this first one should not take <u>over three days.</u>

The next one, folks, is really <u>very</u> difficult, so please concentrate. This one is a woman…a famous Swedish moving-picture star under contract to Metro-Goldwyn-Mayer, who has just returned to her native country for a short vacation. She has starred in such pictures as GRAND HOTEL, MATA HARI and MATA HOOEY….Her first name in Greta…and her last name starts with "G" and rhymes with Cargo…And now to give you a little hint…AY TANK AY GO HOME NOW. Have you got it?.... Now if anybody has Joan Crawford marked down, you might as well scratch it off and start all over again. This one should not take over twenty-minutes….It is tests like these that sharpen the brain and make sponsors advertise on street cars…Oh, well.

Now the next one is even more difficult, but it should carry you into the winter. This man is a very famous statesman…a dictator of a certain European country. It would not be fair to mention the country. However, the first syllables of two of its principal cities are VEE and NAP….If you have <u>Venice</u> and <u>Naples</u>, that's a good start….

And now for the brain twister..the <u>first</u> name of this man is Benito….Of course the last name is up to you. That's <u>your</u> worry…not ours, we can't give out prizes and tell you who it is, too…of course, if you're still in the dark, I might mention that there's a girl up here tonight with a <u>mussolin</u> dress on…Now that's <u>all</u> we can tell you.

And now we will give you a short one. This should be easy – a famous Hollywood moving-picture star…a man. His first name is <u>Clark,</u> and that's all we are going to tell you. Figure this out for yourself if you're <u>GABLE.</u> Now to show you how difficult they really are, will some young lady in the audience kindly step up.

ETHEL SHUTTA: I'll try.

JACK: Thank you…what's your name?

ETHEL: Ethel Shutta.

JACK: Sarah Jones…Now, Miss Jones, here's one for you. This is made-to-order by the glass and sold at all fountains, and everybody's drinking it…It's <u>first</u> name is CANADA and you must guess the second name. It rhymes with PIE and it is <u>not</u> wet. No, what is it?

ETHEL: DAMP.

JACK: No, no…come on now. I'll give you a little hint --- (sings) How dry I am. how dry I am..What's what?

ETHEL: That's awful.

JACK: You see how difficult it is, folks…so just give this test your time and thought. Be sure to have your answers in as soon as possible.

Have you a little elephant running around your house?....Have you a river at your door?...Have you a broken third prize in your china closet?....Well, you can win them all in this test. So go to it, and we're going to bed.

And now Hotcha Gardner will sing, "Old Man Of The Mountain," played by George Olsen and his Gingeralians.

5. OLD MAN OF THE MOUNTAIN   HOTCHA GARDNER AND ORCHESTRA

JACK: That was the last number of the 30th program on the 10th of August. We have had a lot of requests to do another AMATEUR EIGHT, so this will come to you next Monday night…with new stars…new songs…and new pests…And don't forget our prizes!... Say, Ethel, did you see little Mary around tonight?

FRAN FREY: Pardon me, are you Jack Benny?

JACK: Yes.

FRAN: Well, I'm a reporter on the Evening Gazette. I want to ask you a few questions.—

JACK: Oh, You are – eh?

(SOUND EFFECT: TERRIFIC CRASH AND BANG)

Good-night, all. See you Monday.

SIGNATURE---ROCKABYE MOON

ANNOUNCER: Remember you can enjoy Canada Dry, the Champagne of Ginger Ales, anywhere—anytime – for it is now available two ways – either made to order by the glass at soda fountains or in bottles, as always for your home. The new big bottle is particularly economical and convenient. Remember too, that with the exception of a few localities, where freight rates do not permit, you can take back your Canada Dry bottles to the dealer and get a cash refund. You pay for the contents only. Next Monday night at this same time Jack Benny, Ethel Shutta and George Olsen will again entertain you. This is the National Broadcasting Company.

HH

August 15, 1932

Jack and George Olsen trade jokes about who is "cheaper." Jack mentions his "nickel back on the bottle" catch-phrase. Its Opportunity Night, and the program offers amateur performances. Early version of the "Chicken Sisters" skit Jack did for years on radio and in summer stage tours, features the Three Built-Well Sisters, who sing "Would you like to take a walk." Sid Silvers shows up in a bit part, months before he was hired by Canada Dry to spiff up the comedy. Mary does not appear on this episode of the program, but a short letter from her to Jack is read in her voice, at the end of the episode.

STATION WJZ   PROGRAM CANADA DRY GINGER ALE INC.

       AND   DATE MANDAY, AUGUST 15, 1932

       BLUE NETWORK   TIME 9:30 – 10:00

SIGNATURE – JOLLY GOOD COMPANY

OPENING ANNOUNCEMENT

1. RHUMBATISM	GARDNER
	DIALOGUE
2. HONEY SMILE AT ME	SHUTTA
	DIALOGUE
3. IN OLD VIENNA	SHALL
	DIALOGUE
4. ANGEL CAKE LADY	SHUTTA
	DIALOGUE
5. FROM A.M. TO P.M.	FREY
	DIALOGUE

SIGNATURE – ROCKABYE MOON

CLOSING ANNOUNCEMENT

CANADA DRY GINGER ALE INC   MONDAY, AUGUST 15, 1932

SIGNATURE – JOLLY GOOD COMPANY

ANNOUNCER:	Ladies and gentlemen, another half hour of entertainment about Canada Dry – the champagne of ginger ales – now available by the glass at soda fountains, as well as in bottles for the home. You'll find new, large size bottle very economical, and particularly convenient for home use.
	George Olsen, Ethel Shutta, and Jack Benny – the Canada Dry humorist – again perform for your enjoyment. George Olsen opens the program with RHUMBATISM. Hotcha Gardner singing.
1. RHUMBATISM	OCHESTRA & GARDNER
ANNOUNCER:	And now Jack Benny…. just a moment, please, ladies and gentlemen. Say, George have you seen Jack?
OLSEN:	No, he isn't here yet, but I'll take it…. Hello, customers. This is George Olsen speaking…. "Ole" as in Ole Man River… and "Sen" as in Olsen. I am sorry to say that Jack Benny isn't here yet. Something seems to have delayed him, but he should be here any minute. And let me tell you one thing, ladies and gentlemen, Jack is one of the <u>nicest</u> fellows that I've ever worked with. Of course, he's a little bit <u>conservative</u>, but a nice fellow. You know… just a little thrifty. In fact, I <u>could</u> say… Ethel, is Jack here yet?
ETHEL:	No, George.
GEORGE:	There is the <u>cheapest</u> guy I have ever met in my life. Why, he wouldn't give a nickel to see a <u>piano sit on Helen Morgan.</u>
ETHEL:	Oh, I wouldn't say that, George…. especially behind his back. Jack's all right. It's none of <u>our</u> business if he wears the same necktie all your round. Why should <u>you</u> worry if he cuts his own hair? It's unfair.
GEORGE:	I know, Ethel, but you heard the things he's been saying about me. Why, just the other day he told Fran Frey that the tailor who put pockets in my trousers must have a great sense of humor.

ETHEL:	Well Jack's right…. but he should keep it to himself.
GEORGE:	Shh! here he comes.
JACK:	Hello, everybody…. hello. Ethel…how are you, George? Sorry I was late.
GEORGE:	That's all right, Jack. I was batting for you, and I just told the audience that a fine fellow you are.
JACK:	THANKS, George…. Ladies and gentlemen, it was mighty nice of George to help me out. Of course, I don't know what he said about me, but I'm not taking any chances. To keep even with him, let me tell you this: last night Olsen drank <u>three</u> bottles of Canada Dry Ginger Ale in <u>five</u> minutes so he could get the nickels back on the bottles before the store closed…. I guess that evens the score, George. Well, anyway folks, I must apologize and tell you how I happened to be so late this evening.
JACK:	Now don't get alarmed, folks, but I had a slight accident on the way to the studio about fifteen minutes ago.
ETHEL:	What happened, Jack? Anything serious?
JACK:	No, Ethel…. nothing to worry about. You see I am all right. I was walking across the street about a block from here, when a fellow driving a truck ran into me and kept right on going.
ETHEL:	Oh, that's awful, Jack…. are you <u>sure</u> you're not hurt?
JACK:	No, Ethel, I'm fine…just a little nervous, that's all.
ETHEL:	Why, that's terrible. Imagine a fellow hitting you with a truck and then not even stopping. Did you get his number?
JACK:	No, but I'd recognize his laugh <u>any place</u> …. I'll tell you one thing, Ethel … crossing the street in New York is like kissing another man's wife. If you don't do it fast enough, you'll land in the hospital.
ETHEL:	Jack, I can't get over that…. the driver not stopping after hitting you. Why do you suppose he did it?
JACK:	I don't know, Ethel…. unless he heard some of our programs. Oh well, here I am. You can't kill a master of ceremonies.
JACK:	Say, Ethel, who are all those people sitting around with their instruments and everything?
ETHEL:	Hey, those are amateur entertainers. You, remember, this is Opportunity Night.
JACK:	Opportunity Night?
ETHEL:	Yes, Jack…. you announced it last Wednesday. Don't you remember?
JACK:	I did? <u>How time flies</u>… All right, we'll hear from them right after you sing this next number…Ethel will sing, "HONEY, SMILE AT ME," played by Ethel's husband… darn it!

2. HONEY, SMILE AT ME   ETHEL SHUTTA & ORCHESTRA

JACK: And now, folks, I am going to bring to you our amateur entertainers who are here on this night of opportunity…. a chance for newcomers to win fame and fortune on the air… and to be <u>tuned out</u> by some of the best families in the United States. Who knows that amongst our talent tonight there night be another Rudy Vallee…? another Rudy-noff…. another violin……another Mickey Mouse…another Marx Brother…. or another headache? But as I look around at these people, I don't think we need worry.

And now for the entertainers…we will take them in the order in which they arrived. Say, Ethel, who got here first?

ETHEL: Jack, here are three little girls…. Harmony Singers. They've been waiting since six o'clock this morning.

JACK: All right, young ladies. Stop right up to the microphone. How shall I introduce you?

DOROTHY ROSS: We're the Three Built-Well Sisters.

JACK: The Three Built-Well Sisters…that reminds me of <u>another</u> harmony trio, girls.

DOROTHY: You're telling us!

JACK: Of course, you girls are really sisters—aren't you?

DOROTHY: I am… I don't know about the other two.

JACK: What kind of numbers do you girls do? Do you sing <u>close</u> harmony?

DOROTHY: Pardon me?

JACK: I said…do you girls sing <u>close harmony</u>?

DOROTHY: No, we stand about three feet apart.

JACK: I think the further apart you stand, the better it will be for our program. Girls, if I ask any more questions, just ignore me. All right, Miss Builtwell, what are you going to sing?

DOROTHY: You're going to sing the M-M-M song.

JACK: The what?

DOROTHY: The M-M-M song.

JACK: What's the M-M-M song?

DOROTHY: Mm-mm-mm, would you like to take a walk?

JACK: Mm-mm-mm, would you like to take a walk?

DOROTHY: M-M-M Built well.

JACK:	Hmm.
ANNOUNCER:	Those "Mm-mm-mm"'s come to you thru the courtesy of Canada Dry Ginger Ale made to order by the glass and sold at all fountains. <u>And is it good?</u>
ORCHESTRA BOYS:	Mm-mm-mm.
JACK:	All right, George, you know the "Mm-mm-mm" song – don't you?
GEORGE:	Mmm.
JACK:	Ready, girls?
DOROTHY:	Oh, I forgot to tell you that we also whistle and dance in the middle of the chorus.
JACK:	<u>If</u> you get that far.
DOROTHY:	Yes.
JACK:	Go ahead, George.

(ORCHESTRA strikes chord – then into vamp music)

HARMONY TRIO (sing):	Mm-mm-mm, would you like to take a walk?
	Mm-mm-mm, do you think it's gonna rain?
	Mm-mm-mm, ain't you tired of the talkies?
	I prefer the walkies….
JACK (sings):	Nothin' good will come from this.
HARMONY TRIO (singing):	Ah, ah, ah, have you heard the latest song?
	Eh, eh, eh, it's a very pretty strain!
	Mm-mm-mm, how about sarsaparilla?
JACK (sings):	You mean Canada Dry….
HARMONY TRIO (sing):	It's sold at every fountain, too.

(TRIO starts to whistle….)

JACK (ad lib line):	Now they're whistling, folks…go into your dance, girls.

(HEAVY TAP ROUTINE)

Wait a minute, there are people living downstairs.

(DANCING STOPS)

DOROTHY:	Well, how did you like it, Mr. Benny?
JACK:	It would be very good – with Ice cream.

DOROTHY:	Oh, we forgot to tell you something, Mr. Benny. You might not believe it, but that was our <u>first</u> broadcast.
JACK:	Really, girls…. Well, I forgot to tell <u>you</u> something…. you might not believe it, but this is your <u>last</u> broadcast…. How long have you girls been singing?
DOROTHY:	Oh, just a little while. We're really three bathing beauties from Atlantic City.
JACK:	You are? Say, George, do you like bathing beauties?
GEORGE OLSEN:	I don't know…. I never bathed any.
JACK:	George, join the girls…. And now George Olsen and his Non-Bathing Beauties will play, "In Old Vienna". Paul Small will sing while I kick myself for showing up tonight.

3. IN OLD VIENNA   ORCHESTRA & SMALL

JACK:	And now to carry on with our amateurs…. what other people are waiting, Ethel?
ETHEL:	Here's the list, Jack.
JACK:	Oh…three wire walkers…two jugglers…five contortionists…and thirty-two crooners. Tell the crooners not to wait, Ethel. Well, who's next.
SID SILVERS:	I'm next…. I should have been on first.
JACK:	Oh, a fresh guy!... <u>who are you?</u>
SID:	My name's Jessel J. Cantor.
JACK:	Jessel J. Cantor…that's a familiar name, What's the "J" for?
SID:	Jolson.
JACK:	Oh, Jolson…. I see. You left out Richman and Wynn.
SID:	I'll use them later.
JACK:	Well, what do you do in the line of entertainment?
SID:	I'm anemic.
JACK:	You're what?
SID:	I'm <u>anemic</u>… anemic.
JACK:	I know you don't look good…. but what do you do?
SID:	I'm anemic…I <u>imitate</u> people.
JACK:	Oh! you're a <u>mimic</u>.

SID:	Yeah, what's the matter with you?
JACK:	Well, here's your chance. Did opportunity ever knock at your door?
SID:	No, but the wolf has been scratching it.
JACK:	I am only talking to you because I have to…. Well, who will you imitate first? Do you do Chevalier?
SID:	No.
JACK:	Oh, you're the fellow that don't imitate Chevalier. I knew there was one that didn't.
SID:	Who is Chevalier?
JACK:	You'll find him someplace in your name. Well, go ahead with your imitations.
SID:	First, I'll do Eddie Cantor.
JACK:	Eddie Cantor…go ahead.
SID (sings – imitating Chevalier):	I don't care what's down below….
JACK (ad libs over this):	How Eddie has changed.
SID (continues):	Let it rain…let it snow… I am oop on top of ze ranbow, Swipping ze clouds away……
JACK:	Wait a minute, wait a minute, so that's Eddie Cantor?
SID:	Yes.
JACK:	Well, let me introduce myself. I'm Herbert Hoover…. Who else can't you imitate?
SID:	Crosby.
JACK:	Oh, Crosby! Bing Crosby?
SID:	No, his twin brother, Double.
JACK:	Double Cross-by…. Can you imitate Russ?
SID:	Russ who?
JACK:	Russ beef…. now top that one!
SID:	All right, now I'll sing a song like Crosby.
JACK:	Say, wait a minute – this song doesn't start with Mm-mm-mm, does it?
SID:	Oh no, it doesn't start like that.
JACK:	All right, then – go ahead.
SID (sings "Paradise" melody):	And when I hold your hand….Mm-mm-mm….and then I'll…. STOP! you're choking me…stop choking…you're gripping me….

ANNOUNCER: This gripping scene comes to you through the courtesy of Canada Dry Ginger Ale made to order by the glass and sold at all fountains. And now George Olsen and his boys will play, "Angel Cake Lady" sung by Ethel Shutta.

4. ANGEL CAKE LADY   ORCHESTRA & SHUTTA

JACK: That was Ethel Shutta singing, "Angle Cake Lady" …Now who's next?

SEVERAL VOICES (ad lib – together): I was here first, Mr. Benny…. been waiting hours…I'm a juggler…I'd like to sing and dance, etc.…

JACK: Sit down, boys…you'll all get your chance. Maybe not tonight, but remember – everything comes to those who wait.

ETHEL: Say, Jack…. see that gloomy looking fellow over there…with the fur collar on his coat? He hasn't moved or said a word since he came in.

JACK: You mean the fellow with the red nose who needs a shave?

ETHEL: Yes … I feel sorry for him.

JACK: Is he one of the entertainers?

ETHEL: I think so.

JACK: Well, call him over…. Pardon me, <u>young man</u>… are you one of the actors?

RALPH ASHE: <u>WHAT</u>? …What? <u>Me</u> an amateur? <u>Me</u>, a student of Shakespeare? a master of the drama…. a renowned Thespian…. Ye Gods!

JACK: Well, I'm sorry…. what did you come up here for?

RALPH: I'm here to uplift the Theatre.

JACK: Oh, a <u>strong</u> man, eh? Do you think you can do it?

RALPH (explodes): Hah! a <u>tragedian</u>! I have played Hamlet…Richard the Third….and King Lear.

JACK: They haven't got a chance. I got a tip on Burgo King in the fourth race tomorrow. The horse called me up himself…. Play it and get yourself a haircut.

RALPH: Forbear! <u>Cease</u> this hilarity.

JACK: Is there an interpreter in the house? <u>Who are you,</u> anyway?

RALPH: I am Brutus…. I have come here to bury Caesar…not to praise him.

JACK: Caesar isn't here. How about Fran Frey?

RALPH: Ah! Fran Frey looks like Nero…. Here, Nero. (Whistles as to a dog)

JACK: Wait a minute, Brute… <u>I</u> say the funny things on this program. So, <u>you're</u> Brutus, ah?

RALPH:	Forsooth.
JACK:	And two pair of pants…. Brutus, dost thou not recognize me-us?
RALPH:	Nay, nay … for who art thou, stranger-ous?
JACK:	I am Jack-us Benny-us.
RALPH:	Not of Canada Dry-us Ginger Ale-us?
JACK:	So, help us…. Well, proceed, Brutus. What are you going to do?
RALPH:	I shall play Shylock in a scene from Shakespeare's "Merchant of Venice."
JACK:	Ah, Shylock from "Merchant of Venice" …. would you like a little music with this?
RALPH:	If you please.
JACK:	George, play "Shylock, Harvest Moon".
	(ORCHESTRA picks up strain of "HARVEST MOON")
RALPH (starts clearing his throat):	To be or not to be…that is the question….
JACK:	Not to be….is the answer.
RALPH:	Avaunt! and quit my side… let the earth hide me…Thy bones are marrowless… thy blood is cold. Hence, horrible shadow…. unreal mockery…. hence!
	(FRAN FREY goes into terrific laughter)
JACK:	Brutus! thou are brutal. Tell me, have you appeared in any late plays?
RALPH:	Yes, I was in "Grand Hotel-us".
JACK:	Hotel-us what?
RALPH (sings):	Hotel-us, pretty maiden, are there … (SOUND EFFECT: sharp pistol shot)
JACK:	This Closes our Shakespearean series coming to you thru station J-U-N-K. And now, to clear the atmosphere, George Olsen and his Hamlet-and-Egglet Orchestra will play, "From A.M. to P.M.", sung by Fran Frey…. from P.M. to A.M. Isn't this program a mid-summer's night –mare?

5. FROM A.M. TO P.M.   ORCHESTRA & FREY.

JACK:	That was the last number of the 31st program on the 15th of August. Things were so tough on this program that we had to lay off MacDuff …. Oh, Mr. Benny.
ETHEL:	Jack – Jack, here's a telegram for you.
JACK:	Thanks Ethel. Pardon me…. Ethel, this is from Mary in Plainfield…what do you know? It says:

"DEAR JACK: I AM LISTENING HERE TO YOUR AMAREUR NIGHT PROGRAM AND I THINK IT'S SWELL…. FATHER FELL OUT OF A FIFTH STORY WINDOW AND KILLED A CAT…BUT I'LL TRY AND SEE YOU WEDNESDAY. MARY"

Ethel, isn't that sweet? I was wondering why she hasn't been up here… well, folks, I have to leave you now …. See you Wednesday. So good-night …. Good-night, Mary.

MARY'S VOICE: Good-night, Jack.

JACK: Where did that come from?

(ALTERNATE CLOSING IN EVENT MARY'S VOICE IS NOT USED)

(Repeat above speech)

…. to leave you now. See you Wednesday. And as they say in Scotland, <u>sleep tight.</u> Good-night, then.

SIGNATURE – Rockabye Moon.

ANNOUNCER: The next time you stop at a soda fountain for a refreshing drink ask for a glass of Canada Dry, the champagne of ginger ales – it will be made to order for you. And when you buy Canada Dry in bottles for the home, remember that the new big bottle is particularly convenient and economical. Remember too, that with the exception of a few localities, where freight charges do not permit, you can take your Canada Dry bottles back to the dealer and get a cash refund. So that now when you buy Canada Dry you pay for the contents only. Next Wednesday night at this same time Jack Benny, Ethel Shutta and George Olsen will again entertain you. This is the National Broadcasting Company.

August 17, 1932

George Hicks becomes the somewhat-regular announcer, and obnoxiously blares out advertising for Canada Dry. More "nickel back" jokes are made, and Jack and the cast toss around some cute puns about college football season and then-current Broadway productions. Mary, back on the program, offers to be Jack's secretary, but writes a letter to her mother while supposedly taking dictation of Jack's letter to his sponsor. (Another recurring comic bit on the show for years to come). Jack's a football player at the "nickel back" position.

STATION WJZ   PROGRAM CANADA DRY GINGER ALE, INC.

    AND   DATE WEDNESDAY, AUGUST 17, 1932.

BLUE NETWORK   TIME 9:30 10:00 P.M.

SIGNATURE -JOLLY GOOD COMPANY

OPENING ANNOUNCEMENT

1. LIBESTRAUM

DIALOGUE

2. I GUESS I'LL HAVE TO CHANGE MY PLANS   SHUTTA

                                                DIALOGUE

3. I'M YOURS FOR TONIGHT   SHUTTA AND FREY

                                                DIALOGUE

4. AFTER TONIGHT   SMALL

                                                DIALOGUE

5. UP DOWN   SHUTTA

SIGNETURE - ROCKABYE MOON

CLOSING ANNOUNCEMENT

CANADA DRY GINGER ALE, INC.   WEDNESDAY, AUGUST 17, 1932.

SIGNATURE--JOLLY GOOD COMPANY

ANNOUNCER: Ladies and gentlemen. another half-hour of entertainment about Canada Dry, the champagne of ginger ales, now available by the glass at soda fountains, as well as in bottles for the home. You'll find the new large size bottle very economical and particularly convenient for home use. George Olsen, Ethel Shutta and Jack Benny, the Canada Dry humorist, again perform for your enjoyment.

George Olsen opens the program with "LIBESTRAUM".

1. LIBESTRAUM   ORCHESTRA

ANNOUNCER: And now, Jack Benny.

JACK: Hello, followers of this mystery. This is Jack Benny speaking.......George as in Olsen....Ethel as in Shutta...Fran as in Frey....Hotcha as in Gardner....and Paul as in Small....JACK BENNY.

Now tonight, ladies and gentlemen, is the night of nights.... THE BIG NIGHT... in fact, we have been waiting all afternoon for tonight. And here it is <u>yes, sir</u> and <u>ma'am</u>. Now sit back, relax and prepare for this gala occasion.... for tonight we are going to give you exactly what we promised you on Monday night......regardless of expense. Our word is our bond, and you know what bonds are right now. However, when we promise a certain type of program, we give it to you. So tonight we are going to present to you at this time er er --Ethel, what did we promise the folks for tonight?

ETHEL: Nothing, Jack.

JACK: So, ladies and gentlemen, I take great pleasure in introducing to you NOTHING.

(CHORD)

(ROUND OF APPLAUSE)

JACK: Don't worry, folks, that was NOTHING...so you didn't miss anything. But it is still a great night...a night for romance and poetry. The moon is shining...the stars are twinkling...Ethel, do you know any poems that would fit a night like this?

ETHEL: Yes, I know one, Jack.

JACK: Let's hear it.

ETHEL:	twinkle, twinkle, little star, How I wonder what you are, Up above the world so high...
JACK:	Imagine! .... drinking Canada Dry.
ANNOUNCER:	This champagne of Ginger Ales can now be bought by the glass, with the right amount of syrup and especially good in ice cream sodas.
JACK:	I knew that was coming. I knew it...I knew it...Ah, Hicksie, what <u>are</u> we going to do with you? Well, anyway, I'm on time tonight. And <u>oh, yes</u>...say George, do you remember when I was late Monday night and you started the program for me?
GEORGE:	Yes, Jack...why?
JACK:	Well, several of my friends listened in and they told me you made a few wisecracks about me.
GEORGE:	Yeah?
JACK:	<u>Yes</u>....they told me you said I wouldn't give a nickel to see a piano sit on Helen Morgan. Did you say that?
GEORGE:	Yes, <u>I said it</u>.... <u>what about it?</u>
JACK:	Oh, nothing, George. I just wanted to know if my friends were lying-- that's all.... This is Jack Benny taking it. And, Ethel, I'm a little bit surprised at some of the things <u>you</u> said about me, too. I heard all about it.
ETHEL:	What did I say, Jack?
JACK:	Oh, you know what you said, Ethel....that I cut my own hair and wore the name necktie all year round. I heard all about it.
ETHEL:	Well, it was all in the spirit of fun. Why, we're all <u>one, big happy family</u>.
JACK:	I know, Ethel, but <u>I'M</u> supposed to be the master of ceremonies on this program. You know <u>I</u> have to do all the panning.
ETHEL:	Well, Jack, tell me what is the real meaning of "master of ceremonies"?
JACK:	Well, the <u>master</u> of ceremonies is the <u>boss</u> of everything...you know, the <u>head man</u>.... the <u>master</u>. Now I'll show you what I mean, Ethel...HEY, FRAN! Come over here and sing, "LULLABY OF THE LEAVES."
FRAN FREY:	Aw, sing it yourself!
JACK:	There you are, Ethel...<u>I'M</u> the master. One for all....and all on me!
ETHEL:	Jack, isn't there a song...something about a master of ceremonies?
JACK:	Yes, Ethel..."Master's in the cold, cold ground."

ETHEL:	I like that song, and I think there ought to be more masters in the cold, cold ground.
JACK:	And now, ladies and gentlemen, Ethel Shutta will sing, "I GUESS I'LL HAVE TO CHANGE MY PLANS," played by George Olsen and his polite hoodlums.... Say, Ethel......
ETHEL:	Don't bother me.
JACK:	I'm strictly the boss up here.... Go ahead, George.
GEORGE:	I know my business...don't tell me what to do.
JACK (LAUGHS QUIETLY CALLS):	Well, anyway, my dog likes me.... Here, Fido!
(SOUND EFFECT: GROWL OF DOG)	
	You, too?

2. I GUESS I'LL HAVE TO CHANGE MY PLANS   ETHEL SHUTTA & ORCHESTRA

JACK:	Hello, everybody...this is Jack Benny, <u>the Boss</u>, again.
ORCHESTRA:	Shut up.
JACK:	And now, folks--
SADYE:	Stop hollering at Jack like that. You fellows have a lot of nerve. He's doing the best he can. I think Jack is <u>swell</u>, and it's a shame the way you're all picking on him.
JACK:	Mary, Mary....you mustn't interfere like that. Please sit over here and be quiet.
SADYE:	I don't care.... nobody can talk to you like that.
JACK:	Oh, it's all right, Mary, We're all friends. That's what they're supposed to say. We rehearsed it that way.
SADYE:	Yes? Well, I think it's swell. (LAUGHS)
JACK:	All right, Mary, sit down.
SADYE:	Oh, thanks for the peanuts you sent me, and I---
JACK:	All right, Mary see you later...And now, folks, let's see----where was I? .... Oh, yes, yes...
	You know, folks, we are certainly tickled to death with the results we got from the Brain Test last Wednesday night. It was a great success and you'd be surprised how quickly this contest was solved. <u>Hundreds</u> of answers came in the day <u>after</u> the contest and <u>thousands</u>, the day <u>before</u> .... which is quick thinking on the part of our listeners. In fact, we have answers right now to contests that we don't know anything about. So, you see our customers are all alert.

Now as to the winners of our prizes: as we expected, <u>everyone</u> guessed the answers correctly. There were no losers, so we gave the prizes to three of our friends, just as you would.

Our first prize which was a combination <u>fly-and crooner swatter</u>, mind you, went to Mrs. Ima Litvak....92 Blintza Street, Borshton, Mass.......with a cold potato.

The second prise which was a 7-day cruise on a Staten Island Ferryboat went to Captain J. Swaabber Deck of the S.S."Malaria." Our third prize - which was a genuine Olympic hundred-yard dash went to Karl von Schnitzel-Spitzenbergen, the owner of a two-yard <u>dash-hunt</u>.

Congratulations, Schmitz!

Now in conclusion, ladies and gentlemen, let me add that these prizes were given away cheerfully and cannot be returned or exchanged. We did not ask you to win them.

Of course, these educational brain tests have done a great deal for the public.... broadening their minds, hips and shoulders.... It has even helped college students. Here are some of the testimonials we have received so far from our most important schools and colleges. Here is one from Nicholas Murray Butler...<u>three</u> fine fellows. He says:

"IT IS BRAIN TESTS LIKE YOURS THAT KEEP OUR <u>FRESHMEN FRESH</u>...... AND MAKE OUR <u>SOPHOMORES SOPHOR</u>....Now, Nickey.

Here's another one from the professor of Economics, Comics and Pastromics...... at <u>Lafayette</u> U. He says: "YOUR BRAIN TEST OF WEDNESDAY NIGHT WAS A REVELATION. THE DEAN BOUGHT A LOLLIPOP AND STARTED LIFE ALL OVER AGAIN.".......Lafayette! I am still here.

Here is one from the U. of ME....er..<u>MAINE</u>, isn't it?..........It reads: "YOUR BRAIN TEST WAS A HUGE SUCCESS HERE AND WE ARE ALL DRINKING CANADA DRY BY THE <u>STEIN</u>....SONG."...We don't care <u>how</u> you drink it, as long as you drink it.

Of course, we haven't the time to read all of the testimonials, but I would like to acknowledge a few.

We received one from a ladies' school.... from a Professor Helen Kane of Boop-Boop....Purdue, Indiana. And one more from a Chinese college...the U. of <u>WASH</u>.... and so forth and so on. We could read <u>youse</u> about these <u>u's</u> for a long time, but what's the <u>use</u>?.... Thank you, Professors! These testimonials are very encouraging. Seeing that you like this contest, we will have another one in the near future. So stand by, colleges! We won't tell you what the prizes will be...but HARVARD- you like to win a nice <u>live algebra</u>?....You would, eh?... Well, follow our contests and you never can tell when one of our prizes will sneak up and bite you. And now George Olsen and his boys will play......

ETHEL: Say, Jack, did you ever go to college?

JACK: Certainly, Ethel, but I had to quit. I sprained my ukulele finger.

ETHEL:	What school did you go to?
JACK:	I went to the Canada Dry University. I was on the football team.
ETHEL:	Oh, a football player, eh? Were you a half-back or a quarter-back?
JACK:	I was the <u>nickel-back</u> on the bottle.... you know, the quart bottles. And now George Olsen and his half-wits...er, half-backs.... will play "I'M YOURS FOR TONIGHT" .... while I think up some more <u>punts</u>...Oh yes, Ethel and Fran are going to sing...and it's Yale's ball.

3. I'M YOURS FOR TONIGHT   ETHEL, FRAN AND ORCHISTRA

JACK:	Now in contrast to our Monday night's program when we had Amateur Night and you heard some of the world's worst actors, <u>tonight</u> we have with us those who have already <u>made</u> their mark in the theatrical world...those that are right on top. Now don't get anxious, folks.... Garbo is <u>not</u> with us. But you are familiar with those who did show up, and I will now introduce them to you. First, I want you to meet one of the stars from that great New York success, "THE <u>CAT</u> AND THE <u>FIDDLE</u>" .... Now meet <u>The Cat</u>.
VOICE:	Meew!
JACK:	Hold your seats...and now <u>The Fiddle</u>.
	(VIOLIN two bars of "Paradise")
	That's all, boys...thanks for coming up...Now how would you like to hear the <u>Band</u> from "The Bandwagon" .... All right:
	(4-piece orchestra plays a bit from "HI-LEE-HI-LO")
	That sounds more like Olsen's Bandwagon.
	And now who do you think we have here tonight! Sit back and I'll tell you. Ladies and gentlemen, I take great pleasure in introducing to you <u>The Whistle</u> from "Show Boat."
	(SOUND EFFECT: STEAMBOAT WHIATLE)
	We are very fortunate getting all these Broadway stars up here tonight, folks. And now may I present to you <u>the hen</u> from "Eggs (x) Marks the Spot." Meet the hen, folks.
	(SOUND EFFECT: HEN'S CACKLE)
	Pick up these eggs, George. At least we got our breakfast out of this scene. And now, how would you like to meet the <u>Three Little Greeks</u> from "The Greeks Had a Word for It." Folks, I want you to meet.... what's your name?
FIRST GREEK:	Concertino.

JACK:	Concertino....and yours?
SECOND GREEK (BALDWIN):	Banjo.
JACK:	And you? .... I suppose your name is <u>Cornet</u>.
HARRY CONN:	<u>No, Nico</u>las
JACK:	Well, don't forget that you get a <u>nickel</u> back on every quart bottle of Canada Dry. And this goes for you, too, folks. Now, boys, tell us what was that word the Greeks had for <u>it</u>?
HARRY CONN:	Opple dompling.
JACK:	There you are, folks.... What other program gives you this information?
BALDWIN:	Who wants it?
VOICE:	Say, Mr. Benny, you haven't introduced me yet.
JACK:	Who are you?
VOICE:	My name's Alec.
JACK:	Alec who?
VOICE:	Alec-trician.
JACK:	What show are you with?
VOICE:	"Mourning becomes Electric".
JACK:	I see....an electrician from "Mourning becomes Electric"......say something, Alec.
VOICE:	Well, I'm glad you nominated me, and if you'll give me your <u>volts</u>, I'll try to do <u>watts-watt</u>. I am happy to <u>ampere</u> here tonight ….
JACK:	All right, Alec....we have other stars to be introduced. And now, ladies and gentlemen last but not least - I want you all to meet that famous star, MR. LUKE WARM of "Strange Inter<u>luke</u>". Say hello to the folks, Luke.
ANOTHER VOICE (NASAL TONE):	Howdy, folks.... glad to be here tonight, and I just want to say that I always drink Canada Dry --
JACK:	I'm sorry you can't stay with us, Luke. But, ladies and gentlemen, these stars all have to rush back to their respective shows where they are appearing nightly.... Thank you thank you. Next week, folks, we are going to try to bring you the four Marx Brothers -Groucho Sloucho Poucho and No Doubt-cho. And now all our stars will have to get-outcho, while George Olsen plays, "After Tonight", sung by Paul Small.

4. AFTER TONIGHT   SMALL AND ORCHESTRA

JACK: Well, folks, all our celebrities just left us, so we can go on with our regular program. I know that you are all interested------

SADYE: Oh, Jack...Jack....can I talk to you now?

JACK: Certainly, Mary....where did you disappear to?

SADYE: I was sitting right over there. I didn't want to butt in while all those big Broadway stars were here.

JACK: That would have been all right, Mary. I'll bet you were thrilled weren't you?

SADYE: Yeah. I saw all those shows, but I don't remember seeing all those people. Say, Jack, I really stopped up here on my way home to ask you something, if you don't mind.....I.....I.....

JACK: No - go right ahead, Mary. What is it?

SADYE: Well, I was just wondering if.....well....I thought maybe...you might need a secretary or something. You know, Jack....I do that kind of work...that is, I could.....and.... well.....I'd kind a like to work for you.....if you happened to need anybody......and, well.....

JACK: Well, Mary, I don't know -- I really <u>could use</u> a secretary.... even if it is just to answer my fan mail.

SADYE: Well, I mean something <u>steady</u>.

JACK: Oh, I see.....Well, Mary, maybe if you didn't want <u>too much</u> salary, I could take you on as my secretary. Of course, that all depends. Now how much would you want a week?

SADYE: Well, I don't know - on account of this being <u>my first</u> job, would seventy-five dollars a week be too much?

JACK: Why, Mary, that's pretty steep. But I <u>could</u> start you off with <u>twenty</u> dollars a week.

SADYE: What would be swell.

JACK: All right, Mary, it's all set. And you can start working right now. Let's take a letter.

SADYE: Excuse me a minute till I get my notebook and a pencil. (A little away from the "mike") I suppose I'll have to call you <u>Mr. Benny</u> from now on.

JACK: I suppose so......Are you ready, Mary?

SADYE: Yes.

JACK: All right - "Dear sponsors of Canada Dry Ginger Ale, made-to-order by the glass, and sold at all fountains, also good in ice cream sodas and a nickel back on the quart bottles - Now for the letter;

	"Next Monday night we are going to have another novelty program - a Carnival Night -- with sideshows, freaks, bands, popcorn and peanuts .... Imagine, sitting home at your radio and enjoying an <u>outdoor</u> carnival. Well, that's what we're going to give you. I understand, sponsors, that you very seldom listen in to our program, but try not to miss this one."
	That's all, Mary - sign it - never mind, I'll sign it myself. Suppose you read it back to me.
SADYE:	"Mrs. Rebecca Livingston, Plainfield. "Dear Ma, I just got a job as Jack Benny's secretary, and I know I'm going to like working for him as the work is very easy and I think he's swell. Your loving daughter, Mary."
JACK:	That's good, Mary. You didn't miss a word.... Now get here early tomorrow morning, Mary, as I have several mistakes to make and I want you to help me out.
SADYE:	I'll be here.
JACK:	Oh, Mary, if you want to wait a few minutes until after our program, I'll see you home.
SADYE:	Jack, why didn't you say so before?
JACK:	Why, Mary?
SADYE :	I just made a date with Strange Inter<u>luke</u>.
JACK:	That's all right Mary....I think he's swell.... <u>how do you like that</u>, George? ....Play the next number.

5. UP DOWN   ETHEL SHUTTA & ORCHESTRA

JACK:	That was the last number on the thirty-second program on the 17th of August. I'll be seeing you next Monday night...and don't forget our Carnival. Good night, then.... Can you imagine, making a date with Strange Interluke?......
SIGNATURE -- Rockabye Moon	
ANNOUNCER:	Remember you can enjoy Canada Dry, the champagne of ginger ales, anywhere -
	anytime - for it is now available two ways - either made to order by the glass at soda fountains or in bottles, as always, for your home. The new big bottle is particularly economical and convenient.
	Remember too, that with the exception of a few localities, where freight rates do not permit, you can take back your Canada Dry bottles to the dealer and get a cash refund, you pay for the contents only. Next Monday night at this same time Jack Bonny, Ethel Shutta and George Olsen will again entertain you. This is the National Broadcasting Company.

August 22, 1932

Jack and the cast attend a carnival, away from the present-ness of being around the microphone at the radio broadcast studio. They visit a weight guessing booth and encounter an obnoxious hot dog vendor, who throws a great insult at Jack. Jack performs a monologue skit playing a side-show barker. Mary continues to be a part of the show.

STATION WJZ   PROGRAM CANADA DRY GINGER ALE, INC.

      AND   DATE MONDAY, AUGUST 22, 1932

      BLUE NETWORK   TIME 9:30 – 10:00 P.M.

SIGNATURE – JOLLY GOOD COMPANY

OPENING ANNOUNCEMENT

1. CARNIVAL DAYS ARE HERE AGAIN   FRAN FREY

                                                                    DIALOGUE

2. ROCKABYE MOON   SHUTTA

                                                                    DIALOGUE

3. WHAT A SWEET SENSATION   FRAN FREY

                                                                    DIALOGUE

4. AS LONG AS LOVE LIVES ON   SMALL

                                                                    DIALOGUE

5. THE LITTLE GERMAN BAND   ETHEL SHUTTA

CLOSING ANNOUNCEMENT

STATION   PROGRAM CANADA DRY GINGER ALE, INC.

WJZ AND   BLUE NETWORK   DATE MONDAY, AUGUST 22, 1932

                                      TIME 9:30 – 10:00 P.M.

SIGNATURE – JOLLY GOOD COMPANY

ANNOUNCER: Ladies and gentlemen, another half hour of entertainment about Canada Dry – the champagne of ginger ales – now available by the glass at soda fountains, as well as in bottles for the home. You'll find the new, large size bottle very economical, and particularly convenient for home use. George Olsen, Ethel Shutta, and Jack Benny – the Canada Dry Humorist – again perform for your enjoyment.

George Olsen and Fran Frey open the program with "CARNIVAL DAYS ARE HERE AGAIN" – in fact they are and right now we are about to take you with us to the Carnival.

1. CARNIVAL DAYS ARE HERE AGAIN   ORCHESTRA & FRAN FREY

(SOUND EFFECT: START CALLIOPE MUSIC ATMOSPHERIC SOUNDS AND COMPLETE UNDER THE FOLLOWING DIALOGUE -)

ANNOUNCER: And now, folks, here's Jack Benny, the Master of Carnival Ceremonies!

JACK: Hello, fun-seekers…don't be alarmed. This is not a parade passing your house nor a concert in your backyard. This is CARNIVAL NIGHT on the Canada Dry Program. Imagine! Bringing a carnival up to the studio to entertain our customers. Say, if we thought you would like it, we would bring NIAGARA FALLS up here. There is nothing for good for you folks.

ANNOUNCER: This carnival come to you thru the courtesy of Canada Dry Ginger Ale----

JACK: Wait a minute, Hicks…. this is Carnival Night…. a night of fun, so stop talking about Canada Dry Ginger Ale made-to-order by the glass – and good in ice-cream sodas.

ANNOUNCER: Also sold by the bottle at all stores – with a cash refund on each bottle.

JACK: I'll have to learn that…Say, George, get Ethel and we'll go out and have some fun. Have you got any money?

GEORGE: No, Jack – you lay it out and we'll split it later.

JACK: I knew that…that was George Olsen speaking, folks…. All right, come on, Ethel.

ETHEL: Oh boy, do I love carnivals. Let's go!

JACK: You know, Ethel, I haven't been to one since I was ten years old.

ETHEL: Are carnivals *that old*?

JACK: That was Ethel Shutta digging…. Come on, George…there's the merry-go-round over there.

ETHEL: The merry-go-round…. say, that's where George and I used to go round together.

JACK: I see, Ethel…and George hasn't got off yet …. Well, it looks like every thing's opening up, let's go!

(SOUND EFFECT: GONG RINGS. MERRY-GO-ROUND MUSIC IN BACKGROUND, WATER TANK SPLASH. BARKERS YELLING, ETC.)

BALDWIN (WALKING TOWARD MIKE): step up, folks… try your luck …six balls for a dime…knock down the dummy and win one of our handsome prizes…Come on, boys, try your luck…knock down the dummy…knock down the dummy….

HOTCHA GARDNER (WALKING TOWARD MIKE): Get you toy balloons…. something for the kiddies… toy balloons….

JACK: George, do you want a balloon?

GEORGE: No, I want a hot dog.

FRAN FREY (WALKING TOWARD MIKE): All right, Miss, you don't have to go any further. Step right over here…. (into mike) Step right up, folks, get your correct weight …. your weight *free* if I don't guess it within *half a pound*…. Come on. How about you, Buddy?

JACK: Go ahead, George…. I always wanted to know what you weigh.

ETHEL: Go on, George, see if he can guess it.

GEORGE: All right.

FRAN: Let me see…you weigh one hundred and five pounds…one hundred and five…. now sit in that chair, I never miss….

(SOUND EFFECT: SQUEAK OF CHAIR)

There you are…one hundred and ninety…ten cents, please…. come on, folks. Your correct weight here.

JACK: He certainly came close.

ETHEL: Do you know he was eighty-five pounds out of the way?

JACK: Well, he didn't figure on George's pocketbook.

GEORGE: I want a hot dog.

HARRY CONN:	Hot corn…hot corn…popcorn…corn-on-the cob…. cornstarch….and ice cream corns.
JACK:	You forgot <u>corn cure.</u>
HARRY C.:	That's what I'm selling…I couldn't think of it.

          (OBOE STARTS TO PLAY ORIENTAL MUSIC--ACCOMPANIED BY DRUM)

          JACK SHUTTA (WALKING TOWARD MIKE)

          Step this way, folks…the treat you've been waiting for…. the <u>only</u> show of its kind on the Midway…this comes to you once in a lifetime…so (INTO MIKE) STEP RIGHT THIS WAY, Iadies and gentlemen, and see those <u>dancing</u> girls…. see Princess <u>Coochita</u>, the famous little Oriental dancer…She's here…. she's there…she's everywhere…. <u>Princess Coochita.</u>

          (MUSIC GET SOFTER)

HOTCHA GARDNER (RUBE DIALECT):	I saw it, and it's pretty slick.
JACK (IN WHISPER):	Shall we go in, George?
GEORGE:	No, I don't want to see it…. do <u>you</u> want to go in, Jack?
JACK:	Not me…I don't care for that kind of stuff…. a lot of girls dancing.
GEORGE:	I don't want to go in, Jack but, of course, if You want to ---
JACK:	Well, it's up to you, George, I'll go in if you want to.
GEORGE:	I don't care…it's up to you.
JACK:	Say, Ethel – go back and tell the band to play, "ROCKABYE MOON" -- and while you're there, sing it.
ETHEL:	I don't want to go.
GEORGE:	GO!
JACK:	Let's hurry in now, George.

2. ROCKABYE MOON   ORCHESTRA & ETHEL SHUTTA

          (OBOE AND DRUM AGAIN PLAY ORIENTAL MUSIC VERY SOFTLY)

JACK:	What did you think of those dancers, George?
GEORGE:	They were <u>all right</u>…. I'm certainly glad Ethel didn't see us go in.
ETHEL (ENTERS QUICKLY):	Hello boys – I've been looking <u>all over</u> for you.
JACK:	We were over there – watching the sword-swallowers.

ETHEL (WITH UNDERSTANDING):	Yeah? …. Well, those sword swallowers could certainly dance.
JACK:	George, let's get a hot dog.
ETHEL:	I want a drink.
RALPH ASHE (WALKING TOWARD MIKE):	Howdy, folks…get your hot dogs here…step this way … (INTO MIKE) Get your red-hot dogs…red hots…red hots…red hots….
JACK SHUTTA (INTO MIKE):	Get your Canada Dry Ginger Ale By-the-glass…get your Canada Dry made-to-order right here….
ANNOUNCER:	This sparkling beverage can be bought at all fountains—and it's good in ice-cream sodas. Everybody's drinking it.
JACK:	All right, Hicks – get out of the carnival.
RALPH ASHE:	Here you are – get your hot dogs…no cover charge…. hot dogs…do you want a hot dog, mister?
JACK:	What kind have you got?
RALPH:	Fox terriers – <u>what do you think</u>?
JACK:	What I think, has been censored… Give me a hot dog.
GEORGE:	I'll take one, too.
RALPH:	Right!
GEORGE:	and put some mustard on it.
RALPH:	Right!
GEORGE:	Have you got sauerkraut? Put that on, too.
RALPH:	Right!
GEORGE:	And while you're at it, put a slice of onion on it.
RALPH:	Right!
JACK:	George, you don't want the cash register on it – do you? Ethel, what will you have?
ETHEL:	I want a large glass of Canada Dry Ginger Ale.
RALPH:	Here's your hot dog, mister.
	(SOUND EFFECT: BARK OF DOG—WOOF! WOOF!)
JACK:	Hey give this a little more fire. The dog is still barking.
RALPH:	Wait a minute – aren't you JACK BENNY?
JACK:	Yes.
RALPH:	Of the Canada Dry Program?

JACK:	Yes.
RALPH:	Boy! are you rotten!
MARY:	He is not. I think he's swell…. you've got a lot of nerve—
ETHEL:	Jack, there's Mary…Hello, Mary.
JACK AND GEORGE (TOGETHER):	Hello, Mary….
Mary:	Hello, everybody, oh, Jack. I've got the funniest thing to tell you – I just had my fortune told by a gypsy woman.
JACK:	Yeah? ….what did she tell you?
MARY:	She told me that I was going to meet a nice young fellow, and that he would be a master of ceremonies, and that his first name starts with a "J" and that his last name starts with a "B," and that he's on the Canada Dry Program. Now who do you suppose she means?
JACK:	Mickey Mouse.
MARY:	Oh, gee! Can you imagine that? I thought she meant you… and I gave her an extra quarter.
ETHEL:	Say, Mary – why don't you join us? We're having lots of fun.
MARY – ETHEL – JACK – GEORGE – all together:	I think that would be swell.
JACK SHUTTA (WALKS TOWARD MIKE):	Come on, folks…step this way for the biggest thrill on the Midway…something you'll never forget….
ETHEL:	Here's the roller coaster…let's go on that.
JACK SHUTTA (INTO MIKE):	Come on, folks…enjoy yourselves on the longest ride and the biggest thrill

on the Midway. Thirty thrills for fifteen cents. How about you, fellows? Thirty thrills for only fifteen cents.

JACK BENNY:	Wrap me up a couple.
ETHEL:	Aw, let's go on this.
GEORGE:	All right – say, Jack, you lay it out and I'll give it to you later.
JACK BENNY:	You're spoiling my whole day, George.
JACK SHUTTA:	Hurry – hurry, folks …Step right in the car. No waiting.
	(SOUND EFFECT: OF PEOPLE GETTING INTO CAR)
JACK:	George, you sit with Mary. I'll sit with Ethel.
MARY:	No – I want to sit with you, Jack.
JACK:	All right…. Ethel, you sit with George.

GEORGE:	Put your arm around me, Ethel.
ETHEL:	For what?
JACK:	Okay - we're ready.

    (SOUND EFFECT: START OF ROLLER COASTER – HEAR CHAIN GRINDING AS CARS CLIMB UP.

    OVER THIS SOUND EFFECT, WE HEAR

JACK; HERE WE GO! …. Boy, this is a steep climb…Are you scared, Mary?

MARY:	No.

    MARY – JACK – ETHEL – GEORGE – (AB LIB)

    DOROTHY ROSS AND BALDWIN LAUGH AND TALK IN BACKGROUND)

ETHEL:	Oh, boy, … isn't this high!
JACK:	Here we go….

    SOUND EFFECT (GIRLS SCREAM – ROLLER COASTER; TURNED AROUND VERY FAST)

    (OLSEN BLOWS WHISTLE – SEGUE INTO ….

3. WHAT A SWEET SENSATION   ORCHESTRA & FRAN FREY

    (DURING FIRST CHORUS OF NUMBER,

    GEORGE HICKS SPEAKS --

ANNOUNCER:	Well, the boys and girls are certainly getting a real sensation out of that roller coaster. Now you're going to hear Fran Frey sing, "WHAT A SWEET SENSATION."

    (AFTER FINISH OF NUMBER----

JACK:	Hello, folks, this is Jack Benny again…now master of ceremonies for the side show.

    (CYMBAL CRASH)

Step right this way, folks, … and see the <u>greatest</u> collection of freaks in the world… See DURANTE, the nose faced boy…FRAN FREY, the saxophone swallower…and right over here we have CYCO, Half-man and half bicycle…look at those handlebars on his upper lip.

    (CYMBAL CRASH)

We also have with us MISS HONEY DEWA, half-woman and half-cantaloupe…. STEP UP THIS WAY, FOLKS…and see J. EMPIRE STATE –O, the giant….ten feet tall in his stocking feet IF he had stockings….

    (CYMBAL CRASH)

Come in and see them all…and over here we have the fat woman …. TEENY-WEE-NY… weighs five hundred and seventy-five pounds…. count them…five hundred and seventy-five pounds…and two flights of chips, she used to weigh seven hundred and fifty…but you know how times are!

(CYMBAL CRASH)

AND LAST – but not least – the <u>star</u> attraction of our Side Show, the Bearded Lady… MADAME GILLETTA…   (CYMBAL CRASH)

Say something, Gilletta.

PAUL SMALL (GILLETTA): <u>Hair-o</u> everybody.

JACK: Gilletta, now tell us your last name.

PAUL: Smith.

JACK: I see….one of the Smith Sisters…Now tell the folks why you want to be a Bearded Lady.

PAUL: So I can earn my room-and-<u>beard</u>.

JACK: Hmm…. now if we can only get light wines, we'll have light wines and <u>beards</u>… Are you folks. <u>beard</u> with this?...Now tell us, Gilletta, are you married?

PAUL: Yes.

JACK: Who is your husband?

PAUL: John the Barber.

JACK: John the Barber is your husband – and you're a Bearded Lady.

PAUL: That's nothing – my sister is married to a butcher and --

JACK: And she's a vegetarian – I heard that before. How tell us, Gilletta, is that a permanent wave in your beard or transient?

PAUL: Neither – I've been eating noodle soup.

JACK: I see – one more question…. tell the folks how difficult it was to grow that beard.

PAUL: Well, at first I thought it would be impossible – but after a long battle, I finally did it. <u>And I owe it all to</u>----

JACK: Oh, you do, eh?...All right, go inside, Gilletta – and play with Dracula. And now folks, if you'll just step inside you will see some of the world's greatest attractions. Step right up…Only a few seats left. What a crowd!...what a crowd!...Hello, Paul.

PAUL SMALL: Hello, Jack.

JACK: Oh, hello there, Hicks…. what's new?

ANNOUNCER: Canada Dry Ginger Ale is now made-to-order….

JACK:	Nothing new, eh? All right, folks, don't crowd. There's room for everybody…and now while we are preparing for the big show on the inside, George Olsen and his Carnival Orchestra will play "As Long as I Live"

4. AS LONG AS I LIVE   ORCHESTRA & PAUL SMALL

JACK:	And now, folks, step up a little closer – come on, right up to the platform and see TOTO, the Tattooed Boy. Toto is tattooed from toupee to toe…These tattoos on Toto include a great collection of pictures by such artists as Rembrandt, Michelangelo and Ballyhoo…all rare old tattoos… This boy would have reached the dizzy heights of fame, only he had an anchor tattooed on his brain which held him down…Now say something to the folks, Toto ….
HARRY CONN:	Ta-ta, everybody.
JACK:	You should have saved that for the finish…Now explain those different decorations on your body…what does that picture on your forearm represent?
CONN:	Wieners.
JACK:	What?
HARRY:	Wieners.
JACK:	Wieners…you mean little frankfurters?
HARRY:	No, Wieners de Milo.
JACK:	Wait a minute, you mean <u>Venus</u>!
HARRY:	Yes, sir.
JACK:	Well, don't you know that Venus has no arms, and the lady in this picture has <u>both</u> arms.
HARRY:	This was taken <u>before</u> the accident.
JACK:	Well, Toto, it is only the dignity of this program that keeps me from tattooing you with the microphone.
HARRY CONN:	I have no room for that.
JACK:	We'll make room…Tell us, Toto, what is that picture you have tattooed on the palm of your hand?
HARRY:	That's a ham sandwich.
JACK:	It's very pretty – is that <u>mustard</u> you have alongside of it?
HARRY:	No, I was cleaning my ear.
JACK:	That's a nice picture you have on your ankle.

HARRY:	That's Niagara Falls – do you like it?
JACK:	Yes, but that water should be up on your neck – where you need it.
HARRY:	I've got the Sahara Desert up there.
JACK:	You're telling me…The desert is getting close to your ears…. Say, what's that beautiful architecture on your shoulder?
HARRY:	That's President Hoover standing in front of the White House.
JACK:	It looks like the White House all right – but <u>where's</u> the president?
HARRY:	Oh, he's on a fishing trip – haven't you read the papers?
	(SOUND EFFECT – THUD OF BOTTLE ON HEAD)
JACK:	We just put <u>another</u> tattoo on Toto's head.
	And now, folks, if you will just move along to your right- you will see the Original <u>Siamese</u> Twins… LEFTA on the right…and RIGHTA on the left…. Come here, girls, say a few words to the folks before you do your stuff. Now, folks, I don't want to lie to you about these Siamese Twins. Hear what they have to say themselves. Now, girls, you really are from <u>Siam</u> – aren't you?
ETHEL (with German accent):	No – SALEM.
JACK:	Oh, Salem Massachusetts….my error. These girls are the <u>Salem</u>-ese twins. They look more like the <u>Salami</u> Twins…. Now, girls, how old are you?
ETHEL:	I am twenty-two.
DOROTHY (without any accent):	I'm twenty-nine.
JACK:	Seven years difference – what a novelty!
ETHEL:	I've got to go home now…you can talk to my sister.
JACK:	Take your sister with you. I hate to break up a family…. And now for the big <u>free</u> outdoor attraction…George Olsen, the <u>Swede</u>-emese Maestro and his Freak Musicians – will play, "Listen to the German Band", sung by Ethel Shutta.

5. LISTEN TO THE GERMAN BAND   EHTEL SHUTTA & ORCHESTRA

JACK:	That was the last number of the thirty-third program on the 22nd of August. Did you have a nice time at the carnival, folks? …. By the way, George, your boys pretty nearly crabbed our side show business tonight.
GEORGE:	How was that?
JACK:	Well, everybody was looking <u>at them…</u> and they weren't even playing…. Well, folks, we've got to go home now. We're all tired out from walking around…. Say, George, what did we make on the carnival tonight?

GEORGE:	We <u>lost</u> fourteen dollars.
JACK:	Say, didn't you get a nickel back on the large Canada Dry bottle?
GEORGE:	Yes.
JACK:	Then we only lost thirteen dollars and ninety-five cents…that isn't bad…Good-night, George…good-night, Ethel.
GEORGE & ETHEL (TOGETHER):	Good night, Jack, had a nice time.
JACK (to Mary):	Can I take you home, Mary?
MARY:	Hotcha Gardner just asked me the same thing.
JACK:	GOOD NIGHT, MARY.

SIGNATURE – ROCKABYE MOON

ANNOUNCER: The next time you stop at a soda fountain for a refreshing drink ask for a glass of Canada Dry, the champagne of ginger ales – it will be made to order for you. And when you buy Canada Dry in bottles for the home, remember that the new big bottle is particularly convenient and economical. Remember too, that with the exception of a few localities, where freight charges do not permit, you can take back your Canada Dry bottles to the dealer and get a cash refund. So that now when you buy Canada Dry you pay for the contents only. Next Wednesday night at this same time Jack Benny, Ethel Shutta and George Olsen will again entertain you. This is the National Broadcasting Company.

August 24, 1932

Jack is hiding from his tailor and other creditors to whom he owes money, and broadcasts while hiding in the cellar. Fan mail is read from Jack's father, who asks to hear him play the violin, but during Jack's performance, the announcer reads the commercial over the music. The Benny program's first melodramatic parody skit is performed, "She Loved, She Loved, She Learned." Jack plays the lover who must hide in the closet (singing a few bars of "Just a Gigolo,") when the husband unexpectedly returns home. Ethel plays the woman, and George is the cuckholded husband. Mary does not appear on this episode.

STATION WJZ   PROGRAM CANADA DRY GINGER ALE, INC.
        AND   DATE WEDNESDAY, AUGUST 24TH, 1932
    BLUE NETWORK   TIME 9:30 – 10:00 P.M.

SIGNATURE – JOLLY GOOD COMPANY

OPENING ANNOUNCEMENT

1. THOU SHALT NOT   GARDNER
                                         DIALOGUE

2. ALWAYS IN MY HEART   SHUTTA
                                         DIALOGUE

3. TWO POOR PEOPLE   FREY AND SHUTTA
                                         DIALOGUE

4. MOONLIGHT ON THE RIVER   SMALL
                                         DIALOGUE

5. I'M THAT WAY ABOUT BROADWAY   SHUTTA
                                         DIALOGUE

SIGNATURE – ROCKABYE MOON

CLOSING ANNOUNCEMENT

CANADA DRY GINGER ALE INC   WEDNESDAY, AUGUST 24, 1932

SIGNATURE – JOLLY GOOD COMPANY

ANNOUNCER:	Ladies and gentlemen, another half hour of entertainment about Canada Dry – the champagne of ginger ales – now available by the glass at soda fountains, as well as in bottles for the home. You'll find the new, large size bottle very economical, and particularly convenient for home use.
	This is request night and George Olsen, Ethel Shutta, and Jack Benny – the Canada Dry Humorist – again perform for your enjoyment. George Olsen opens the program with "THOU SHALT NOT," Dick Gardner, singing.

1. THOU SHALT NOT   ORCHESTRA

ANNOUNCER:	Where's Jack Benny? …. George, have you seen Jack?
GEORGE:	No – not yet.
ANNOUNCER:	There are three men here waiting for him…. I'm sorry, folks, but Jack seems to be late again. Somebody will have to say something till he gets here
DOUG COULTER:	I'll say something…hello, people. This is Jack Benny's tailor talking. He bought two suits from me last year, and hasn't paid for them <u>yet</u>. You folks may think he's all right, but I do <u>business</u> with him. I'm waiting <u>right here</u> – program or <u>no</u> program.
FRAN FREY:	Yeah….and let me say something…I'm Jack Benny's <u>barber from Sayville</u>…. I have shaved that mug for a year, and he keeps putting it on the cuff. I'd like to get my money or shave him <u>once more.</u>
DOROTHY ROSS:	Here…let me get a word in I'm Jack Benny's landlady. He lived at my house for <u>seven years</u>…. Then, when he finally got work, he <u>scrammed</u>, and owes me <u>seven years' rent</u>. I'll get my money or know the reason why.
ANNOUNCER:	These bills come to you thru the courtesy of Canada Dry Ginger Ale made-to-order by the glass.
HARRY CONN:	Is Jack Benny here yet?

ANNOUNCER:	NO.
HARRY C.:	Well he borrowed my full-dress suit last week, and I want it back. I'm getting married tonight, and I hate to call it off on account of the suit.
JACK (WHISPERS – GET EFFECT, AS FROM ANOTHER LOCATION):	Hello, people…. this is Jack Benny <u>broadcasting</u> from a rat hole in the cellar…do you blame me, hmmmm? There seem to be a few friends of mine around here whom I don't want to see…. It looks like I'll have to do the whole program down here…. Well, folks, this is <u>Request</u> Night. You have just heard my creditors <u>requesting</u> their money, which will be paid in <u>due</u> time…but not when <u>due</u>. I can't please everybody. I'm here to entertain <u>my</u> <u>listeners</u>…<u>not</u> my creditors….
	Gee, it's dark down here.
FRAN FREY:	Say, Jack…Jack!
JACK (QUICKLY):	Who is it?
FRAN:	It's me…. Fran Frey.
JACK:	Oh…. do you owe bills, too?
FRAN:	No…. George told me to tell you that they have all gone. You can come up now.
JACK:	All right, folks…. see you upstairs any minute.

2. ALWAYS IN MY HEART   ETHEL SHUTTA & ORCHESTRA

(GEORGE OLSEN MAKES ANNOUNCEMENT DURING NUMBER)

JACK:	Hello, folks…I'm back up in the studio again…with a beard on. Don't let on that you know me.
	Say, George, one of our sponsors showed me a letter this morning…. from a man in Illinois, asking me to play another violin solo. You remember the last time I played one, George?
GEORGE:	DO I?
JACK:	On the level, George…. whom would you rather hear play the violin – me or Rubinoff?
GEORGE:	Well, Jack, you play all right…but when Rubinoff plays, you can….
JACK:	I see – never mind, George…. but regardless of what <u>you</u> think, let me road this letter. It says:
	"DEAR CANADA DRY…M.T.O. …. B.T.G. …. SOLD AT ALL FOUNTAINS AND UTGAY IN ICE CREAM SODAS" …. ISN'T that a subtle way of advertising, George? …. Well, anyway, it reads:

"PLEASE ASK JACK BENNY TO PLAY ANOTHER VIOLIN SOLO. I THINK HE IS ONE OF THE GREATEST ARTISTS I HAVE EVER HEARD IN MY LIFE, AND HIS VIOLIN PLAYING POSITIVELY THRILLS ME. WHY DOESN'T HE PLAY MORE? IT'S MUSIC LIKE HIS THAT MAKES LIFE WORTH LIVING."

Isn't that a wonderful letter, George?

GEORGE: It certainly is – who is it from?

JACK: My father… he is sweetest guy you've ever met in your life…. Well, George, I'm going to make my old Dad happy.

GEORGE: That's a nice thought, Jack – but what about all the other people listening in?

JACK: Say, a lot of them are fathers, too…. George, can I borrow a violin from one of the boys?

GEORGE: Sure – any particular one?

JACK: I'd like a second violin – if you don't mind.

(JACK TAKES VIOLIN FROM MUSICIAN)

Thanks, George.

(STARTS TO TUNE UP)

A little flat…. guess it's been standing too long…Now, folks, my first selection will be Reuben's "Second Hungarian Dinner."

GEORGE: Are you going to play all of it?

JACK: From soup to nuts…Or would you rather hear something else?

ETHEL: I think you'd better play that number you've been practicing for six weeks.

JACK: That's right, Ethel – something impromptu …. George, "Soft Lights and Sweet Music."

GEORGE: Would you like to have the piano accompany you on this?

JACK: Yes – and stick with me…oh, wait just a minute.

(PLAYS EXERCISES ON VIOLIN)

Ma! what time is it? Ah, those were the happy days, George. Many's the time I played hooky from school just so I could practice my violin. I'll never forget when my father bought me my first violin and a monkey wrench.

GEORGE: What was the idea of the monkey wrench?

JACK: He didn't want me to take any chances as plumbing is not a bad business, either… Let's go, George…" Soft Lights and Sweet Music".

(STARTS TO PLAY – AD LIBS)

	I'll bet you'd rather hear something new….it took me long enough to learn this.
ANNOUNCER:	Canada Dry Ginger Ale can now be bought at all fountains, with the right amount of syrup – and good in ice cream sodas.
JACK:	He picks out a fine time to advertise.
	(AT START OF SECOND CHORUS—
ETHEL:	Say, George, that carpenter is here to fix the platform.
GEORGE:	Yes…. right here, mister. These boards are loose again.
FRAN FREY:	Okay. (SOUND EFFECT: LOUD HAMMERING)
	There you are…anything else?
GEORGE:	No, that's fine.
FRAN:	So long.
JACK:	Thousands of people out of work, and that guy found a job here!
	(AT FINISH OF NUMBER – ONE MAN APPLAUDS)
	Well, anyway, thank you. I'm glad there is one music-lover applauding me.
PAUL SMALL:	Applauding? I'm killing flies!
JACK:	The next number, ladies and gentlemen, is entitled," TWO POOR PEOPLE" …. sung by Ethel Shutta and Fran Frey …. without the carpenter.

3. TWO POOR PEOPLE   ETHEL SHUTTA – FRAN FREY & ORCHESTRA

JACK:	Well, folks, here is another request – a rather unusual one. Let me read you this letter from Mr. J. Thespian Legit ….no doubt, an actor. He says:
	"I HAVE BEEN LISTENING TO YOUR PROGRAM EVERY MONDAY AND WEDNESDAY, AND HAVE FAILED TO RECOGNIZE ANYTHING FROM THE PENS OF SUCH PLAYWRIGHTS AS SIR JAMES BARRIE – EUGENE O'NEILL – OR GEORGE BERNARD SHAW. WHY DON'T YOU GIVE US SOME OF THE MODERN PLAYS…. GIVE US 'LIGHTNING'…. GIVE US 'RAIN'…. GIVE US A CLOUDBURST…. GIVE US 'THE BARRETTS OF WIMPOLE STREET'"
	…. I'm sorry, Legit, the best we can do is The Olsens of 110th Street….
	"GIVE US 'WAY DOWN EAST'….'UNCLE TOM'S CABIN'" ….
	Well, we could give him the ice, George, but he'll have to buy the Canada Dry himself…….

"NOW UNTIL YOU PEOPLE ON THE CANADA DRY PROGRAM PUT ON SUCH PLAYS AS THESE, I WILL NOT CONSIDER YOU ACTORS, AND YOU ARE ONLY CLOGGING UP THE AIR."

Can you imagine that, George? So, we're not actors – eh? All right, Mr. Legit, we will give you plays…. we will give you Drama… and if we see you, we'll give you punch in the nose. However, if you're over six foot, that last crack don't go….

Boy! dust off one of our plays…We are going to present to you this evening a one-act play that won the Wurlitzer Prize for its organ-ality… I mean, its originality. It is entitled, entitled, "She Lived... She Loved...She Learned... She Loafed…He Left… and She Laughed…or "That's Why Darkies were Born." Here is a brief outline of the plot:

Prologue – a demure maiden – is very much in love with Sy-nopsis...Sy ... who has just made a non-stop flight…down a flight of stairs after visiting her father …. is very angry with Exit, his rival…..Now Mezza Nine …. who lives on the floor above … warns Prologue of the impending duel between Sy and Ex…. Meanwhile, Prologue's brother, Epi, who was way out West returns with an Indian friend, Chief Standing-Room-Only and his brother, One-on-the-Aisle….Do you follow the continuity?

Now the next scene is in front of a theatre – where you see Chief Standing-Room-Only scalping tickets.

Then we take you to the third plot – which lies in the Cemetery – right next to the author – as it should be. Of course, there is no use giving away the thrilling climax of this drama, so I will now introduce the cast of characters….

Seneca, the wife, will played by Ethel Shutta….and George Olsen will play Abercrombie, the husband…while I, Jack Benny, will play the part of T. Twombley Twilliams, the sweetheart…. The "T" stands for Twedward….

Oh, I almost forgot to mention the other character – a Butler – who will be played by Parker T. Van Van-Van-Van …. an actor who has just finished a thirty-two-year run with "ABIE'S IRISH ROSE" – starting in as the child in the play – finishing as the grandfather – and retiring on a pension, who is also in the cast…. " ABIE'S IRISH ROSE," as you know, was written by Anne Nichols --

ANNOUNCER: Don't forget, folks, that you get your nickels back on all quart bottles of Canada Dry Ginger Ale.

JACK: I knew it…I knew it…The minute you give that guy Hicks an opening, he takes advantage of it.

(SOUND EFFECT: MOVING CHAIRS AROUND, ETC.)

JACK: And now, while we're setting the stage for our play, George Barrymore Olsen and his Shake-Spear Carriers, will play, "MOONLIGHT ON THE RIVER" sung by Paul Small…. Fall in, Paul!

4. MOONLIGHT ON THE RIVER   PAUL SMALL AND ORCHESTRA

JACK: That was Paul Small singing. "MOONLIGHT ON THE RIVER." And now to get on with our play…. Ladies, kindly remove your hats…park your gum and, remember folks, no <u>hissing</u> and no trying to get <u>other</u> stations.

The scene is the Living-Room… the time, <u>six</u>…. place, <u>two</u>…and <u>even</u> to show…So on with the <u>Parlay</u>…. or, the play….and let George be unrefined, CURTAIN

(ORCHESTRA PLAYS CURTAIN MUSIC – OPENING BARS OF "JOLLY GOOD COMPANY)

ETHEL: (HUMS SOFTLY OPENING BARS OF "JOLLY GOOD COMPANY") …. Oh, this married life is driving me mad…<u>diamonds</u> – <u>cars</u> – <u>yachts</u>…but no freedom…. (hums another bar) Parker! PARKER!

PAUL SMALL: Yes, Milady.

ETHEL: What detained you? You're the slowest butler we've ever had.

PAUL (WITH AFFECTED ENGLISH ACCENT): I was packing the <u>master's</u> luggage, Milady…He starts on his journey today.

ETHEL: (HUMS ANOTHER BAR OR TWO):That's right…this <u>is</u> the twenty-fourth. All right, Parker, put Fido to bed…. feed the canary…wash the cat and send my husband in.

BUTLER: Yes, Milady.

ETHEL: That's all, Parker….

(SOUND EFFECT: DOOR CLOSES)

(SOUND EFFECT: DOOR OPENS)

GEORGE: Hello, Seneca darling.

ETHEL: Oh, Abercrombie, I see you have your grips all packed…Just think, we have been married <u>only twelve years</u>, and you're leaving me already.

GEORGE: It's business, my dear. I must leave for Havana today.

ETHEL:	<u>Must</u> you go?
GEORGE:	Yes.

ETHEL (HUMS ANOTHER BAR OF "JOLLY GOOD COMPANY")

GEORGE:	Aw, don't cry, dear.
ETHEL:	How can I help it? I'm going to miss you <u>so</u> much.
GEORGE:	There – be a brave little woman. I won't be gone long. But I must hurry now, dear. The boat sails in half an hour…. Kiss me, darling.
ETHEL:	Oh, I'm tired. Wait till you get back…. Good-bye, dear.
GEORGE:	Good-bye, sweetheart…. Quit pushing….
ETHEL:	I don't want you to miss your boat.
GEORGE:	<u>Good</u>-bye.

(SOUND EFFECT: DOOR SLAMS)

ETHEL:	<u>Good-bye.</u>

(SINGS) I'm All Alone…so All Alone. (goes into jazz tempo). There's no one else but you…boop-poop-a-doop.

(SOUND EFFECT:	KNOCK ON DOOR)

Who is it?

JACK:	Can I come in?
ETHEL:	Yes, yes…<u>who is it</u>?
(SOUND EFFECT:	DOOR OPENS)
JACK:	It is I…. Twombley, your heartache.

ETHEL: Oh, Twombley dearest, I'm so happy to see you. I thought you'd never get here. I've been alone for almost a <u>minute</u>.... Tell me, do you love me, Jack?

JACK: It's <u>Twombley</u>.

ETHEL: Do you love me, Twombley?

JACK: Wait a minute....is Walter Winchell around?

ETHEL: No.

JACK: Oh, I do love you, Seneca darling.

ETHEL: Shall we play a rubber of bridge?

JACK: <u>You said it</u>.

ETHEL: Parker!

BUTLER: Yes, Milady.

ETHEL: Bring in the bridge table...and tell Fifi to have dinner for two.

BUTLER: Very good, ma'am.

JACK: Oh, Parker.... I mean, Oh, Seneca...ever since I met you, I <u>can't think</u> .... I <u>can't sleep</u>... I <u>Can't eat</u> --

ETHEL: And why not, dearest?

JACK: I'm <u>broke</u>!

ETHEL: Oh, Twombley...why didn't you tell me? Let me help you...Take this money.

JACK: I can't, dearest.

ETHEL: <u>Please</u> take it...(pause)...What's the matter, Twombley?

JACK: (SINGS) I'm just a gigolo...Every place I go... Olsen knows the part I'm playing... Paid for every dance....

(SOUND EFFECT: LOUD KNOCK AT DOOR)

JACK:	What's that? (SECOND KNOCK)
	What's that knock?
ETHEL:	My heavens! <u>My</u> husband!
JACK:	My hat! (sings) If I had wings of an angel…. (THIRD TERRIFIC KNOCK)
ETHEL:	Hide, Twombley…<u>quick!</u> if he finds you here, he'll kill us both.
JACK:	Where shall I hide?
ETHEL:	Under the table -- no, behind that statue. No, <u>in the closet</u>.
JACK:	Well, make up your mind, Ethel…er, Seneca.
ETHEL:	IN THAT CLOSET!
	(SOUND EFFECTS: FOOTSTEPS AND DOOR CLOSING) (ANOTHER KNOCK IS HEARD)
ETHEL:	Come in – come in – (SOUND EFFECT: DOOR OPENS) ---Hello, darling…I thought you had gone to Havana.
GEORGE:	It's raining in Havana, and I came back for my umbrella. <u>I</u> <u>left</u> <u>it</u> <u>in</u> <u>that</u> <u>closet.</u>
ETHEL:	Wait, I'll get it, Abercrombie.
GEORGE:	No, Seneca. <u>I'll</u> get it.
ETHEL:	No – let <u>me</u> get it.
GEORGE:	Ha, ha! …. Just as I thought. There's a <u>man</u> in that closet.
ETHEL:	Why no, dear…how can you say that?
GEORGE:	Don't lie to me…. there's a <u>man</u> in that closet…Open that door or I'll shoot. (PAUSE) I MEAN IT…. OPEN THAT DOOR OR I'LL SHOOT! (SOUND EFFECT: DOOR OPENS)

Just as I thought-----What are doing here? …(PAUSE) <u>What are you doing in that closet</u>?

JACK: Believe it or not – I'm selling Canada Dry Ginger Ale made-to-order by the glass!

(SEGUE INTO….)

5. I'M THAT WAY ABOUT BROADWAY   ETHEL SHUTTA AND ORCHESTRA

HARRY CONN: Hey! Where is Jack Benny! We were listening to this program across the street. We know he's <u>here</u>.

FRAN FREY: Yes…and we want that money he owes us.

JACK (AWAY FROM MIKE FOR PROPER EFFECT): Hello, everybody…this is Jack Benny in the cellar again…<u>without the beard</u>. That was the last number on the thirty-fourth program on the twenty-fourth of August. I have to sneak out of here now, so I'll see you Monday night – which will be <u>Sports Night</u>. indoor and outdoor. Be sure to listen in and will have a lot of fun…I had better get out now…Good-night, all.

SIGNATURE – ROCKABYE MOON

ANNOUNCER: Remember you can enjoy Canada Dry, the champagne of ginger ales, anywhere, anytime, for it is now available two ways – either made to order by the glass at soda fountains, or in bottles, as always, for your home. The new big bottle is particularly economical and convenient.

Remember, too, that with the exception of a few localities, where freight rates do not permit, you can take back your Canada Dry bottles to the dealer and got a cash refund. You pay for the contents only. Next Monday night at this same time Jack Benny, Ethel Shutta and George Olsen will again entertain you. This is the National Broadcasting Company.

August 29, 1932

Jack opens this episode with an introspective monologue that sounds like one of writer Harry Conn's early "Labor Day" stanzas, and mentions the Depression troubles "of these last 2 years." It's Sports Night. A female golfer is interviewed, and Jack calls play-by-play on a wrestling match. Mary appears at the end of the program, and types a letter that Jack dictates, but there is no ribbon in the typewriter.

STATION WJZ PROGRAM CANADA DRY GINGER ALE, INC.

       AND DATE MONDAY, AUGUST 29, 1932

BLUE NETWORK TIME 9:30 – 10:00 P.M.

SIGNATURE – JOLLY GOOD COMPANY

1. WEDDING OF THE PAINTED DOLL	ORCHESTRA
2. WHEN MOTHER PLAYED THE ORGAN	ORCHESTRA & SHUTTA
3. ALL AMERICAN GIRL	ORCHESTRA & PAUL SMALL
4. MY BABY'S GONE	ORCHESTRA & PAUL SMALL & ETHEL SHUTTA
5. YEAH MAN	ORCHESTRA & DICE GARDNER

SIGNATURE – ROCKABYE MOON

CANADA DRY GINGER ALE INC MONDAY, AUGUST 29TH, 1932

SIGNATURE – JOLLY GOOD COMPANY

ANNOUNCER: Ladies and gentlemen, another half hour of entertainment about Canada Dry – the champagne of ginger ales – now available by the glass at soda fountains, as well as in bottles for the home. You'll find the new, large size bottle very economical, and particularly convenient for home use. Once more we present George Olsen, Ethel Shutta, and Jack Benny – the Canada Dry Humorist, who will perform for your enjoyment. George Olsen opens the program with the WEDDING OF THE PAINTED DOLL.

1. THE WEDDING OF THE PAINTED DOLL   ETHEL SHUTTA, JACK BENNY & ORCHESTRA

ANNOUNCER: And now we bring to you our master of ceremonies!

JACK: Hello, John Q. Public…this is er…. this is er……

ANNOUNCER: Jack Benny.

JACK: Yeah, Jack Benny…. this is Jack Benny talking…isn't it funny how we forget names? And, after all, how many people really <u>know</u> themselves? It's a strange world – isn't it? We're <u>here</u> today and <u>gone</u> tomorrow. In fact, some of us are <u>here</u> <u>today</u> and <u>gone</u> <u>tomorrow</u>…. or vice versa. It certainly is a funny world. Tchk…. tchk…. tchk…. why, do you know when I got up this morning, my mind was absolutely a blank. In fact, I had to look in the mirror <u>to see</u> who I was. And do you think it was me? <u>No</u>! …. So you see, folks, I'm not <u>my</u>-<u>self</u> today. I even told that to the landlord this afternoon. I said "Landlord. I'm <u>not</u> myself today." And he said, "<u>Whoever</u> you are, either pay the rent or get out!" …. So I paid the rent…and even <u>he</u> was a new man. It's a strange world………Why, these last two years have made everybody look like somebody else. <u>And what does it</u>? WORRY……that's it…worry. In the older days, a man's hair used to turn gray at the age of sixty-five or seventy. Now you see kids <u>two</u> and three years old running around, looking like Hoover… And what can you do with little kids nowadays? They <u>won't</u> listen. To give you an illustration, I gave my little nephew, aged four, <u>ten cents</u> yesterday for spending money, and what do you think he did? He went right down to Wall Street and bought more stock! …. What a world!

GEORGE: Don't worry about it, Jack.

JACK: How do you feel, George?

GEORGE: I feel fine, Jack. Have a cigar.

JACK: WHAT A STRANGE WORLD!

(SOUND EFFECT: TELEPHONE RINGS)

ETHEL: Hello…. hello…yes, this is the Canada Dry Ginger Ale program. I'm sorry, I can't tell you, Madame. I don't know what he's talking about myself…. Jack, a lady on the phone wants to know what you're talking about.

JACK: There you are, folks…. I was speaking perfect English and nobody knows what I'm talking about.

ETHEL: All right, Madame, just a minute and I'll ask him……. the lady wants to know what became of Sports Night. She said you promised on last Wednesday's program that tonight we would have Indoor and Outdoor Sports.

JACK: Has she got any witnesses that I said it?

ETHEL: Yes, her whole family.

JACK: All right, Ethel, there is <u>nothing</u> we can't do on these programs. You sing the next number, and I'll go out and dig up some sport champions.

(SEGUE INTO—

1. WHEN MOTHER PLAYS THE ORGAN   ORCHESTRA & ETHEL SHUTTA

(GEORGE OLSEN MAKES ANNOUNCEMENT DURING NUMBER)

JACK: This way, boys. Take seats right here …. put down your golf bags and hockey sticks. You can put your wrestling mat right over there. That dumb bell goes over here.

MARY: Anything you say, Jack.

JACK: Not you, Mary…. the <u>iron</u> dumb bell.

MARY: Oh!

JACK: Now, folks, the sport season is on the wane. Most of the big golf tournaments here already been played…the baseball season will soon be over…and, of course, the Olympic Games are thru. It was our intention to bring to you the winners of these various sports, but – as you know – Sharkey is up in New England….the Olympic champions have all gone back to their respective countries….So you see, ladies and gentlemen, not being able to get the <u>cream</u> of the sporting world, we have brought you the <u>sour</u> cream….and vegetables. Of course, if you like a hot potato with it, you've got the <u>wrong</u> station. Tonight, we are not only going to present these different champions to you – but also award a medal to each of them....not gold, mind you, nor silver....but made of fresh Hamburger....with their names beautifully inscribed with sliced onions....so that later, when they have nothing left but their medals, they can – at least – eat them.

FIRST – we want you meet a lady champion of that popular outdoor sport, Golf. Meet Miss er …. Miss er…what's the name, please?

MISS KELCEY: Miss Zen.

JACK: Miss Zen… and what's the first name?

MISS KELCEY: Sara.

JACK: Sara Zen…a very familiar name. Tell us, Miss Zen, what was your latest victory?

MISS KELCEY: I came in third in the Northern Hoboken Open Tournament.

JACK: Oh! the Open tournament.

MISS KELCEY: Yes, it was open from nine a.m. to five p.m.

JACK: I see…you came in third. That's very nice. How many were in the tournament?

MISS KELCEY: Three.

JACK: Well, you made a fine showing. Who came in first?

MISS KELCEY: Equipoise.

JACK: Equipoise…. that must have been the Belmont Park Country Club…. May I see your score-card, Miss Zen?

MISS KELCEY: Certainly – there you are.

JACK: Hmmm…. very nice. I see you got a birdie twelve on the sixth hole.

MISS KELCEY: Oh, that's nothing…I made a hole-in-one on the thirteenth.

JACK: A hole in one? You got a seven marked down here.

MISS KELCEY: Well, I missed the first six off the tee.

JACK: I wish you'd have missed this program…. Tell us something about your game. Miss Zen…. How is your putting?

MISS KELCEY: Oh, I make finest rice putting you ever ate in life.

JACK: I see – I suppose you have mashie niblick potatoes with it.

MISS KELCEY: Oh yes…and you must try some of my baked divets.

JACK: Oh, by the way, I notice you have a zero marked on the ninth hole, which is a par five. How can you make a hole in zero?

Miss KELCEY: Well, I was shooting the eighth hole, and the ball fell in the ninth one.

JACK:	Here's your medal, Miss Zen…. Now you don't mind a little advice from an old golfer – do you?
MISS KELCEY:	Oh no – not at all.
JACK:	Well, have a shaft put on your head…it will make a fine brassie.
MISS KELCEY:	Thank you.
JACK:	Good-bye……. Say, Ethel, who is that boy sitting over there? He keeps getting up all the time.
ETHEL:	I don't know, Jack --- Mary brought him in from Plainfield.
JACK:	Say, young man, what are you doing here among all these athletes?
BOY:	I came here because it's <u>Sports</u> <u>Night</u>. I'm a champion in my line. If you got any medals, I'll take one.
JACK:	Well, you don't look very muscular to me, and you don't seem to – say, <u>what</u> line of sports are you in?
BOY:	Hockey.
JACK:	Oh, I see – you play <u>ice</u> hockey.
BOY:	No, hockey from school.
JACK:	Kvetch, punch a medal on this boy…. And now, ladies and gentlemen, a big surprise to you dyed-in-the-wool baseball fans. We have in this studio tonight the Cleveland Indians who have been playing great ball this year and have been a menace to their rivals….May I present to you the <u>Cleveland</u> <u>Indians</u>.
	(ORCHESTRA GOES INTO INDIAN MUSIC ---
	DAGGER DANCE – THEN BOYS MAKE NOISE WITH HAND AND MOUTH)
	What a team! What a team! Every game a feather in their caps………. And now – last but not least – we bring to you the <u>Yankee</u> <u>Stadium</u> …. Boys! bring in the stadium.
	(<u>SOUND</u> <u>EFFECT</u>: A LOT OF BOARDS DROPPING)
	Well, they dropped it and broke it. What a clumsy gang. Say, Jimmy, see that we get better help around here…. Announce the next number, George.

GEORGE OLSEN (ANNOUNCE NUMBER)

3. ALL AMERICAN GIRL   PAUL SMALL & ORCHESTRA

JACK:	That was "All American Girl". sung by Paul Small.

	Ah, your lucky people listening in tonight. What a thrill we have in store for you. A wrestling match right here in the studio for the short-weight championship of the world……. between those two well-known grapplers…. first – The Great and only Ali Pasha Pisha Paysha Pusha Hamid Kamel……the terrible Turk. Kamel looks as tho he has already gone eight days without water…and Kamel has walked a mile to get here…Say, George, wouldn't that be a great joke for a certain cigarette program? But let them get their own jokes – this is the Canada Dry Program…. Anyway, Pasha Kamel wishes to say a word to you.
FRAN FREY:	Abadaba…. corona…. panatela…. a la carte…. palooka-----
JACK:	No doubt, Pasha. He's a real Turk, ladies and gentlemen, so you see we spare no expense.
	And now may I present his opponent and room-mate Stanislaus…. Voislaus Slobiske……the ferocious Lith….. Say something, Slobbey.
2ND WRESTLER:	Ad libitum Cognito …. non de plume …. e pluribus
JACK:	How about the Fifth Avenue bus?
2ND WRESTLER:	Yes.
JACK:	Atta-Lith, and now, folks, let me give you the records of these two wrestlers. Pasha started wrestling in 1892 at the Union Depot in Constantinople, where Pasha was baggage smasha. In his first bout, he threw a wardrobe trunk with a snaplock…… and handle-held in exactly twenty-two minutes…. His next tussle was in a tailor-shop in London, where he threw Sir Corduroy Pants…with a half-crotch and scissor hold, and had the crowd in stitches. He then came to this country to commercialize his fame and, immediately after his first bout is the West, he served two years for wrestling cattle or rustling cattle and was thrown for the first time……in jail, where he learned some new lockholds and discipline. There is only one thing that Pasha insists on before wrestling… and that is, Pasha Mustapha glass of Canada Dry before entering the ring.
ANNOUNCER:	Thanks, Jack.
JACK:	You're welcome, Jimmy…. And now little Stanislaus Slobiske's record is not quite as good. He has met the best men in Europe……and they are still the best men. However, Stanislaus is very muscular and, if all his muscles were placed end-to-end, they would reach from Mussolini to Mussel-toff. While the boys are preparing for this match, Olsen and his boys – not a muscle in carload – will play, "MY BABY'S GONE", sung by Ethel Shutta and Fran Frey…. George! get that arm lock off Ethel.

4. MY BABY'S GONE   ETHEL SHUTTA, FRAN FREY & ORCHESTRA.

JACK:	Ladies and gentlemen, prepare for this great wrestling match. (ORCHESTRA – LOUD FANFARE)

	George, this is not a prize contact…. it's a <u>wrestling</u> <u>match.</u> On our right, we have Pasha, the Terrible Turk and from where I'm standing the Lith looks terrible – too. This promises to be a great <u>battle</u> –
ANNOUNCER:	And don't forget, folks, you get your nickel back on each quart <u>battle</u> of Canada Dry….er, bottle of Canada Dry.
JACK:	Say, Jimmy, this is not the <u>bottle</u> of the century – it's the <u>battle.</u>
ANNOUNCER:	But, Jack, Canada Dry is the <u>bottle</u> of the century.
	(<u>ROUND</u> OF <u>APPLAUSE</u>)
JACK:	All right, Jimmy, you win. Time was 2 and 2/5 seconds.

And now, folks, for the Tussle of the Century. Let me give you a hold-by-hold description of this terrific what-chuma-call it.

(SOUND EFFECT: SWEET CHIME – DUM-DUM-DA, DUM –DUM-DUM-DA)

That's very pretty. Can you play, "Holding My Honey's Hand?"

(REAL GONG IS HEARD)

The wrestlers are now in the center of the ring.

(SOUND EFFECT: SLAPPING SOUND)

They are slapping each other on the back and are sparring for a <u>grip</u>……which seems to be leaking at the bottom……. STANI just got a new hold.

(SOUND EFFECT: SLAP AND GRUNT)

Pasha has the same hold

(SOUND EFFECT: SLAP AND GRUNT)

They are both holding for a long pull…. This is a bout to the finish, and will probably go into the next four programs.

(SOUND EFFECT: SEVERAL THUDS AND MORE GRUNTS)

Pasha is now on one knee, but forgot to bring the dice, so they continue wrestling.

(SOUND EFFECT: THREE BUMPS)

Just as rehearsed – Pasha is now playfully bumping Stani's head to the floor – and not doing the floor any good. Now Stani gets a toe-hold on Pasha.

(MORE GRUNTS)

Pasha seems to be suffering, but doesn't give up. He finally pulls away and leaves four toes in Stani's hand…They are both on their feet again – locked in each other's arms.

(ORCHESTRA PLAYS "PARADISE") (WRESTLERS GRUNT IN TEMPO)

Ten cents a dance…. get your tickets right here…….

(TERRIFIC NOISE OF SLAPPING, GRUNTING AND FALLS)

The dance is over, and Pasha is very mad…. he picks up Stani with a half-Nelson and a quarter ice-tong hold and spins him in the air…Stani is dizzy – aren't we all?

(TERRIFIC GRUNT)

Pasha throws Stani completely out of the ring – there he goes over Newark (BUMP) – Trenton (BUMP) – Camden (BUMP) – into PHILADELPHIA…. but Stani is not hurt and rushes back by fast train --

(ORCHESTRA DOES IMITATION OF FAST TRAIN – WHISTLE AND EFFECT)

(CROWD CHEERS)

Here he is again – what a game guy!

(GONG IS HEARD)

They are now back in the center of the ring. Stani makes a pash at Pasha…. Pasha makes a pass at Olsen…. Olsen makes a lunge at Fran Frey…Fran Frey grabs Paul Small---

(CHEERING GETS LOUDER)

	This is Jack Benny broadcasting from under <u>forty</u> people.
ANNOUNCER:	(GROANS) Ooh! …. Ooh….
JACK:	What's that?
ETHEL:	Jack!….. Jimmy Wallington is terribly hurt. Somebody gave him the flying mare-hold-----
	(CROWD MURMURS)
JACK:	Get out of the way, everybody…give him air, fellers…give him air.
	Jimmy!….Jimmy!…. for Heaven's sake, speak to me…. speak to me…. you're not badly hurt – are you? … Oh Jimmy, please – say something.
ANNOUNCER (VERY WEAKLY):	Canada Dry Ginger Ale is made-to-order by the glass and sold at all fountains. (SEGUE INTO NEXT NUMBER.)

5. YEAH MAN   "HOTCHA" GARDNER & ORCHESTRA

JACK:	Hotcha Gardner sang the last number of the thirty-fifth program on the 29th of August. Well, we have had quite an exciting evening, didn't we? …. Oh, Mary…Mary….
MARY:	Yes, Jack.
JACK:	We have a little work to do now……You're my secretary – remember?
MARY:	Oh yes, <u>Mr. Benny</u>. I almost forgot about it. You see I haven't been paid yet. <u>When</u> is pay day?
JACK:	You'll get your pay, Mary. Don't worry. (LAUGHS) Now take a letter direct on your typewriter.
	(SOUND EFFECT: HEAR CLICK OF TYPEWRITER AS HE SPEAKS)
	"Dear appreciative Canada Dry audience---"
MARY:	How do you spell "DRY"?
JACK:	And you want to know when pay day is! …. Well, let's continue. "Tonight we brought to you our Outdoor Sport Champions, and if you will listen in next Wednesday, we will bring you a program of <u>Indoor</u> Sports. So be a <u>good</u> <u>sport</u> and listen in Wednesday night." …. Have you got that, Mary?

MARY:	(STARTS TO GIGGLE) Can you imagine? There was no ribbon in my typewriter.
JACK:	Better run out and get one. Say, while you're out, Mary, stop at the post-office and get me ten cents' worth of three-cent stamps…. then bring me a ham and egg sandwich…. buy next Sunday's paper with tomorrow's baseball results….and, if the weather is nice, bring some in. Can you remember that?
MARY:	Funny, I can remember everything but the ham and egg sandwich.
JACK:	All right, Mary, bring me that…. Oh, Mary, do you want to hear a good riddle?
MARY:	Sure – what is it?
JACK:	What's the difference between a ham sandwich… a typewriter…and a feather duster?
MARY:	(LAUGHS) I think it's swell!
JACK:	Good-night, folks.
ANNOUNCER:	The next time you stop at a soda fountain for a refreshing drink, ask for a glass of Canada Dry, the Champagne of Ginger Ales – it will be made to order for you. And when you buy Canada Dry in bottles for the home, remember that the new big bottle is particularly convenient and economical. Remember, too, that with the exception of a few localities, where freight charges do not permit, you can take back your Canada Dry bottles to the dealer and get a cash refund. So that now when you buy Canada Dry you pay for the contents only. Next Wednesday night at this same time Jack Benny, Ethel Shutta and George Olsen will again entertain you. This is the National Broadcasting Company.

August 31, 1932

It's Indoor Sports Night. Jack got a speeding ticket and is late to the broadcast. Jack and Jimmy Wallington, the announcer *du jour*, make "nickel back on the bottle" jokes. They perform a skit called "Three O'clock in the Morning," about parents up all night walking around with a cranky baby. At the end is an odd little skit about the Sun and Moon conversing that will remind you of the "New Year's Fantasies" that Jack and company would perform during World War II and the later 1940s' episodes.

STATION WJZ   PROGRAM   CANADA DRY GINGER ALE, INC.

       AND   DATE   WEDNESDAY, AUGUST 31, 1932

BLUE NETWORK   TIME   9:30 – 10:00 P.M.

SIGNATURE – JOLLY GOOD COMPANY

1. WEDDING OF THE PAINTED DOLL   ORCHESTRA

2. WHEN MOTHER PLAYED THE ORGAN   ORCHESTRA & SHUTTA

3. ALL AMERICAN GIRL   ORCHESTRA & PAUL SMALL

4. MY BABY'S GONE   ORCHESTRA & PAUL SMALL & ETHEL SHUTTA

5. YEAH MAN   ORCHESTRA & DICE GARDNER

SIGNATURE – ROCKABYE MOON

CANADA DRY GINGER ALE INC   WEDNESDAY, AUGUST 31TH, 1932

SIGNATURE – JOLLY GOOD COMPANY

[Ed. cover page is missing]

ANNOUNCER: Ladies and gentlemen, another half hour of entertainment about Canada Dry – the champagne of ginger ales – now available by the glass at soda fountains, as well as in bottles for the home. You'll find the new, large size bottle very economical, and particularly convenient for home use. Once more we present George Olsen, Ethel Shutta, and Jack Benny, the Canada Dry Humorist, who will perform for enjoyment. George Olsen opens the program with "LET'S HAVE A PARTY," vocal chorus by Fran Frey.

1. LET'S HAVE A PARTY   ORCHESTRA & FRAN FREY

ANNOUNCER: Say, what's the matter with Jack Benny? Looks like he's late again…Grab the mike, Ethel.

ETHEL: This is Ethel Shutta, coming to you thru the courtesy of Jack Benny who is not in the studio…. This is Indoor Sports Night, and we have a great program lined up and ---- (coughs louder)

GEORGE OLSEN: This is George Olsen, coming to you thru the courtesy of a bad cold which Ethel just caught. As you know, this is Indoor Sports Night and…. (SOUND EFFECT: FALLING OFF PLATFORM)

ANNOUNCER: This is Jimmy Wallington coming to you thru the courtesy of a bad fall which George Olsen just took from the band stand. This is Indoor Sports Night -

JACK BENNY: Hello, everybody. This is Jack Benny, coming to you thru the courtesy of the motorcycle cop who stopped me for speeding and made out a ticket in time for me to get here

HARRY CONN: Hello …. this is the motorcycle cop who came here thru the courtesy of a warrant which I have for Jack Benny's arrest ----

FRAN FREY: And I am here thru the courtesy of being a mechanic who built the motorcycle which this cop used in chasing Jack Benny

SEVERAL VOICES (TOGETHER): I came here thru the courtesy of etc. etc.

JACK:	All right, boys. Don't overdo it. What the folks are trying to say, is that this is <u>Indoor Sports Night</u>. Well, we are not going to waste time tonight by introducing John Q. Whoozis and Meyer H. Whatsiz-name …. we're going to get down to <u>Joe T. Business</u> and give you the essence of indoor sports, just as we promised. Of course, these are numerous. We all like different things. For instance, Olsen's favorite indoor sport is playing <u>solitaire with marked</u> cards…. Fran Frey sits and looks the mirror all day, trying to improve himself… while Captain Jimmy Wallington belongs to the Indoor Yatch Club and sails boats in his bathtub.
ANNOUNCER:	What is your favorite Indoor sport, Jack?
JACK:	Breakfast, dinner and supper…Ah! What sports – what's yours, Jimmy?
ANNOUNCER:	Drinking Canada Dry Ginger Ale, made-to-order by the glass.
JACK:	What else can you say? --And sold at all fountains.
ANNOUNCER:	And good in ice cream sodas.
JACK:	And don't forget you get the nickel back on the big bottle.
ANNOUNCER:	That's right, Jack – but let me show you how to say that correctly. It's the nickel back on the big <u>bottle</u>. See? Emphasize <u>bottle</u>.
JACK:	What did <u>I</u> say, Jimmy?
ANNOUNCER:	You said, "A <u>nickel</u> back on the bottle." Now it should be, a nickel back on the <u>bottle</u>.
JACK:	But, Jimmy, you should emphasize the <u>nickel</u>. That's the important thing.
ANNOUNCER:	But Jack you must tell the people what the nickel is for …… it's the nickel back on the <u>bottle</u>.
JACK:	No, Jimmy, you're wrong. It's the <u>nickel</u> back on the bottle.
ANNOUNCER:	Bottle on the <u>nickel</u>.
JACK:	<u>Nickel</u> on the bottle.
ANNOUNCER:	Bottle!
JACK:	Nickel!
ANNOUNCER:	Bottle!
JACK:	Nickel!

(SEGUE INTO MUSICAL NUMBER-----

2. WHEN THE SUN KISSES THE WORLD GOOD-BYE   ETHEL SHUTTA & ORCHESTRA

(OLSEN MAKES ANNOUNCEMENT DURING NUMBER)

JACK:	Jimmy, how you can say "it's the nickel back on the <u>bottle</u>" – when it's the <u>nickel</u> you're talking about.
ANNOUNCER:	<u>You're</u> talking about the nickel – <u>I'm</u> talking about the <u>bottle.</u>
MARY:	Jack, Jack – you're wasting the whole program arguing. <u>This is Sports Night</u>.
JACK:	Well, look, Mary…. which do you think it should be: a <u>nickel</u> back on the bottle – or a nickel back on the <u>bottle</u>?
MARY:	I think it should be <u>five cents</u> back on the <u>fountain</u>.
JACK:	I don't know why I asked you… Well, let's go on with our program. Mary, what's your favorite indoor sport?
MARY:	Well, we have a new game at our house – it's called: "Rent – Rent – Who's Get the Rent?"
JACK:	How does it go, Mary?
MARY:	Well, we play it on the first of the month. The landlord comes and knocks at the door. We all run and hide, and he looks for us.
JACK:	I see….and the one he finds has to pay the rent.
MARY:	Yes – but so far hasn't found anybody. Isn't that a great game?
JACK:	All right, Mary – sit down and take care of the correspondence.
MARY:	Oh yes – I meant to tell you something. Here's a letter from a woman in Philadelphia who says she doesn't like you.
JACK:	Oh, yeah? …. did you answer it?
MARY:	No – but I'm going over there tomorrow and <u>slap her face</u>. I have the address right here. I think you're swell – don't you think so, Mrs. Tagenblatt?
JACK (SPEAKS ON WORD CUE "SWELL"):	Now the first of our indoor sports is that healthful, blood-circulating game of Puss-in-the-Corner…. Remember when you were children and played Puss-in-the-corner? Well, that is still the national indoor game. And we have in our studio the <u>original</u> Puss-in-the-Corner…Come here, Kitty. Say hello to the folks.
BRAD BARKER:	(PURRS)
JACK:	Imagine having a Malt-ese cat on the Canada Dry Program! Now, pussy-pussy, will you sing for us?
BARKER:	Nowwwwww?
JACK:	Yes, now.
BARKER:	Not nowwwww.
JACK:	Say, what's your name, pussycat?

BARKER:	Meriah.
JACK:	Meriah – I expected that…it would be hard for a cat to say "Helen" …… What's your husband's name?
BARKER (IN NATURAL VOICE):	TOM.
JACK:	Tom…. stick to your dialect…. Do you like pictures?
BARKER:	Yeah.
JACK:	Who is your favorite picture star?
BARKER:	Mickey Mouse.
JACK:	Now, Meriah, do you know <u>Mrs. Katz</u> at 110th Street?
BARKER (DOG IMITATION):	(Bark) woof-woof!
JACK:	Cat FIGHT. You better beat it, Meriah.
BARKER:	(DOES CAT-AND-DOG FIGHT BIT)
JACK:	Well, it looks as tho we are going to lose our cat. It's hard to keep good talent these days…. And now, ladies and gentlemen, you know that other famous indoor sport… I'll give you five seconds to guess what it is…. <u>you said it</u>! …. <u>Swatting the fly</u>. Well, we have with us tonight our little pet, a house-fly…. a domestic animal and a pal. This fly has just completed a non-stop flight from a grain of sugar to a dish of chocolate ice cream, without refueling…. now I'm going to ask him a few questions. Listen to these <u>fly</u> remarks…George, chase that fly over here.
GEORGE:	Where is it?
JACK:	On your right ear.
GEORGE:	You call him…you brought him in.
BARKER (DOGS FLY IMITATION):	Buzz, buzz …. buzz.
JACK:	Come right over here, and sit down my little finger. Now tell us, Fly, when you are not busy working, where do you play?
BARKER:	Buzz …. buzz. buzz.
JACK:	I see…you play on bill-of-fares in restaurants…Tell us how did you manage to escape the fly swatter up to now?
BARKER:	Buzz…buzz.
JACK:	He says that a swatter hit him three times, but he can take it. This little fellow has a cauliflower ear…. Which shows that he's game…. Now, one more question, where do you flies go in the wintertime? BARGER: Bzzzz …. Bzzzzz
Jack:	He says they hide in <u>raisin cake</u>…. Listen, Insect, I'll tell the jokes on this program…. All right, you can go now. Go over there and annoy Olsen.

BARKER:	(BUZZES AWAY INTO DISTANCE)
JACK:	Wait a minute – you forgot your specks….
	Say, Mary, you haven't seen a little germ around here that wants to be introduced – have you?
MARY:	No, but I'll look around.
JACK:	Sit down, Mary – go ahead, George.
	(SEGUE INTO NEXT NUMBER –

3. MARIELLA   PAUL SMALL & ORCHESTRA

(OLSEN MAKES ANNOUNCEMENT DURING NUMBER)

JACK:	One of the best-known Indoor Sports today is "Walking the Baby." This is generally played at three o'clock in the morning, after being awakened out of a sound sleep, by your little baby who doesn't care <u>what</u> time it is. So now we are going to offer a little playlet called, "Three O'clock in the Morning." ……. The Cast of Characters is as follows:
	Mr. Gum Unt-heit, a successful business man, will be played by yours truly, Jack Benny…Ethel Shutta will play, Mrs. <u>Cachoo</u> (sneeze) Gus Unt-heit, the wife. And little Sneezer Gus Unt-heit, the baby, will be played by Babe Ruth – The scene takes place in the <u>Broken Arms</u> Apartments, Irvington-on –the-Cuff. This apartment has six rooms and eleven baths for sixty-five dollars a month … or you can get eleven baths with <u>no</u> rooms for fifty cents a bath…or if you don't like baths, you can get three living-rooms with <u>no baths</u> or <u>four baths</u> with <u>no</u> dining-room for twenty dollars. Drive out Sunday and look them over. Not that I'm trying to rent you an apartment…. this is the Canada Dry Program.
	Well, anyway, this scene takes place in the parlor, bedroom and pump in the backyard. Now follow the play closely…the continuity will kill you. READY – <u>CURTAIN</u>!…. Say, George, we'll have to have music with this. You know, it's three o'clock in the morning and everybody's asleep. Give us some appropriate music…. you know what to play…something soothing and dreamy…
GEORGE:	All right, boys.
	(ORCHESTRA PLAYS FEW MEASURES OF "HAPPY DAYS ARE HERE AGAIN")
JACK:	That's it…now, George, give us the chimes. (CHIMES STRIKE 5 TIMES)
	George, it's supposed to be <u>three</u> o'clock. You struck it <u>five</u> times.
GEORGE:	Well it's <u>five after three</u> now.
JACK:	Now folks, let me described this scene to you. It's three a.m. The husband and wife are both asleep in twin beds…the husband on the third floor…the wife on the

fifth…..and the lawyer sleeps on the fourth….The baby is asleep on a <u>davenport</u>, by special permission of Iowa…The uncle, who came over to spend ten week-ends, is fast asleep on the doormat right where it says, "Welcome"….And you folks will no doubt be asleep long before this playlet is over, if you know what's good for you.

Now, boys, give us a little sound effect of a man and his wife asleep.

(ETHEL AND BARKER SNORE)

And now – the baby.

(<u>SOUND EFFECT: LION'S ROAR</u>)

That must be a <u>baby lion</u>…. George, you better announce the next number while the cast stands by for the play.

GEORGE OLSEN: The next number, ladies and gentlemen, is ANOTHER NIGHT ALONE.

4. ANOTHER NIGHT ALONE   ORCHESTRA

JACK: All right…. all right…everybody in their positions. On with the show! Curtain…music…and chimes.

(ORCHESTRA PLAYS FEW MEASURES OF "HAPPY DAYS" – CHIMES STRIKE THREE TIMES – SNORING AND WHISTLING)

(BRAD BARKER DOES BABY'S CRY THROUGHOUT FOLLOWING SCENE.)

ETHEL: Oh, dear, dear – there goes that child crying again…Gus..Gus..Unt-heit.

JACK (YAWNS):   Aw, what do you want, darling? Why don't let a fellow sleep?

ETHEL: Will you <u>please</u> stop that child crying.

JACK: Aw, let her cry.

ETHEL: You mean – let <u>him</u> cry.

JACK: Yes.

ETHEL: Can't you see he's waking up all the neighbors. What will they think?

JACK: I don't care what they think…he's <u>our</u> child.

(<u>BABY CRIES LOUDER</u>)

JACK: What will I do with him?

ETHEL: Give him his bottle of milk.

JACK: All right…Sneezer, come here…. Don't cry…here's your bottle.

<u>BARKER</u>:   I <u>don't</u> want the <u>bottle</u>…I want the <u>nickel back.</u>

JACK:	Now, now, Sneezer…Let Poppa be the master of ceremonies. Come and sit on Poppa's back and play horsey.
BARKER (LAUGHS):	Look, Momma…Poppa Jack-ass.
ETHEL:	You said it.
JACK:	Now no wisecracks of Poppa break little leggee.
ETHEL:	Now dare you talk that way to our one child? It's a fine way to educate our boy.
BARKER:	It's all right, Mom – don't worry about me – I read "Ballyhoo."
JACK:	Oh, yeah?....I'll show you.
ETHEL:	Don't you dare raise a hand to that child.
	(BABY CRIES IN DISTANCE DURING NEXT LINE)
JACK:	There…there, don't cry little Sneezer. (STARTS TO SING) Rock-a-bye, Baby, on the Tree Top…dum-da-dum-da Canada Dry…. (wait.)
BARKER:	That's rotten, Pa. Sing something hot. (STARTS TO CRY AGAIN)
JACK:	What are you crying about now?
BARKER:	It's in the script. (Cry longer.)
JACK:	Here, Mom – take your child.
ETHEL:	Come here, angel… (starts to hum "Jolly Good Company" – baby continues crying)
BARKER:	I'm sick of that, too. (cry)
ETHEL:	Tell Momma what did Poppa do to you?....Give him his bottle of milk, you brute!... here's your bottle, dear.
BABY:	I don't want a bottle.
ETHEL:	What on earth do you want?
JACK – ETHEL & BARKER (TOGETHER):	Canada Dry Ginger Ale made-to –order by the glass (and start to cry)

SEGUE INTO NUMBER --

5. HARLEM MOON　　　　　　　　　　EHTEL SHUTTA & ORCHESTRA

(OLSEN MAKES HIS ANNOUNCEMENT DURING NUMBER)

JACK:	That was the last number of the 36th program on the 31st of August. Altho this is Indoor Sports Night, we must present to you the stars of the great outdoor event that happened today – the Eclipse of the Sun. We have the two principals of that

outstanding event up here tonight. What other program can offer such a treat? What other program gets all of the stars first – not only the stars, but the Sun and the Moon….And now it gives me great pleasure in introducing to you MR. MOON… who has finally come over the mountain…passed the sun and was severely burned. But he came up here just the same. And now it is a great honor and a pleasure to introduce to you MR. MOON.

(ROUND OF APPLAUSE)

FRAN FREY: How do you do, ladies and gentlemen…I had the pleasure of passing the Sun at 4: 28 this afternoon, and I am very happy to be up here this evening as this will not occur again until 1963 – when I hope to be here again – with Jack Benny – to say hello.

JACK: And don't forget, folks – it will be at 9:30 P.M……Tell me, Mr. Moon, how do you like night work?

FRAN: I don't know – I'm just so used to it that it doesn't bother me at all.

JACK: I notice you have quite a sun-tan. Did you have any difficulty in passing the sun this afternoon?

FRAN: I was prepared for it – I had on my sunglasses and a parasol. Besides, he's not so hot.

JACK: All right, Mr. Moon, thank you very much…. And now, folks, we will bring to you his opponent THE SUN!....Oh, Sol….SOL…….

HARRY CONN (WITH ACCENT): Vat do you want?

JACK: Well, folks, you figure it out….Good night…We will see you on Monday – on our Special Labor Day program…Come on, Sol…..

ANNOUNCER: The next time you stop at a soda fountain for a refreshing drink, ask for a glass of Canada Dry, the Champagne of Ginger Ales – it will be made to order for you. And when you buy Canada Dry in bottles for the home, remember that the new big bottle is particularly convenient and economical. Remember, too, that with the exception of a few localities, where freight charges do not permit, you can take back your Canada Dry bottles to the dealer and got a cash refund. So that now when you buy

Canada Dry you pay for the contents only. Next Monday night at this same time Jack Benny, Ethel Shutta and George Olsen will again entertain you. This is the National Broadcasting Company.

September 5, 1932

There's a big Labor Day parade that Jack describes as the marchers go past. Mary reads her first "Labor Day" poem, which is oddly morose rather than like the humorously dippy poems she would read out in later years. Jack and the cast talk about their appearances at New York's Capitol Theater (which the sponsor had objected to as they weren't getting an advertising plug). Jack accuses George with being cheap, and brags that his white Palm Beach suit cost $90 (a boast Jack Benny would never make in the years afterward). Jack jokingly name-checks Garbo and Gable, Frankenstein and Dracula (even if the latter two were characters in Universal films, Benny wants to mention then-popular films playing at movie theaters).

STATION WJZ	PROGRAM	CANADA DRY GINGER ALE, INC.
AND	DATE	MONDAY, SEPTEMBER 5, 1932
BLUE NETWORK	TIME	9:30 – 10:00P.M.

SIGNATURE – JOLLY GOOD COMPANY

1. LET'S K-NOCK K-NEES	ORCHESTRA, ETHEL SHUTTA & FRAN FREY
2. GOODBYE TO SUMMER LOVE	ORCHESTRA & PAUL SMALL
3. I CAN'T BELIEVE IT'S TRUE	ORCHESTRA & ETHEL SHUTTA
4. "I LOVE A PARADE	ORCHESTRA & FRAN FREY
5. YOU'RE TELLING ME	ORCHESTRA & FRAN FREY

SIGNATURE – ROCKABYE MOON

STATION WJZ	PROGRAM	CANADA DRY GINGER AIR, INC.
AND	DATE	MONDAY, SEPTEMBER 5, 1932
BLUE NETWORK	TIME	9:30 – 10:00

SIGNATURE – JOLLY GOOD COMPANY

ANNOUNCER: Ladies and gentlemen, another half hour of entertainment about Canada Dry – the champagne of ginger ales – now available by the glass at soda fountains, as well as in bottles for the home. You'll find the new, large size bottle very economical, and particularly convenient for home use. Once more we present George Olsen, Ethel Shutta and Jack Benny – the Canada Dry humorist – who will perform for your enjoyment. George Olsen opens the with "Let's K-nock K-nees," Ethel Shutta and Fran Frey singing.

1. LET'S K-NOCK K-NEES   EHTEL SHUTTA, FRAN FREY & ORCHESTRA

ANNOUNCER: And here is our Master of Ceremonies---

JACK: Hello, atmosphere customers…. remember me? …the fellow who hangs around here Monday and Wednesday nights – hmmm? You remember – the fellow with Robert Montgomery <u>features</u>….and Laurel and Hardy <u>shorts</u>? you know, the fellow who walks to the microphone sort of <u>Garbo-ish</u>…. with that <u>Pathetic</u> Weekly smile? standing here like an adagio dancer waiting for his mate, hand on hip, elbow out? You know me now – Jack Benny? Sure – how are you? This is <u>Jack Benny</u> – that representative American youth and Heaven's gift to the wave --

GEORGE: Say Jack – Jack – why don't you talk about yourself for a change?

JACK: That was George Olsen – the big <u>sharp</u>-<u>and</u> <u>flat</u> man from Sweden…Say, George, I want to congratulate you on your appearance at the theatre this week…. You know, ladies and gentlemen, George, Ethel, the boys and I are all playing at the Capitol Theatre, having a lot of fun – and I wish you could all come to see us. In fact, George invites all of you ever. <u>His name</u> and the price of admission will get you in – in fact, you don't even have to mention <u>his name</u>…. But, George, you do look like a million dollars on the stage, and I like that full dress suit you <u>hired</u>.

GEORGE: <u>I hired!</u> …Why, that's <u>my</u> suit. I was married in that suit eight years ago.

JACK: Well, George, the least you can do in <u>shake the rice</u> out of it…. You certainly didn't get stuck with it…. your tailor gave you <u>plenty of pants</u>.

GEORGE:	Hey, Jack, these pants are all right…. they're just <u>loose and roomy</u> – that's all.
JACK:	Yeah – <u>roomy</u>…. you can get the whole hand in them.
GEORGE:	I want you to know that I had that suit made-to-order in <u>London</u>.
JACK:	You did, ah? …. you must have been <u>in Paris</u> at the time.
GEORGE:	Well, let me tell <u>you</u> something, Jack. You didn't look so hot yourself.
JACK:	How about that nice white Palm Beach suit <u>I</u> wore?
GEORGE:	All you needed was a helmet, a broom and a shovel.
JACK:	George, that shows what you know about <u>style</u>. They wear those suits at <u>Newport.</u>
GEORGE:	Well, they have <u>street cleaners up there</u>, too.
JACK:	George, you'd be very much surprised to know the price of my suit. That suit costs <u>ninety</u> dollars.
GEORGE:	<u>Ninety</u> dollars? I don't believe it.
JACK:	You don't ah? Well, I'll show you the <u>summons</u>…. I'll tell you who did look gorgeous, tho, George – that was <u>Ethel</u>. She looked beautiful in that blue gown.
ETHEL:	Oh, thanks Jack. I'm as glad you liked that new gown of mine. Did you like the "V" in the back?
JACK:	That must have been capital "V" … I never saw such a <u>big</u> "V." What a spot for a Canada Dry ad!
ETHEL:	You know <u>George</u> bought me that gown as a little present.
JACK:	He did?... He really <u>paid</u> for it?
ETHEL:	Yes, I was with him.
JACK:	Say, Ethel, let me ask you something – is it true or not, then, that George is a little bit <u>tight</u>…. you know, <u>close</u>.
ETHEL:	Why, Jack, of course not – it's greatly exaggerated…. He's very liberal, really at least, <u>he is with me.</u>
JACK:	I had a hunch that everyone else must be wrong. But, Ethel, how is it, then, that I never see you two together anywhere? He never seems to take you any place.
ETHEL:	Why, Jack, he does, too. Why, only last Wednesday he took me to see the – to see the –
JACK:	The <u>eclipse.</u>
ETHEL:	Yes.
JACK:	I know, Ethel – I had seats for that, too…. You could have gone with me. Wasn't that a wonderful sight?

ETHEL: YES – isn't science amazing?

JACK: I wonder if that was really an eclipse – or Fran Frey eating a slice of watermelon…. Just think of that <u>sun</u> getting in front of the moon!

ETHEL: Jack, you mean the <u>moon</u> getting in front of the sun.

JACK: Well, I must have seen the <u>second</u> show…. George, you better play the next number. Ethel and I will be talking for hours.

2. GOODBYE TO SUMMER LOVE   ORCHESTRA & PAUL SMALL

(GEORGE OLSEN MAKES ANNOUNCEMENT DURING NUMBER)

JACK: Well, ladies and gentlemen, today is <u>Labor Day</u> – and it is the aim of this program to keep ahead of the times. So we are going to give you not only a Labor Day program, but that little something extra that we all like – that little <u>sprig of parsley</u> on your omelet – or that <u>little olive</u> with your favorite sandwich…..Tonight, we will bring your our usual Guest Star—<u>officer take the handcuffs</u> off our Guest Star and bring him in….Better keep the <u>strait jacket on that guy</u> who thinks he's Napoleon…. Ah! we certainly get a lot of <u>Frankensteins</u> and <u>Draculas</u> up here….Now here's a guy standing up – say, what's <u>your</u> name?

GEORGE HICKS: I'm George Hicks, the announcer.

JACK: Oh, <u>Hicks</u>! Pardon me…. hello, Hicks, I haven't seen you in two weeks. I didn't know you were back.

HICKS: Oh, yes, I was away on a little vacation.

JACK: Is that so? Did you have a nice time?

HICKS: <u>Did I</u>! … I was up in the mountains – and let me tell you, Jack, <u>everybody</u> up there was talking about this program.

JACK: Is that so? …What did they say?

HICKS: Canada Dry Ginger Ale made-to-order by the glass, and sold at all fountains.

JACK: <u>No</u>.

HICKS: <u>Yes</u>.

JACK: You can't get away from it – can you, Hicks?

HICKS: Well, Jack I want to tell you I had a swell time up there. I was visiting a friend of mine way up in the Maine woods – a very wealthy fellow –

JACK: Really!

HICKS: Yes, sir – he owns <u>over eight hundred</u> large Canada Dry bottles.

JACK:	Can you imagine that? .... A <u>nickel</u> back on each …. Gee! that means a fortune nowadays…. Well, Hicks, what make you come back so soon?
HICKS:	Well, Jack I spent my last Canada Dry bottle – and I had nothing left.
JACK:	Are you <u>broke</u>, Hicks? I can let you have a few bottles until tomorrow.
HICKS:	Thanks, Jack –
JACK:	There you are!
HICKS:	Ladies and gentlemen, Canada Dry bottles are as good as the cash itself.
JACK:	It's all right, Hicks. They get the idea. Don't make this program <u>so commercial</u>…. Wait a minute, what are we selling – Ginger Ale or bottles? Well, send our guest Star over here to the microphone…Ladies and gentlemen, I want to introduce to you a <u>great personality</u> who boasts of an excellent record for the advancement of Labor – our guest of the evening -- (ROUND OF APPLAUSE) Now, young fellow, your audience awaits you.
HARRY CONN:	Yeah! – what do you want from me?
JACK:	WELL, <u>before</u> we kick you out of here, I want to find out a few things about you.
HARRY:	Well, go ahead – I'm in a hurry.
JACK:	Hey, what have you got to do?
HARRY:	I have three days to kill and I want to get it over with.
JACK:	You probably won't live that long…. Now, not that it matters, but what's your name?
HARRY:	My name is <u>Walker</u>.
JACK:	Not <u>Mayor Walker</u>.
HARRY:	No – <u>Meyer</u>.
JACK:	Oh, I see <u>Meyer</u> Walker.
HARRY:	Yes, I'm <u>Meyer of Schenectady</u>.
JACK:	Oh, you're the <u>Mayor of Schenectady</u>.
HARRY:	No! I'm <u>Meyer of Schenectady</u>…… you've beard of <u>Helen of Troy</u>, haven't you?
JACK:	Yes.
HARRY:	Well, I'm Meyer of Schenectady.
JACK:	Don't tune out, folks. We'll straighten this thing out very soon. Now let me get this thing straight – is your name <u>Meyer Walker</u>?
HARRY:	No – my first name is <u>McKee</u>.

JACK:	Oh, McKee… <u>McKee Walker</u>…… So, <u>you're</u> the fellow who's going to fight Schmelling.
HARRY:	Well, if you want it that way, all right. <u>I'm tired</u>.
JACK:	McKee Walker – eh? …. Listen, do you think you can stop <u>Schmelling</u>?
HARRY:	Sure.
JACK:	Well, how would you like to stop <u>Breathing</u>?
HARRY:	What's <u>his</u> weight?
JACK:	Wait a minute – what did you come up here for?
HARRY:	I don't know. Someone gave me a dollar and a half and told me not to tell anybody.
JACK:	Well, I think you're going to be our <u>last</u> Guest Star…. Say, Meyer, will you take the advice of an old-timer?
HARRY:	What?
JACK:	Go on a hunting trip with Frank Buck and let him bring everything back alive <u>but you</u>…. Now get out of here!
HARRY:	<u>What</u> a joint this is to bring a gentleman.
JACK:	<u>SCRAM</u>! …And now George Olsen and <u>his</u> Guest Stars will play" I Can't Believe it's True," sung by Ethel Shutta.

3. I CAN'T BELIEVE IT'S TRUE   ORCHESTRA & ETHEL SHUTTA

JACK:	And now, ladies and gentlemen, for our big surprise of the evening…. Every city of any size throughout the country has had their big Labor Day Parade today. So, for the benefit of those of you who live in the rural districts and remote spots, we are not going to let you miss anything. We will stage our own Labor Day Parade for your pleasure. <u>Imagine a hundred thousand</u> men in this Studio! You think it's impossible – eh? …. Well, <u>nothing</u> is impossible on this program. And that isn't all. We expect to have a <u>hundred and fifty</u> thousand people here for the Army-Navy game this Fall…. Of course, we'll have to move out the piano…. There is nothing too good for our customers. Believe me and see where you get…. All right, George, take the mike while I get the boys in formation.
	(START DRUMS HERE – BACKGROUND CONFUSION)
	All right, boys, straighten out those horses…. Come on, Carpenters, get behind those Plumbers…. Hey! you Butchers, got behind those Bakers….and <u>you</u>, Bakers, follow those Candlestick-Makers. Come on – line up there, Rich Man – Poor Man – Beggar Man – Thief…Doctor – Lawyer - Indian Chief…. I'm glad I remembered that…. Hey, you Watchmakers, you're all out of <u>time</u>…. Everybody – stand by!

4. "I LOVE A PARADE" ORCHESTRA & FRAN FREY

(MUSIC FADES OUT BUT DRUM CONTINUES--

JACK: Look at that parade coming down the street---

HICKS: This is the Studio, Jack.

JACK: All right, the studio – here they come, folks…. what a parade!.......This is Jack Benny standing on the curb --

(SHUFFLING OF FEET MARCHING – ALSO DRUMS)

Ah! What is that group? …. The Ice Men! …. the ice men have been marching all morning, and here they are…. with their tongues hanging out……These boys work all year round, selling stiff pieces of water…. What a job! … what a parade! And here come their enemies – twenty thousand electric iceboxes filled with Canada Dry…. next in line are the Shoemakers…there they come, walking on their heels…. What kindly souls. Here is the head shoemaker. Say something, Boss.

HARRY CONN: Heel-o, everybody!

(BRASS BAND PLAYS)

JACK: What a crowd…what festivity! Here come the Matzoh Ball Makers … and now come the Sculptors from Greenwich Village…two thousand of the finest chiselers in the world…and right behind them are the Pinochle Kibitzers…. Hello, Kibitzers. Say something to the gang.

PAUL SMALL: You should not have led that Ace of Spades.

JACK: Thank you, Kibby – I'll play out this hand. There are more Kibitzers than anything else.

(BAG PIPES IN DISTANCE – INCREASES IN VOLUME)

And the Scotch Highlanders in close formation…. Say something, Scotties.

PAUL – BALDWIN – HANNA (SPEAK IN TURN): Hello Olsen…. Hi, George……How are you, Olsen?

JACK: All the Scotchmen know Olsen – And It's a bran brich moonlich nicht wi' Olsen tonight…they're all going on a party…and what a deadlock…. Next come the Crooners – headed by Bing – Rudy – and Russ.

FRAN – PAUL AND GARDNER (SING TOGETHER): When the blue of the night Meets the gold of the day….ba, ba, bee, ba, ba…

JACK: Look at them – all marching with their megaphones…And now some the Tailors who press everybody's pants but their own…and the Barbers… all big, strooping men…. Don't forget I'm next, boys…. Ah! here come the Masters of Ceremonies……. What a fine gang of Laboring men……how they toil! Look at their worn faces. It's a shame that most of them wind up without a nickel.

HICKS:	Oh, but if they had a large Canada Dry bottle, they would wind up <u>with a nickel</u>…... You get a nickel back on each large Canada Dry bottle.
JACK:	Hey, Hicks, wait a minute. I thought I had this parade fixed so that you couldn't butt in…. And now for the tag end of the Parage…. The <u>Gigolos</u>…. Here they come, lighting their cigarettes. Say something. Gig!
PAUL SMALL:	Business is awful.
JACK:	People know the game you're playing.
	(DRUM AND FIFE CORPS – SHINE INTO FINISH OF "I LOVE A PARADE)
JACK BENNY:	Now, ladies and gentlemen, wasn't that thrilling sight? Did you ever <u>see</u> such a parade?
	(HEAR DRUMS AND MARCHING FEET IN DISTANCE SOFTLY)
	Hey, wait a minute – what are <u>you</u> <u>fellows</u> doing here, marching alone? Don't you know the parade is over?
HARRY CONN AND FRAN FREY (TOGETHER):	We're the <u>Street</u> <u>Cleaners</u> …. we follow every parade. (START SINGING: "WE LOVE A PARADE" --
JACK:	Take it, George, while I join the boys.

(SEGUE INTO –

5. YOU'RE TELLING ME   ORCHESTRA & FRAN FREY

JACK:	What was the last number of thirty – seventh program on the 5th of September. <u>What</u> an exciting time we had in the studio!
SADYE:	Jack – oh! Jack!
JACK:	What is it, Mary?
SADYE:	Jack, I made up a little poem for Labor Day, which I think is swell. I think it would fit this program – do you mind if I read it?
JACK:	No, of course not.
SADYE (STARTS TO SNIFFLE):	Jack, it's awfully sad.
JACK:	Go ahead, Mary – that's all right. Read it.
SADYE (READS POEM):	As thru life we wander – often even as we go Troubles – worry – care – endure us yet Something listens in our ear as oft it was – and <u>still</u> Isn't it the truth as what you get? When the night begins each morn or afternoon we feel

>
> Those times are not just what they used to be.
> Labor Day – Oh, Labor Day!......
> It just seems to reveal
> That a rolling stone is not your friend at all,
> Old pal of mine....... <u>Isn't that sad</u>?

JACK: Much sadder than I expected.

MARY: Oh, I have another one –

JACK: <u>Goodnight</u>, everybody – I'll see you Wednesday.

SIGNATURE – ROCKABYE MOON

ANNOUNCER: The next time you stop at a soda fountain for a refreshing drink, ask for a glass of Canada Dry, the Champagne of Ginger Ales – it will be made-to-order for you. And when you buy Canada Dry in bottles for the home, remember that the new big bottle is particularly convenient and economical. Remember, too, that with the exception of a few localities, where freight charges do not permit, you can take back your Canada Dry bottles to the dealer and get a cash refund. So that now when you buy Canada Dry you pay for the contents only. Wednesday night at this same time Jack Benny, Ethel Shutta and George Olsen will again entertain you. This is the National Broadcasting Company.

September 7, 1932

George Hicks again is the obnoxious Announcer, and he keeps breaking into others' dialogue to tout Canada Dry. Jack says the jokes he tells on stage are old, but were good enough for Lincoln and Washington (an early instance of the regular associations Benny would make with these two presidents who were also born in February, and whom make Jack appear very old himself). Mary appears at the end of the episode in a funny dialogue exchange with Jack, in which she asks if he has sent her flowers.

STATION WJZ	PROGRAM	CANADA DRY GINGER ALE, INC.
AND	DATE	WEDNESDAY, SEPTEMBER 7, 1932
BLUE NETWORK	TIME	9:30 – 10:00 P.M.

SIGNATURE – JOLLY GOOD COMPANY

1. YOU'RE JUST ABOUT RIGHT FOR ME	ORCHESTRA & DICK GARDNER
2. ALWAYS IN MY HEART	ORCHESTRA & ETHEL SHUTTA
3. I PLAYED FIDDLE FOR THE CZAR	ORCHESTRA & FRAN FREY
4. THREE'S A CROWD	ORCHESTRA & PAUL SMALL
5. ANGELCAKE LADY	ORCHESTRA & FRAN FREY & ETHEL SHUTTA

SIGNATURE – ROCKABYE MOON

CANADA DRY GINGER ALE, INC.   WEDNESDAY, SEPTEMBER 7, 1932

SIGNATURE – JOLLY GOOD COMPANY

ANNOUNCER: Ladies and gentlemen, another half hour of entertainment about Canada Dry – the champagne of ginger ales – now available by the glass at soda fountains, as well as in bottles for the home. You'll find the new, large size bottle very economical, and particularly convenient for home use. Once more we present George Olsen, Ethel Shutta and Jack Benny – the Canada Dry Humorist – who will perform for your enjoyment. George Olsen opens the program with "You're Just About Right for Me," vocal chorus by Dick Gardner.

1. YOU'RE JUST ABOUT RIGHT FOR ME　　　　ORCHESTRA AND GARDNER

ANNOUNCER: And now our master of ceremonies, Jack Benny.

JACK: Hello, more people than last week…. this is Jack Benny welcoming you back from your vacations. Did you have nice time- hmmm? And say, girls, did you meet a swell feller on the porch whom you promised to marry as soon as he gets a raise, or are you going back your Winter feller? I know all the tricks, girls. I used to sit on porches myself…. And how were the meals at the hotel you stopped at? Not bad, eh? Did you get up at eight o'clock just so you wouldn't miss breakfast because you were paying for it? Well anyway, I'm glad you're all back, feeling rested and all tanned up, and now is the time to get down to hard work and serious thought. And don't worry about anything as I was here all summer, and I want to tell you that you didn't miss a thing. Everything is the same – prosperity is <u>still</u> around the corner…" Happy Days are here again" is <u>still</u> a great song….and Olsen is <u>still</u> dodging unnecessary expenses. So, you see, you had a nice time - you missed nothing – and now you're back, ready to knuckle down to work.

ANNOUNCER (GEORGE HICKS): And don't forget, you get a <u>knuckle</u> back on each large Canada Dry bottle.

JACK: Close that door. (SOUND EFFECT: DOOR BANG) Keep Hicks out of here…. A knuckle back on the bottle…But I must say this, folks, things are going to be much better, and the outlook is brighter already. Why, only the other day I read in the paper where a rosy future for this country is predicted by Senator Glass, and Glass knows what he's talking----

ANNOUNCER (INTERRUPTING ON WORD "<u>KNOWS</u>"):	Speaking of <u>glass</u>. Canada Dry Ginger Ale is made-to-order by the glass, and sold at all fountains.
JACK:	I'm sorry it wasn't Senator <u>Borah</u> who said that…. George, how can we stop Hicks from talking about Canada Dry on this program?
GEORGE OLSEN:	Why shouldn't he? Everybody's drinking it.
JACK:	Well, why talk about it, then? Ethel, will you do me a favor – sing a song. Please change the subject and don't mention Ginger Ale.
ETHEL:	All right, Jack.
JACK:	What song are you going to sing?
ETHEL:	'Ail, 'Ail, the Gang's All Here!
JACK:	I see, Ethel, it's a plot---- You can see, ladies and gentlemen, this is the National Nut and Bolt program. <u>Now</u> Olsen will play while I make a <u>bolt</u> for the next room…. and Ethel will probably sing "Rivet, Keep Away from My Door," or whatever she'll sing…. I'm mad …. everything happens to me….

(SEGUE INTO –

2. ALWAYS IN MY HEART   ETHEL SHUTTA AND ORCHESTRA

(GEORGE OLSEN INTORDUCES NUMBER)

ANNOUNCER:	All right, Jack, the number is over. Take the mike.
JACK:	No, I don't want to play. I'm still mad.
ETHEL:	What are you mad about now, Jack?
JACK:	Aw, I always have a lot of jokes to tell, and all I hear is Canada Dry Ginger Ale made-to-order by the glass-----
ANNOUNCER:	And sold at all fountains----
JACK:	And good in ice-cream sodas…. <u>some</u> nerve!
ETHEL:	Jack, don't be mad. Come on – talk to the folks.
JACK:	NO!
ETHEL:	I'll give you a lollipop.
JACK:	Yeah? …. what color?
ETHEL:	Yellow.
JACK:	I don't want yellow.

ETHEL:	Here's a nice <u>red</u> lollipop.
JACK:	Thanks, - gee, it's a big one. What does it cost?
ETHEL:	They're a <u>nickel</u> apiece.
ANNOUNCER:	Which is exactly what you get back for each large Canada Dry bottle.
JACK:	You see, Ethel…. there he goes again – always starting something.
ANNOUNCER:	I am not.
ETHEL:	Now, Hicks, stop it…. Leave Jack alone.
JACK:	Yeah, he's always picking on me…Say, Ethel, you know what I was just thinking? Here we are playing at the Capitol Theatre this week, telling a lot of jokes and I think our jokes are too good to keep away from our air customers. Don't you think we ought to tell some of them tonight?
ETHEL:	That's a good idea, Jack – do you remember them all?
JACK:	Do I remember them? Ethel, those jokes have been with me for years. Say, if they were good enough for <u>Lincoln</u> and <u>Washington</u>, they're good enough for me.
ETHEL:	All right, Jack, let's tell them.
JACK:	All right, folks, get into the mood for these witty sayings and puzzling riddles…… Now Ethel, I'll say to you …. <u>you must be a very popular girl</u>. Then you say to me – why? And I'll tell the answer.
ETHEL:	All right, Jack.
JACK:	Here we go – Joke number one …. Ethel, I see you're a very popular girl.
ETHEL:	Why, Jack?
JACK:	Because your name is in front of every gas station.
ORCHESTRA BOYS:	(IN DISGUST) BOOOOO!
JACK:	Of course, folks, it isn't the jokes alone. You should see the expression on our faces. <u>That's</u> what counts…All right, Ethel. Joke number two. What is it that has four eyes – is half-male and half-female, and don't care for peanuts?
ETHEL:	I give up, Jack. What is it that has four eyes and is half-male and half-female?
JACK:	Sophie Tucker and her son.
ETHEL:	But where do the peanuts come in?
JACK:	In little paper bags, Ethel.
ORCHESTRA BOYS:	(IN DISGUST) BOOOOO!
JACK:	Well, we got them laughing.

ETHEL:	Let <u>me</u> tell one now.
JACK:	All right, Ethel – go ahead.
ETHEL:	Now, I'll ask the question, but let me tell the answer, too.
JACK:	Okay – go ahead.
ETHEL:	What's the difference between Station W-E-A-F and W-I-F-E?
JACK:	I don't know – what is the difference between Station W-E-A-F and W-I-F-E?
GEORGE OLSEN:	You can tune out W-E-A-F…. I know <u>that</u> one. This is George Olsen speaking.
JACK:	That's pretty good, George, I got it.
GEORGE:	Say, let me play this time, Jack. I've got a peach of a riddle.
JACK:	What is it?
GEORGE:	It's not your father – it's not your mother, It's not your sister or your brother. It's not your uncles nor your aunts, It's not your coat – nor vest – nor pants…. <u>What is it?</u>
JACK:	I don't know – do you know, Ethel?
ETHEL:	No.
JACK:	Do you know, Hicks?
ANNOUNCER:	<u>Yes</u> – it's Canada Dry Ginger Ale made-to-order by the glass.
JACK:	I knew it…. I knew it…. there he goes again…. I'm not going to play any more <u>–</u> NO!
ETHEL:	Come on, Jack…. See what you did, Hicks?
ANNOUNCER:	I didn't mean anything
ALL (AD LIB) –	

(SEGUE INTO NEXT NUMBER –

5. I PLAYED THE FIDDLE FOR THE CZAR   ORCHESTRA AND FRAN FRAY

JACK:	Well, folks, it isn't enough that I'm mad at Hicks and everything, but to top it off here's a letter I just selected at random from a batch of fan mail. It's a letter from Cincinnati, <u>O'Dayton</u>…. It reads:

"DEAR PROGRAM:

I LISTENED TO YOUR PROGRAM LAST MONDAY NIGHT WHEN YOU HAD YOUR LABOR DAY PARADE AND I DON'T BELIEVE YOU HAD A HUNDRED THOUSAND MEN MARCHING IN YOUR STUDIO. YOU CAN POOL SOME OF THE PEOPLE ALL OF THE TIME....AND ALL OF THE PEOPLE SOME OF THE TIME, BUT YOU CAN'T .... WHATEVER ELSE LINCOLN SAID.... I HAD AN ARGUMENT WITH MY HUSBAND – THE BRUTE!.........WHO WILL BE LISTENING IN FROM THE HOSPITAL TONIGHT.... HE CLAIMS YOUR PROGRAM IS A FAKE AND I CLAIM IT'S A FRAUD.... NOW KINDLY TELL US WHICH ONE IS RIGHT?

PLEASE SEND ME A PHOTOGRAPH OF SOMEONE WHO IS NOT ON YOUR PROGRAM

(SIGNED) MRS. GEFILTO FISH."

Well, Mrs. Fish, those are the things that hurt.... people doubting our programs. Let me tell you something, lady and fifty thousand others that send us the same stereotyped letter, we had more than a hundred thousand men in the Studio. As a matter of fact, we had two hundred and fifty thousand people present during the Sharkey-Schmeling Fight.... which you remember was held up here.... Let me tell you what this studio is like. It is exactly the size of the wide-open spaces out West, and you know that runs from here to there.... Why, this building is so tall that we had to look down at the Eclipse last week.... Mrs. Gefilto – no doubt Italian – you are dealing with a large institution when you are listening in to our program....and at some future date we are going to reproduce the World War up here with the original cast, at no advance in price.... Now don't let's hear from you soon again.... PLAY, GEORGE!

ETHEL: Jack, did you really get that letter?

JACK: No, Ethel.... I had to fill in a few minutes.

(GEORGE OLSEN ANNOUNCES NEXT NUMBER)

4. THERE'S A CROWD   ORCHESTRA & PAUL SMALL

JACK: Hello, late customers.... take your seats, remove your hats. You didn't miss anything. This is J.B. again, doing the telling....... And now for our big, supreme.... colossal.... stupendous surprise. In fact, I could almost say "Gigantic." What a surprise! Even I don't know what it is...Ethel, did you see a surprise around here?

ETHEL: Well, Jack, Paul Small got a haircut.

JACK: I know, Ethel, but that's not enough for a swell program like this. What we want are attractions, names, addresses.... Well, anyway, while we're waiting, we will entertain you with an ordinary offering. We have right here in this Studio the aviator who has just returned from the Cleveland Air Meet – where he broke all speed records. This man flew at the rate of three hundred and ten miles an hour, as the crow flies – and you know how the fly crows…er…..I mean – the crow flies….<u>I don't</u> ….incidentally, during this last flight, his mechanic fell out of the plane from a height of six thousand feet at the rate of <u>four hundred and fifty miles</u> an hour….as an apple falls, only stopping <u>once</u> to think it over…..So <u>now</u> we take pleasure in introducing to you first – The Flying Farmer, <u>Hy</u> Droplane…and his mechanic, <u>J. Refuel Tank.</u>

(ROUND OF APPLAUSE)

Refuel Tank…that's a <u>Swedish</u> name – isn't it?

PAUL SMALL: <u>Ay tank</u> so.

JACK: Say the usual something, boys.

(SOUND EFFECT: AIRPLANE PROPELLOR)

JACK: That's the stuff, fellers…. it's remarks like that that enlighten our young aviators…. Now, tell us, Mr. Tank, how did you feel when you fell out of the aeroplane?

PAUL: I was a little nervous at first, but on the way down I thought it over and gained confidence.

JACK: What happened when you landed?

PAUL: What could happen? <u>I got killed.</u>

JACK : Oh, that's a shame….And now, ladies and gentlemen, these boys will do a little flying for you – not much…just a little spin around the world to demonstrate the smoothness of their engines…they might throw in a few aerial somersaults….nipups… and loop-the-loops…The boys will leave immediately and expect to make this trip around-the-world in <u>two minutes and thirty-five seconds</u>….stopping only at the <u>key cities</u>….Like Milwau<u>kee</u>….Czecho-Slova<u>kee</u>….Mc<u>Kee</u>sport….<u>Key</u> West and <u>Key</u>-uba…They are now stepping into their <u>Kadensky-Sorensky</u> Tri-plane, which – as you know – has <u>four</u> meters…..Well, boys, are you ready?

PAUL: Okay…spin 'er!

(SOUND EFFECT: PROPELLOR)

JACK: Now, boys, before you hop off, I want to give you a few last-minute instructions… beware of all air pockets.

PAUL: What are <u>air pockets</u>?

JACK: Olsen's pockets any time you ask him for something…. Of course, I know the fog won't bother you fellers as you're both in a fog now…. Are you ready to hop off?

PAUL: Yes, sir.

JACK: How is your propeller?

PAUL: Fine – but my neuritis is bothering me terribly.

JACK:	Well, just fly <u>above</u> the clouds and keep out of the rain...By the way, if you see the Eclipse around anywhere, say hello for me.

(SOUND EFFECT: HEAVY PROPELLOR NOISE)

The boys are now hopping off the Canada Dry Air Field...Ah! They took off nicely and cleared an <u>ant hill</u> by four inches...Look out for that window sill! There they go – (SOUND EFFECT: PROPELLOR FADES AWAY) across the Atlantic, travelling like a bullet.... Ah! they're out of sight, thank Heaven...<u>Brave men,</u> I calls it...I wonder where they are now.

HOTCHA GARDNER:	Cable for Mr. Benny.
JACK:	Let's have it...Hmmm, from <u>Ireland</u>.... It says...GOT HERE IN FORTY-FIVE SECONDS...DELAY CAUSED BY HEAVY NORTH WINDS.... FORGOT OUR MOTOR...RUSH SAME TO TOKYO IMMEDIATELY."

Boys, quick – mail that motor! <u>What</u> heroes.

GARDNER:	Cable for Mr. Benny.
JACK:	Right here....Hmmmm, from <u>Moscow.</u> It says.... "GLIDED IN HERE FROM IRELAND.... TIME THIRTY-TWO SECONDS...LOST FOUR SECONDS IN BERLIN.... MOSCOW TREATS US ROYALLY...THINGS HERE ARE ON THE <u>BOMB</u> AND THE PRESIDENT IS <u>STALLIN</u>.... WE'RE VERY HUNGRY <u>SO-VIET</u>"

(signed) HYDRO AND TANK

What liars...I mean, <u>flyers</u>.... Boy! it looks like they're going to make it.

GARDNER:	Cable for Mr. Benny.
JACK:	Let's have it...Hmmmm, from <u>Tokyo</u>. It says – "JUST ARRIVED TOKYO...TIME ONE AND THREE-FIFTHS SECONDS...PICKED UP <u>MOTOR</u>.... <u>FATHER</u> ALSO WAITING...WILL BE BACK SOON...YOU CAN <u>JAPAN</u> ON US...DONT <u>MANCHU</u> IT TO ANYBODY...WELL WE GOT <u>TOGO</u> NOW.... (signed) HYDRO AND TANK

Don't forget, folks, I'm reaching out to the Orient for these jokes --

GARDNER:	Another cable for Mr. Benny.
JACK:	Here. boy...Hmmm, from <u>Hawaii.</u> it reads.... "ARRIVED IN HAWAII.... <u>ALOHA</u> EVERYBODY...EVERYTHING IS <u>WICKY WACKY</u> HERE.... LEAVING FOR SAN FRANCISCO"

Well, I guess they must be taking their time.

GARDNER:	Telegram for Jack Benny.
JACK:	Ah! from Chicago.... It says....

"LEFT SAN FRANCISCO TEN SECONDS AGO.... WILL BE BACK SOON LEAVE WINDOW OPEN AS WE ARE COMING FULL SPEED"

	(SOUND EFFECT: PROPELLOR HEARD IN DISTANCE – GETS LOUDER)
	Here they come, folks…. OPEN THAT WINDOW, HICKS! They're coming ---
	(SOUND EFFECT: TERRIFIC GLASS CRASH)
	Ah! here they are…What heroes…what a trip!
	(CROWD YELLS "HOORAY" AND APPLAUDS)
	(MARCHING FOOTSTEPS AND DRUM BEAT)
	They are now marching down Broadway to the plaudits of the multitude --
	(STILL HEAR DRUM BEAT AND FOOTSTEPS)
	This sounds like last Monday's program.
BALDWIN:	Hooray!
JACK:	People are cheering and throwing confetti…. ticker tape and office furniture… but the boys can take it…. Now they have arrived at City Hall to receive the McKee to the city…Say something, City Hall…I mean, Somebody.
FRAN FREY (IN OFFICIAL VOICE):	Boys, I must congratulate you…you have set up a new world's record. Tell us how you did it!
PAUL:	Did what?
FRAN:	Flew around the world.
PAUL:	Aw, we didn't start yet…I couldn't find my hat.
JACK:	The next number, ladies and gentlemen, will be "Angel Cake Lady" sung by Ethel Shutta and Fran Frey.

5. ANGELCAKE LADY   ORCHESTRA, ETHEL SHUTTA & FRAN FREY

JACK:	That was the last number of the 38th program on the 7th of September. I hope you'll all listen in next Monday night --
SADYE:	Jack – oh, Jack.
JACK:	What is it, Mary?
SADYE:	Jack, did you send me some flowers last night?
JACK:	No, Mary – what kind did you get?
SADYE:	I don't know, Jack – I like roses and chrysanthemums.
JACK:	I know, Mary – but what kind of flowers did you get last night?

SADYE: I don't know, Jack – maybe I didn't get any.

JACK: But you must have – you asked me if I sent them.

SADYE: I didn't see any flowers.

JACK: Then why ask me if I sent them?

SADYE: Because I stayed in town with my aunt last night…and if you sent flowers to my home in Plainfield, I'd like to know about it.

JACK: Mary, it must have been three other fellers…Good-night, folks, see you Monday.

SIGNATURE – ROCKABYE MOON

ANNOUNCER: Remember you can enjoy Canada Dry, the Champagne of Ginger Ales, anywhere – anytime for it is now available two ways – either made to order by the glass at soda fountains or in bottles, as always, for your home. The new big bottle is particularly economical and convenient.

Remember, too, that with the exception of a few localities, where freight rates do not permit, you can take back your Canada Dry bottles to the dealer and get a cash refund. You pay for the contents only. Next Monday night at this same time Jack Benny, Ethel Shutta and George Olsen will again entertain you. This is the National Broadcasting Company.

September 12, 1932

Jack starts a continuing segment on the show as "The Earth Galloper," reading news headlines that make puns about MGM movie stars and other celebrities. He will continue this bit for several years. Jack announces a new contest to unscramble cut-up pictures of movie stars. Lilyan Tashman arrives to say a few words. She is one of the first guest stars on the program, as she appears in the onstage review with Benny, Olsen and company. This is also the first time the cast performs a "School Days" skit.

STATION WJZ   PROGRAM   CANADA DRY GINGER ALE, INC.

AND   DATE   MONDAY, SEPTEMBER 12, 1932

BLUE NETWORK TIME   9:30 10:00 P.M.

SIGNATURE – JOLLY GOOD COMPANY

1. MARCH ON TO OREGON   ORCHESTRA

2. HARLEM MOON   ORCHESTRA & ETHEL SHUTTA

3. SO ASHAMED   ORCHESTRA & PAUL SMALL

4. IT'S GONNA BE YOU   ORCHESTRA

5. AND SO TO BED   ORCHESTRA & ETHEL SHUTTA & PAUL SMALL

SIGNATURE – ROCKABYE MOON

CANADA DRY GINGER ALE, INC.   MONDAY, SEPTEMBER 12, 1932.

SIGNATURE—JOLLY GOOD COMPANY

ANNOUNCER: Ladies and gentlemen, another half hour of entertainment about Canada Dry – the champagne of ginger ales – now available by the glass at soda fountains as well as in bottles for the home. You'll find the new, large size bottle very economical and particularly convenient for home use. Once more we present George Olsen, Ethel Shutta and Jack Benny, the Canada Dry humorist, who will perform for your enjoyment. The American Legion opens their convention in Portland, Oregon, today. In commemoration of this event George Olsen begins the program tonight with "MARCH ON TO OREGON," the official theme song of the Legion.

1. MARCH ON TO OREGON   ORCHESTRA

ANNOUNCER: And now Jack Benny, our Raving Reporter.

JACK BENNY: Hello, scandal seekers! this is Jack Benny, the Earth Galloper, coming to you with the late news events, thru the courtesy of the <u>Morning Grapefruit</u>…. the news that's first to reach your <u>eye.</u> Do you get it? or do you like cantaloupe, hmmmm? The dispatches I will read come thru the Unreliable News Service…. which sees all, knows all and tells different ……Here goes!

HOLLYWOOD, CALIFORNIA…. There is no truth in the report that the famous movie director, J. <u>Boudoir Smock</u> will (hums) da-da-da-da-da-da down the aisle with the new Danish film star, Miss <u>Retach Grebsa</u>…. when interviewed, she said they were <u>engaged</u> for laughs only.

EASTPORT, MAINE …. Five hundred sardine packers leave for New York to seek work in new subway.

NEW YORK CITY…. Walter Winchell kidnapped and held for <u>transom</u>……. Word comes to us from CENTRAL PARK, NEW YORK…. Three Park benches destroyed in spectacular fire. Olsen's band homeless…. I've been waiting weeks to get that in….

Here's a late news dispatch from BOWLING GREEN, KENTUCKY……Society debutante, IMA LITTLESTIFF from Bowling, announces her engagement to one of the Smith Brothers of Coffing-ton……

They are honeymooning in <u>Paris</u>……which is also in Kentucky.

BRYANT PARK, NEW YORK…. Five thousand pigeons were seen feeding peanuts to pedestrians…. which proves that time are getting better.

PELHAM, NEW YORK…. Roadhouse chandelier falls on free-lunch counter. Three of Olsen's fingers smashed. No other casualties……Well, that's the brightest news of the day.

PHILADELPHIA, PA…. Nothing happened here today…or yesterday…. or the day before…or even before that.

Here's a message from <u>Five Corners,</u> Now Jersey……No prosperity around here…. And now for the sporting results of the day…. Result of baseball game at the Bronx Zoo…. <u>Cubs,</u> three …. <u>Tigers,</u> two…. FOREST HILLS, LONG ISLAND…. Ellsworth Vines beats Henry Cochet in three straight sets in Championship Tennis Match----

ANNOUNCER: Speaking of <u>tennis,</u> folks, you get <u>tennis cents</u> back on two large Canada Dry Bottles…. a nickel back on each one.

JACK: One more gag like that, Hicks and we'll both be out of work….

And now for the foreign news…. LAUSANNE, SWITZERLAND…. Three people <u>shot</u> at Disarmament Conference…. Ah! Here's a report from the <u>Peace</u> Conference, GENEVA…. Spain wants a <u>piece</u> of Italy…. Italy wants a <u>piece</u> of Turkey…. Turkey wants a <u>piece</u> of Russia…Russia wants a <u>piece</u> of herring….

ANNOUNCER: And speaking of <u>piece</u>, you get <u>five cents</u> back on each large Canada Dry bottle.

JACK: Hicks if you didn't say that, you'd surprise all of us…. This is Jack Benny <u>Headache Hunter</u>, talking…. Now please stand by until <u>November ninth</u>…. when we will again bring you the latest news items…This is the voice of the Earth Galloper, bringing you <u>hot</u> news while it is <u>cold</u>…. And Now George Olsen and his boys will play "Harlem Moon," sung by Ethel Shutta which, of course, is not news…. Go ahead, Ethel.

2. HARLEM MOON ORCHESTRA & ETHEL SHUTTA

JACK: That was Ethel Shutta singing "Harlem Moon" …. Say, Ethel.

ETHEL: Jack, I'm busy right now.

JACK: Oh, pardon me…George, do you think we ought to --

GEORGE: Sorry, Jack – I've got to arrange this music.

JACK: Oh! Say, Fran, do you think that -

FRAN: Jack, can't you see I'm trying to -

JACK: Well, folks, it looks like it's every man for himself…. So, I, personally, want to apologize to you folks for not giving anything away these past few weeks during the hot weather. By that I mean, <u>prizes.</u> But really it was no use, because when we <u>did</u> send prizes to you, they all came back some marked, "<u>NOT IN</u>" – others marked," IN <u>–</u>

BUT WE DON'T WANT THEM" ……. However, we are not easily discouraged, and tonight we will start a new contest and give away some more valuable things. The idea of this contest was sent to us by three people – one signing himself NAPOLEON…the other, QUEEN ELIZABETH…and the third one who happens to be the Keeper. Of course, he's all right, the handwriting some to be very clear, considering the fact that they were all in straight jackets…….

So, our test for tonight will be something new and different. All you need to enter this mental Olympic Game is a picture of celebrity…a pair of scissors…lots of time….and no brains. Of course, if you already have been cutting paper dolls, you will have no difficulty at ail…. Here are the simple rules for the contest if you are still listening. Of course, if you are ready to tune out, don't forget that Canada Dry Ginger Ale is a good drink…. Ah, I got that in, Hicks, I'm no fool!......

Now listen closely, folks. First, take a picture of John Barrymore …. then take your shears and carefully cut off John's ear…. then take your old favorite William S. Hart and cut off the William S. leaving the Hart. Now if the proper pieces are put together, you will have a beautiful picture of Miss Earhart…. you remember Amelia…. get the idea? Of course, if you can't get a picture of William S. Hart, use the Ace of HEARTS or Hearts of Lettuce…. but don't tell anybody……….

Now for the second one…. take your popular favorite, Clark Gable…cut off the "E" from Gable, which he doesn't need, anyway…. then take a picture of Ina Claire…cut off the Ina, leaving the Claire…and if placed properly together, you will have a nice chocolate éclaire…that is, Of course, if you can find a picture of Kid Chocolate. This is very good with whipped cream…. And now for the next one…this may prove difficult, folks…. Get a picture of Louis the Seventeenth…. take your shears and cut out the Louis, leaving the Seventeenth. Then take Frederic March, the movie star…. cut out the Fredric….and if the right pieces are placed properly together, you will have beautiful picture of the Seventeenth of March….

And now for our fourth and last one …. Concentrate, now…take a picture of Zazu Pitts and cut out the Zazu, leaving the Pitts….then take a picture of that famous movie producer, Thalberg…. cut out the Thal, leaving the Berg—put them together and you will, no doubt, have a round-trip ticket to Pittsburgh…. of course, folks, you understand that these are only suggestions. It is us to you to make up your own stars and buy your own scissors. Come on – be the little cut-up in your neighborhood, By the way, you must have these problems in to us before tonight's program is over

Our prizes will be as follows: First prize – a baseball pass good for the World Series of any of the Twenty Thousand Leagues under the Sea …. Second prize – a gallon of handsome gasoline to fit your car – yacht – or aeroplane … and …. Our Third prize will be the first two prizes after you return them to us…All right, folks…get into this profit-shearing plan…. And now George Olsen and his Schneiders will play, "SO ASHAMED", sung by Paul Small.

3. SO ASHAMED   ORCHESTRA & PAUL SMALL

JACK:	Well, folks, you know today is the first day of school in most places, so we are not going to wait <u>until Christmas</u> to let you know that the schools are open. We start ours as quick as anybody else…All right, Hicks, get the class together.
	(SOUND EFFECT: BELL RINGS)
	Come on, children – step inside and take your seats.
	(PIANO VAMPS – THEN INTO "SCHOOL DAYS")
MIKE VOICES (SINGS)	
	School days – school days – dear old golden rule days, Readin' and ritin' and 'rithmetic, Taught to the tune of the hickory stick --
ETHEL (ALONE):	You were my beautiful, barefoot guy
FRAN:	Remember! – I bought you Canada Dry
JACK:	And you get a nickel <u>back</u> on the bottle
VOICES:	When we were a couple of kids.
	(SOUND EFFECT: GAVEL RAP ON DESK)
JACK:	Good-morning, Ethel… Hello, Paul…Good morning, Mary…Fran ---
VOICES:	Good-morning, teacher….
JACK:	Johnny! Get your <u>beard</u> off your desk…Well, children, I'm glad to see you here so bright and early, anxious to learn something. Now, Fran Junior, take that saxophone out of your mouth…. Hotcha! Put down that putty-blower.
GARDNER:	That's a <u>flute</u>.
JACK:	Pardon me – now, kiddies, our first subject will Grammar. Take out your Text Books…. Tommy! Tell me – what does the word "hotcha" mean?
GARDNER:	Was you out last night?
JACK:	You.
GARDNER:	Well, <u>hotcha</u> get home?
JACK:	Right…that's fine, Tommy. Now name two great rivers in the United States.
GARDNER:	OLD MAN <u>RIVER</u> and RIVER! STAY AWAY FROM MY DOOR.
JACK:	Now about the <u>Hudson</u> and the <u>Mississippi</u>?
GARDNER:	<u>They're</u> good songs, too.
JACK:	Hey, Paul – Paul, tell us – where is Lake Erie?
PAUL:	The same place it always was.
JACK:	Well, one more question before I dislocate your arm…where is the Atlantic Ocean?

PAUL:	You can search me.
JACK:	Oh, yeah?
PAUL:	Ow! teacher…. Leave me alone…. I ain't got it…. honest, I was sitting right here all the time.
SADYE:	Teacher…. teacher! I know where the Atlantic Ocean is.
JACK:	All right, Mary – you tell us. Where is the Atlantic Ocean?
SADYE:	Well, if you go to Atlantic City, you will find it lying right on the beach… You can't miss it – if you don't see it, ask somebody.
JACK:	Thanks, Mary Willy, stand up.
FRAN:	Yes, teacher.
JACK:	Now, Willy, tell me where is the <u>capital</u> of the United States?
FRAN:	In George Olsen's pocket.
JACK:	Right, Willy! …. you can move up to the head of the class. Now you – little girl over there – what's <u>your</u> name?
ETHEL:	Ethel Shutta.
JACK:	I mean – in the school-room.
ETHEL:	Ethel.
JACK:	All right, Ethel – tell us how many days there are in the different months of the year?
ETHEL:	Thirty days hath September – April, June and November.
	All the rest have thirty-one – excepting Canada Dry, which is made-to-order and sold at all fountains.
SADYE:	Oh no, teacher – she's wrong.
JACK:	All right, Mary – suppose <u>you</u> tell us.
SADYE:	It should be – thirty days hath September – April, June and November. All the rest have thirty-one – except my uncle, who will be thirty-five on his next birthday.
JACK:	All right, Mary – sit down…. Now Sam<u>uel</u>…Sam<u>uel</u>….
HARRY CONN:	My name is <u>Sam</u> – cut out the <u>mule</u>.
JACK:	Now before I break this slate over your head – tell us, who discovered electricity?
HARRY:	Benjamin <u>Frankenstein</u>.
JACK:	Frankenstein! I suppose radio was discovered by Jekyll and Hyde.
HARRY:	No – by Jessel and Cantor.

JACK:	Right! now, children, turn to page twenty-four of your Ballyhoo Reader…Sam, suppose you tell us – what did the first settlers do when they came to America?
HARRY:	They sold <u>settlers'</u> powders.
SADYE:	That's wrong, teacher…that's wrong. They bought New York from the Indians.
JACK:	You're right – Mary…How much did they pay the Indians?
SADYE:	I don't know the amount, but they seemed to be satisfied because I spoke to some Indians the other day and they told me
JACK:	Never mind, Mary – it isn't important…Now, Ethel, stand up – can you recite your poem today?
ETHEL:	Yes, teacher.
JACJ:	Go ahead.
ETHEL:	Old Mother Hubbard – went to the cupboard To get her poor doggie some pie. And when she got there, the cupboard was bare-
JACK:	I know – so she bought him some Canada Dry…sit down, Ethel. And now the <u>minerals</u> – Sam, you seem to be the smartest one in the class. Tell us what is <u>steel</u>?
HARRY CONN:	Steel is forty-eight and a half today.
JACK:	Went up a point – eh? have you got any stock?
HARRY:	Just a little <u>gas</u>.
JACK:	What will you take for it?
HARRY:	Bicarbonate of soda.
JACK:	Sold! now you – young man, what is <u>copper</u>?
GEORGE HICKS:	It's a mineral used in making pennies and telegraph wires.
JACK:	Correct! now what is <u>nickel</u>?
GEORGE HICKS:	<u>Nickel</u> is what you get back on the Canada Dry bottle.
JACK:	Wait a minute – who are you?
GEORGE HICKS:	I am George Hicks, <u>Junior.</u>
JACK:	Oh, you are – eh?... Well, Junior, get out this class.
GEORGE HICKS:	Oh yeah, teacher – I heard father say that Canada Dry is sold by the <u>class</u>.
JACK:	That's all I wanted to know. (SOUND EFFECT: GAVEL) Before the class is dismissed, has anybody else a boost for Canada Dry?
VOICES:	No – no.

JACK:	All right, then – school is over for today.
VOICES:	Good-bye, teacher … good-bye.
	(PIANO PLAYS "SCHOOL DAYS" SOFTLY)
SADYE:	Oh, Jack – I mean, teacher…
JACK:	What is it, Mary?
SADYE:	This being the first day of school, I thought I'd bring you a little present.
JACK:	What is it?
SADYE:	A wet sponge.
JACK:	A wet sponge – what did you bring me that for?
SADYE:	I think it's swell.
JACK:	Go, Mary! George, stay after school and practice the next number – SEGUE INTO –

4. IT'S GONNA BE YOU   ORCHESTRA

JACK:	And now, ladies and gentlemen, I'm going to be serious for just a moment. We really have a celebrity here tonight who is honoring us with her presence. She is a moving picture star, appearing with us at the Capitol Theatre this week and is known as the <u>beat dressed</u> lady of the screen…and I am very, very happy to introduce to you now – and for once, this is on the level – a great artist – <u>MISS</u> LILYAN TASHMAN. (APPLAUSE)
MISS TASHMAN:	How do you do, ladies and gentlemen.
JACK:	Miss Tashman, I want to thank you very much for appearing on this Canada Dry program this evening.
MISS TASHMAN:	The pleasure is all mine.
JACK:	And I also want to take just a moment to tell you how much I have enjoyed your excellent work on the screen.
MISS TASHMAN:	Thank you very much, Mr. Olsen.
JACK:	Fran Frey is the name.
MISS TASHMAN:	Oh, I know it's Mr. Benny – but I'm just a little bit nervous appearing in front of the microphone…Mr. Benny, I want to tell you how much I have always enjoyed your work both on the stage and on the air.
JACK:	Thank you, Miss Tashman – let's stand here and complement each other for fifteen or twenty minutes. (BOTH LAUGH) But really, it's my opinion that the finest work you have ever done on the screen was in that picture, "Girls About Town".

MISS TASHMAN:	I'm so glad you liked it – because I enjoyed doing it.
JACK:	Yes, I could tell that by the way you worked in the picture.
JACK:	Is there anything you would like to say, Miss Tashman?
MISS TASHMAN:	Well, I would just like to say that I am very happy to have this opportunity to talk to so many people – and I'm going back to Hollywood soon to continue with my work in pictures. I certainly hope that (ad lib) Well, goodbye.
JACK:	Good-bye – and thank you very much, Miss Tashman…Well, folks, you heard what she just said about Canada Dry Ginger Ale….and it was certainly very sweet of her to appear on our program this evening. Of course, I have known Miss Tashman a long time. We are old friends – dating back to the days when I was in Hollywood making picture myself. (Ad lib)
	But really, Miss Tashman has a marvelous sense of humor. I know she won't mind it if I tell this. (DROP-THE-TRAY gag)

5. AND SO TO BED   ORCHESTRA- ETHEL & PAUL

(GEORGE OLSEN MAKES ANNOUNCEMENT)

JACK (SPEAKS OVER MUSIC):	This is the last number of the 39th program on the 12th of September. Be sure to listen in Wednesday night as we are going to have a new thrill for you – the Canada Dry R_o_deo or Rod_e_o…Well, goodnight, then.
ANNOUNCER:	The next time you stop at a soda fountain for refreshing drink, ask for a glass of Canada Dry, the Champagne of Ginger Ales – it will be made-to-order for you costs only five cents for a regular glass or ten cents for an extra-large glass. Remember, too, that with the exception of a few localities where freight charges do not permit, you can take back your Canada Dry bottles to the dealer and get a cash refund. So that now when you buy Canada Dry you pay for the contents only. Next Wednesday night at this same time, Jack Benny, Ethel Shutta and George Olsen will again entertain you. This is the National Broadcasting Company.

September 14, 1932

Jack performs a long monologue calling play-by-play of a rodeo extravaganza, with cowboys, trick riders and thousands of steers. Jack discusses the "Shearing" Contest, which involves asking fans to snip out pictures of celebrities and combine their various body parts. Mary asks George Olsen for romantic advice.

STATION WJZ	PROGRAM	CANADA DRY GINGER ALE, INC.
AND	DATE	WEDNESDAY, SEPTEMBER 14, 1932
BLUE NETWORK	TIME	9:30 – 10:00 P.M.

SIGNATURE – JOLLY GOOD COMPANY

1. ALL AMERICAN GIRL	ORCHESTRA & FRAN FREY
2. STUCCO IN THE STICKS	ORCHESTRA & ETHEL SHUTTA
3. TEN HOURS A DAY	ORCHESTRA & FRAN FREY
4. IT'S FROM HUNGER	ORCHESTRA & ETHEL SHUTTA
5. KEEP AWAY	ORCHESTRA & DICK GARDINER

SIGNATURE – ROCKABYE MOON

CANADA DRY GINGER ALE, INC.   WEDNESDAY, SEPTEMBER 14, 1932

SIGNATURE – JOLLY GOOD COMPANY

ANNOUNCER: Ladies and gentlemen, another half hour of entertainment about Canada Dry – the champagne of ginger ales – now available by the glass at soda fountains, as well as in bottles for the home. You'll find the new, large size bottle very economical and particularly convenient for home use. Once more we present George Olsen, Ethel Shutta and Jack Benny, the Canada Dry humorist, who will perform for your enjoyment. George Olsen opens the program tonight with "All American Girl" – Fran Frey singing.

1. ALL AMERICAN GIRL   ORCHESTRA AND FRAN FREY

ANNOUNCER: And now I turn the mike to Jack Benny!

JACK: Hello, if I'm not intruding……(COUGHS) This is Jack Benny, the voice of <u>no sleep</u> last night…coming to you thru the courtesy of Sylvester's Invisible <u>Vest</u> Sleeves…. are you going <u>Vest</u> this year? If you are, take along a pair of Sylvester's <u>Vest</u> Sleeves of <u>Vest</u> Virginia……..Remember the name – Sylvester's <u>Vest</u> Sleeves of <u>Vest</u> Virginia……And now the little <u>Vest</u>ern girl, Miss <u>Vest</u>a Shutta, will sing SHINE OF HAR<u>VEST</u> MOON".

ETHEL: Jack, I don't think I even know that song.

JACK: You don't – eh? …. Well, then, sing something, Ethel – like "LULLABY OF THE <u>SLEEVES</u>".

ETHEL: I don't know that, either.

JACK: Ethel, sing something about our <u>Vest</u> <u>Sleeves</u>…our product needs a theme song.

ETHEL: Maybe George can help us out. He knows all kinds of theme songs.

JACK: That's right – may, George, do you know any theme songs about a <u>vest</u>?

GEORGE: How about "MY LITTLE GRAY HOME IN THE <u>VEST</u>?"

JACK: No, that's a good song for a <u>moth</u>…. well, a moth made a home in my little <u>gray</u> <u>vest</u> last summer…. (laughs) Am I starting out <u>good</u> tonight!

157

GEORGE:	Well, Jack, how about" VESTI LA GIUBBA" from Pagliacci?
JACK:	No, this is the Sylvester's Vest Program. Let Pagliacci boost his own product…I know there was no sense asking George. You know, Ethel, every human being has seven senses, but George only uses one.
ETHEL:	You mean – five senses.
JACK:	No, seven…. there's hearing…seeing…walking…talking --
ETHEL:	Talking isn't a sense. There are only five – hearing…seeing…smelling…tasting…. and feeling –five sense.
GEORGE:	And don't forget, folks, you get five senses back on each large Canada Dry bottle.
JACK:	Oh, for Heaven's sake! …. I thought there was something wrong here…. this in the Canada Dry program.
ETHEL:	You, Jack – you must have been reading the wrong script.
JACK:	Can you imagine that? …. I must have picked up that script. Who leaves these things lying around here! …. I'm sorry, ladies and gentlemen…this in the Canada Dry Ginger Ale program – made-to-order, by the glass and sold at all fountains – and everybody's drinking it…. Imagine me boosting Sylvester's. Why, I wouldn't give a pair of Sylvester's Sleeves to my dog… Play, George – (SEGUE INTO NUMBER) I wish people wouldn't leave their scripts lying around….it gets me into more trouble – (ad lib)

2. STUCCO IN THE STICKS   ORCHESTRA & EHTEL SHUTTA

(GEORGE OLSEN MAKES HIS OWN ANNOUNCEMENT DURING NUMBER)

JACK:	Well, folks, I have some good news for you. Our Shearing Contest was a big success…. You remember our Contest on Monday night, when we told you to get pictures of celebrities, cut out part of one celebrity and put it with part of another, and it would give you a picture of something or other? Well, I'm standing here up to my neck – mind you – in answers to this contest…. Now here's one answer from Mrs. Lika Riddle, Pump Handle, Vermont…She says: "I HEREBY ENTER YOUR CONTEST. I FOLLOWED YOUR RULES CLOSELY. I TOOK A PICTURE OF THE GREAT GARBO…. THEN I CUT OUT THE GREAT…. THEN I TOOK A PICTURE OF MARLENE DIETRICH AND CUT OFF HER LEGS….AND WHEN I PUT THEM TOGETHER, I FOUND A BEAUTIFUL PICTURE OF THE GREAT LAKES….AM ENCLOSED SAME IN THIS LETTER. DOES THIS WIN ANYTHING?" Yes, lady…it wins the seventh prize…. which is a one-way trip over a curbstone….

Now here's another one from Miss <u>Ima Scot</u>.... <u>Free</u> Wheeling, West Virginia. She writes—

"YOUR CONTEST IS RIGHT IN MY BACKYARD. I HAVE BEEN SAVING PICTURES FOR YEARS FOR A CONTEST LIKE THIS....SO I TOOK A PICTURE OF <u>CONSTANCE BENNETT</u> AND CUT OUT THE <u>CONSTANCE</u>.......THEN I TOOK A PICTURE OF <u>RIN-RIN-TIN</u>....CUT OUT THE <u>TIN</u>, WHICH NEARLY RUINED MY SHEARS.....THEN I GOT A PICTURE OF <u>POLLY MORAN</u> AND CUT OUT THE <u>POL</u> FROM HER FIRST NAME.....I PLACED THEM ALL TOGETHER AND AM SENDING YOU THE PICTURE OF <u>CONSTANCE – TIN-OPLE</u>.....a city in Turkey. . Well, what do <u>you</u> think?"

Well, Ima, what do <u>you</u> think? .... that was very good work, Ima, and it's people like <u>you</u> that make people like <u>us</u> hate people like <u>you</u>.... I am going to read just one more, as time limits us to nonsense and we can't be bothered with facts.... This letter is postmarked Things-are-picking-up, New Jersey.... from Miss <u>Iona Washboard.</u>

She says—

"I LISTENED TO YOUR RULES CLOSELY. I TOOK THE PICTURES YOU SENT ME OF ETHEL SHUTTA, GEORGE OLSEN AND JACK BENNY AND CU THEM UP VERY, VERY FINE – IN THOUSANDS OF LITTLE PIECES.... THEN I PLACED THEM ALTOGETHER AND MADE THE NICEST <u>CRAZY QUILT</u> YOU EVER SAW.... HOPING YOU'RE THE SAME...P.S. DO I WIN A PRIZE?"

<u>No, we're mad</u> .... Now, folks – those of you who have sent in these letters are entitled to three honor marks each. When you get four marks, you will have the <u>Marx</u> Brothers.....then take your shears, cut out <u>Harpo</u>...put him in a pot till he boils... then you add <u>Amos</u> of Amos 'N Andy – and when it is finished, you will have at least three good dishes of <u>Harpo-Pot-Amos stew</u>.... and don't ask us why .... And now George Olsen and his boys will play, and Fran Frey will sing, "TEN HOURS A DAY"....and no wisecrack about the title.

3. TEN HOURS A DAY   ORCHESTRA AND FRAN FREY

JACK: Well, well, well, ladies and gentlemen – if I ever had good news for you, I have it <u>right now.</u> We have secured for our customers tonight <u>another</u> great attraction – not the usual melodrama we have been giving you nor the grand opera singers you have been hearing. <u>No, sir – and ma'am!</u> What we have for you tonight – <u>and tonight only</u> – is a blood-curdling .... rootin!.....tootin! Western rodeo ......Imagine a r<u>o</u>deo on the <u>radio</u> ......or a <u>raddio</u> on the rod<u>e</u>o .... I know how to pronounce it, folks. I just want to get the jokes in....

Anyway, we have brought you this great outdoor game of the West from the wide-open spaces where men are men – and the crooners are tuned out....and we are starting (a la Chevalier) not tomorrow.... not today...but <u>right now!</u> ......and no advance in prices.... come on, boys! Clear out the arena.

	(SOUND EFFECT: MOVING STUFF AROUND – GENERAL NOISES)
	All right – you can let the horses in now…. Here they come, folks.
	(SOUND EFFECT: HORSES HOOFS – BRAD BARKER DOES NEIGH)
	Fifty bucking bronchos from the Bronx …er, Arizona….
	(SOUND EFFECT: BUCK DANCE)
	And one bucking, buck-dancer from Layoff, Montana…. Boy! You should see these horses buck.
GEORGE HICKS:	And you also get nickel buck on each large Canada Dry bottle.
JACK:	Say, Hicks, get back in your stall…. Now here come the cowboys---- the champion riders of the world! …. all ready to make whoopee….
CROWD (YELLS):	Whoopee! …. Yippee! …. Yippee! …..
	(SOUND EFFECT: STOMPING OF STEER)
JACK:	Twenty-five thousand head of Texas steer….do you see them, Mary?
SADYE:	Yes, steer.
JACK:	Mary, keep your mind on the program…. Here come the steers …. Say something, steer!
	BRAD BARKER (DOES DOG IMITATION): Woof! …woof!
JACK:	A steer - not a dog.
BRAD BARKER:	Oh, ox-cuse me.
JACK:	And now, ladies and gentlemen, to show you that we are not giving you the wrong steer, we will introduce to you the Champion Rider of the World…. Arsenic Pete…. of Delancey Gulch, Vyoming…. What a he-man! Now, Arsey, as the greatest cow-puncher of the world – tell us a few of your secrets.
HARRY CONN:	In the first place, I don't punch cows – I just slap them.
JACK:	I can see that…. But isn't there a trick in rounding-up cattle?
HARRY:	No, on the contrary – it's oodles of fun.
JACK:	Say, Hicks, hold my coat until I bull-dog this guy…. Now, tell us, how do you round-up cattle?
HARRY:	Well, we all get on our noble steeds….and we play ring around-a-rosy…. then we make a ring around the cattle…and when we tag them – they're it!
JACK:	Tell me – are you really a cow-puncher?
HARRY:	Well, you don't think I'm wearing this big, black moustache for nothing – do you?

JACK:	Were you ever in a "Vanities" chorus?
HARRY:	Oh, certainly - that's where I met you.
JACK:	Get out of here…. get out of here!
SADYE:	Oh, Jack! …. Jack! …He's not a cowboy…he's a book-salesman and he's been here since Monday.
JACK:	Watch that door, Mary – and now bring in a real cowboy.
SADYE:	Yes, Jack…. Mister! …Mister!
RALPH ASHE:	Yes?
JACK:	Before going any further – who are you?
RALPH:	I'm a cowhand from the wild and wooly west.
JACK:	Yes, I notice you have Western teeth.
RALPH:	Yeah – wide open spaces.
JACK:	Read your own script – I was supposed to say that…What's your name?
RALPH:	Cayenne Pepper…from Cayenne, Wyoming.
JACK:	You look more like a plumber to me.
RALPH:	Yes. I'm from a monkey ranch…. who be you, tenderfoot?
JACK (DIALECT):	Well, ah'm Rattlesnake Benny….from O-Ranch, New Jersey.
RALPH:	Rattlesnake Benny …. Well, how be you, Rat?
JACK:	Put 'er thar, pardner…are you ready to do your stuff?
RALPH:	Yes. sir.
JACK:	All right, ladies and gentlemen – we will now take you to the Gold Room of our stables…. where George Olsen and his not-so-rough riders will play – George, play something soothing for the horses, so we can get them in a nice mood….

SEGUE INTO

4. IT'S FROM HUNGER   ORCHESTRA & ETHEL SHUTTA

(OLSEN MAKES HIS OWN ANNOUNCEMENT)

JACK:	All right, folks, come right into the arena and get the thrill of your life. See our man-eating horses and our horse-eating men…. we're all set for the rodeo….

Now our first event will be <u>Cactus Myer</u>...of the Columbus Circle Ranch.... riding <u>Double</u> <u>Pneumonia</u>...a horse that's never been ridden before. In fact, this is the <u>first</u> horse that Myer ever rode...so they will start in together...They both look confident and are in the <u>punk</u> of condition

(SOUND EFFECT: HORSE'S HOOFS)

Myer has only his spurs – but the mustang has a <u>horse shoe</u> in each glove!

(CROWD YELLING   Whoopee!.......Yippee.... Whoopee!

(SOUND EFFECT: MORE HORSE'S HOOFS)

JACK: Ride 'em, cowboy! .... Look at that horse go! ...but <u>Myer</u> stays right with him....

CROWD YELLING: Whoopee! .... Yippee!...

JACK: There goes the horse – snorting and tearing down the arena.... But <u>where</u> is Myer?

RALPH ASHE: Oy! ...Oy!....

JACK: The <u>horse</u> is now riding Myer...Stay with him, Horse! ...This is a horse on Myer....

CROWD YELLING –   Hooray! ...Whoopee!...Hooray!...

(ROUND OF APPLAUSE)

JACK: The horse is the winnah...and still <u>Champion!</u>

(MORE APPLAUSE AND CHEERS)

And now Myer's <u>widow</u> will say something.

DOROTHY ROSS (SPEAKS RAPIDLY):   Hello, everybody...I am very happy to be here on this gala occasion, and I am sorry that I have only <u>one</u> husband to give to this rodeo.

JACK: Thank you, Widow Myer...won't you stay for the rest of the program?

DOROTHY: Oh, I'd love to (LAUGHS GAILY)

JACK: And now for next event...the champion <u>lady rider</u> of the world!

SADYE: <u>Me</u> – Jack?

JACK: You aren't a <u>rider</u>.

SADYE: I am, too   I'm a <u>type-rider.</u>

JACK: Sorry, you're not the type...Go over there and play with the capital letters.... Ladies and gentlemen, we bring to you now the <u>greatest</u> event on our entire program – another riding feat. I want to introduce to you the most remarkable roughrider that ever lived – the <u>man who rides to work every morning in the subway</u> ....and has scars and bruises to prove this.... So tonight, for the first time <u>on any air</u>.... he will ride the Fifth Avenue Bus...without spurs.... saddle .... <u>or even a dime</u>....and it looks as the he will be thrown...He is now waiting on the corner for the Bus and rarin' to go. Here comes <u>the Bus</u>......

	(SOUND EFFECT: AUTO HORN AND MOTOR NOISE)
	Uh! The bus didn't stop…so stand by, folks – till another one comes by.
	(SOUND EFFECT: AUTO HORN & MOTOR NOISE)
	Here she comes…he jumps on the step of the bus….
RALPH ASHE:	Yippee! …. Yippee!
JACK:	Ride 'em, <u>bus boy</u>…er, cowboy.
	(SOUND EFFECT: MOTOR AND AUTO HORN AGAIN)
	There he goes, folks…<u>what</u> a ride he is giving that bus.
FRAN FREY:	Fare, please!
JACK :	Ride 'em, cowboy…<u>stay on.</u>
FRAN:	Fare, please!
JACK:	Hang on, cowboy…<u>ride'em</u>…. Oh-oh….
	(SOUND EFFECT: TERRIFIC <u>GLASS CRASH</u>)
CROWD:	Ooooh!
JACK:	What a shame! He was <u>thrown</u> at Fourteenth Street…. I didn't get the time, but it was darned fast…. Say something. <u>Bus.</u>
	(SOUND EFFECT: BREAK WITH HORN)
JACK :	And now for the grand finale….steering a bulldog…er, bulldogging a steer….The steer runs out into the arena…the rider fellows him, leaps to the steer's neck from his saddle, grabs him by the ears…by the horns….throws him and then ties him up….That is what we call <u>steering a car</u>…er, <u>staring a bull</u>-<u>dog</u>….er, I mean bulldogging a steer….<u>Here they come</u>.…..
	(ALL THRU THE FOLLOWING WE HEAR <u>CROWD NOISE</u>)
	The rider is twirling his rope, but the steer says its <u>oxtail soup</u> for him---
	(<u>BRAD BARKER</u> DOES SNORT SOUND)
	Get him, cowboy! …. Now he has the bull by the horns…Say something, <u>horns.</u>
	(<u>CORNET</u> BLAST)
	Atta, boy! …. He is now tying the steer into knots…what a cowboy!
FRAN FREY:	Ow! Ow! …let me go…ow, get off me…. ow!...
JACK:	What's this? …. Stand by, please, till I find out…. Pardon me, there's a slight mistake…. The cowboy bulldogged Fran Frey by mistake….
FRAN FREY:	I'll kill the guy that started this…. <u>Where's</u> Jack Benny?

JACK:	See you later, folks…Play, George.

(SEGUE INTO –

5. KEEP AWAY   ORCHESTRA & DICK GARDINER

(OLSEN MAKES HIS OWN ANNOUNCEMENT)

JACK:	That was the last number of the fortieth program on the 14th of September…. Try to be with us on Monday night if you---
SADYE:	Oh, Mr. Olsen…Mr. Olsen…can I talk to you a minute?
GEORGE:	Yes, Mary – what is it?
SADYE:	I was listening to your music tonight, and I thought it was swell.
GEORGE:	Thanks, Mary – I'm so glad you liked it. Which number did you like the best?
SADYE:	The violinist – I think <u>he's</u> swell.
GEORGE:	Well, personally, I thought the drums were my best number…Say, Mary – how are you and Jack getting along?
SADYE:	Oh, fine…he gave me a present today.
GEORGE:	What was it?
SADYE:	A nice paper box to keep candy in…. Wasn't that sweet?
GEORGE:	Very sweet…he's always giving things away…. He'd give you a <u>banana peel</u> any time.
SADYE:	That's funny – he never gave me one.
GEORGE:	Say, Mary – you must like Jack pretty well.
SADYE:	I sure do--- but at times he doesn't seem to care for me…. Mr. Olsen, I wish you would say something to him about me sometime – you know – just a little word while you're talking.
GEORGE:	Sure, Mary – I'll be glad to.
SADYE:	See, if I thought he didn't like me – I wouldn't know what to do. I'd be just heart-sick….
JACK:	Hello, Mary.
SADYE:	Oh, hello, Jack.
JACK:	Mary, I've been looking for you…. Can I take you home tonight?
SADYE:	See, I'm sorry, Jack – but I just promised Hotcha Gardner that he could take me…. Come on, Hotcha…good-night, Jack.

JACK: Which way are you going, George?

GEORGE: Uptown.

JACK: Come on, George….

SIGNATURE – ROCKABYE MOON

ANNOUNCER: Remember you can enjoy Canada Dry – the champagne of ginger ales – anywhere, anytime, for it is now available two ways – either made to order by the glass at soda fountains or in bottles, as always, for your home. The new big bottle is particularly economical and convenient.

Remember too, that with exception of a few localities, where freight rates do not permit, you pay for the contents only, that is twenty cents for the large five glass bottles, plus a five cent deposit which is refunded when you return the bottle, and twenty-five cents for two of the regular twelve ounces bottles plus two cents deposit on each bottle. Next Monday night at this same time Jack Benny, Ethel Shutta and George Olsen will again entertain you. This is the National Broadcasting Company.

September 19, 1932

Jack and Ethel talk about his work in the movies, dating back to 1929's "Hollywood Revue" and "Chasing Rainbows." (This could be a creative re-use of his old vaudeville monologues about his early "talkie" appearances.) Jack calls the MGM studio "Macgum." Jack asks a talent agency to send up guest stars, but they are flops. Mary talks up Jack's romantic appeal, and she begins to leap into other performers' discussions with a sly joke, a device she would increasingly use in future years. Jack mimics Mary's distinctive laughter. First mentions are made of "Grand Hotel," the new MGM blockbuster film that Jack and the cast would parody on subsequent episodes.

STATION WJZ   PROGRAM CANADA DRY GINGER ALE, INC.

     AND   DATE MONDAY, SEPTEMBER 19, 1932.

BLUE NETWORK   TIME 9:30 10:00 P.M.

SIGNATURE JOLLY GOOD COMPANY

1. EALINOR   ORCHESTRA & FRAN FREY
2. ALWAYS IN YOUR HEART   ORCHESTRA & ETHEL SHUTTA
3. MICKEY MOUSE   ORCHESTRA & FRAN FREY
4. NIGHT FALL   ORCHESTRA & BORGER
5. TIGER RAG   ORCHESTRA & FRAN FREY

SIGNATURE ROCKABYE MOON

CANADA DRY GINGER ALE INC.   MONDAY, SEPTEMBER 19, 1932.
SIGNATURE JOLLY GOOD COMPANY

ANNOUNCER: Ladies and gentleman, another half hour of entertainment about Canada Dry the champagne of Ginger ales now available by the glass at soda fountains, as well as in bottles for the home. You'll find the new, large size bottle very economical and particularly convenient for home use.

Once more we present George Olsen, Ethel Shutta and Jack Benny, the Canada Dry Humorist, who will again perform for your enjoyment. George Olsen opens the program with a beautiful song by Jesse Ball called "EALINO

ANNOUNCER: Now, Jack, it's up to you.

JACK BENNY: Hello, entertainment seekers.... this is <u>Jack Benny</u>...not a talking picture...not a phonograph record...not a double.... but appearing in <u>person</u>...right here in the flesh at this microphone...Yes, sir and <u>Mrs</u>. Yes, sir! .... the same <u>Eugene O'Neill</u>-Benny that wrote "Strange Interlude"...the same <u>Fritz Kreisler</u> Benny you've heard on the violin...the same <u>Roosevelt</u>-<u>Hoover</u>-Benny who is running for President...and, in conclusion, I will say - commonly known to the public as <u>Jack Benny</u>.

GEORGE HICKS: Speaking of Benny, you get <u>five Bennys</u> back on the large Canada Dry bottle or <u>one nickel</u>.

JACK: Gee, Hicks, you certainly reached for that one...That was George <u>Nickel-back</u> Hicks...a very charming fellow...I might say a <u>gentleman</u>...I might say – a <u>scholar</u>.... I <u>might</u> say - has he gone, George?

OLSEN: Yes, Jack.

JACK: Then I might say a <u>pest</u>! .... I 'm getting fed-up with these interruptions. Everybody knows that Canada Dry Ginger Ale is sold at all fountains, with the right amount of syrup and is good in ice-cream sodas...people don't have to be told that every minute.... Say, George, where are all the Guest Stars we invited here tonight?

OLSEN: I don't know, Jack. Nobody has shown up yet.

JACK: Can you imagine that?

GEORGE: Well, Jack, what do you think we ought to do?

JACK: I don't know, George. What do <u>you</u> think we should do?

GEORGE: I don't know.

JACK:	I certainly don't know, George.
GEORGE:	That's <u>your</u> headache, Jack.
JACK:	I know but we need <u>talent</u>, George.
HICKS:	This <u>shortage of talent</u> comes to you thru the courtesy of Canada Dry Ginger Ale- made-to-order by the glass, and sold at all fountains.
JACK:	Good old Hicks...well, you can always depend on him.... we'd better get some entertainers over here...Mary! …. OH, MARY!
SADYE:	Yes, Jack - oh, pardon me Hotcha.
JACK:	I see - Mary, look up the telephone number of the Sure-Fire Radio Talent Agency.
SADYE:	In the telephone directory?
JACK:	No, no in Webster's Dictionary - <u>some</u> <u>secretary</u>.
SADYE:	Well, Jack there's nothing here but the telephone book.
JACK:	Yes, Mary that's where you look up phone numbers.
SADYE:	Let me see - Sure Fire...Sure Fire....it isn't a fire insurance company is it?
JACK:	No – it's the Sure-Fire Radio Talent Agency.
SADYE:	Oh! here it is...funny, I couldn't find it because I had my finger on it all the time.... (LAUGHS)
JACK (MIMICS HER LAUGH):	Give me the phone.

(SOUND EFFECT: CLICKING OF RECIVER)

Hello, operator...operator! …. give me Bronx two eight one herring...Hello...hello....is this the Sure Fire Radio Talent Agency?...Who is this <u>Sure</u> or <u>Fire</u>?...Oh, it's <u>you</u> Ginsburg......Say, <u>Gin</u>...send me some radio talent. Our guest stars didn't show up tonight...you know, singers...dancers...musicians...mix them up...Yes, send over anything but trained goldfish. The little devils got the studio all wet last time.... Yeah, this is Jack Benny....So long....say, <u>operator</u>...<u>operator</u>...

(SOUND EFFECT: JIGGLING HOOK)

I didn't get my number...Give me my nickel back....MY NICKEL BACK........Hicks.... Hicks!!.... where are you? ... I said <u>nickel back</u>.

HICKS:	Oh, I'm sorry…. And don't forget, folks, you get a nickel back on each --
JACK:	It's too late now, Hicks......just when I needed you, you left me flat.... And now Ethel Shutta will sing that very beautiful number, "<u>ALWAYS IN YOUR HEART</u>".... while Jack Benny is <u>always</u> in your ear...and George Hicks is <u>always</u> getting a nickel back on the bottle.

September 19, 1932

2. ALWAYS IN YOUR HEART   ORCHESTRA AND ETHEL SHUTTA

JACK (APPLAUDS ALONE): Gee, Ethel, that's a beautiful number.... Say, Ethel, I was just watching you while you were singing. Really, I think you're beautiful. I can't understand why you aren't in pictures.

ETHEL: Well, Jack, I can't be every place. I have to be wherever George is.

JACK: Oh, yes....tchk....tchk....tchk....

ETHEL: Say, Jack, how does it happen you didn't stay in pictures? I thought you were great in all those I saw.

JACK: Well, I don't know, Ethel...you see, Clark Gable came out to Hollywood and there wasn't room for both of us...so I got out.

ETHEL (LAUGHS): What company were you with, Jack?

JACK: Oh, I was with the er....Macgum Studios.

ETHEL: Macgum?

JACK: Yes, M-G-M... you know, the picture that always starts out with a big lion roaring.

ETHEL: Oh, was that you? .... Gee, you were marvelous.

JACK: No, Ethel that's the trademark...But I made a couple of good pictures for them. I was in one called, "The Hollywood Revue," I was M.C. in that.

ETHEL: Oh yes and Marie Dressler and Joan Crawford were in it, too weren't they?

JACK: Yes, they helped out a little bit...then I made another picture called, "Chasing Rainbows." That was quite good.

ETHEL: Oh, yes I saw that.

JACK: Oh, You're the one that saw that...I knew someone had seen it.... But, Ethel, I have a contract to go back to Hollywood in a few months.... I'm going to be in a new picture with Greta Garbo.

ETHEL; Isn't that splendid! .... But I thought Garbo was in Sweden.

JACK: Yes but she's just resting up for this picture...That shows how good it's going to be.

ETHEL: That's wonderful, Jack....Who's going to direct the picture?

JACK: Jim Londos, the wrestler.... You know, they sent me the story last week to read. It's an awfully good story, too......particularly for me. I know when the picture first opens, I am found dead in the bathroom. It's a novel idea.... As I remember reading it, I'm found in a bathtub on a Wednesday night.

ETHEL: Oh! I see, it's a sort of mystery picture.

JACK (laughs): yes, wait a minute......you know, Ethel, I was supposed to have been in that other

	Garbo picture...."Inspiration." Do you remember that one?
ETHEL:	Yes, very well.
JACK:	I was supposed to have been in that one, too but they finally gave the part to Robert Montgomery. You Know politics.... And the funny part of it is, I am really much younger than Montgomery.... Say, Ethel, I'm going to ask you something confidential, and I want you to be absolutely frank with me. You know you're a woman, and I'm sure you can explain it to me.
ETHEL:	Why sure, Jack - what is it?
JACK:	Ethel, if I was so good in those pictures, why didn't they make me a star?
ETHEL:	Well er I don't know, Jack.
JACK:	But there must be some reason for it.
ETHEL:	Well, Jack maybe I could tell you but I wouldn't want to hurt your feelings.
JACK:	No go ahead, Ethel I won't be offended. I would really like to know what was the trouble with me.
ETHEL:	Well, Jack to be a great success on the screen, you must have a romantic appeal to women. JACK: Well?
ETHEL:	Jack, you lack that certain something that packs women into the theatre.
JACK:	I see, Ethel.
ETHEL:	You see, Jack what I mean is, you're not a Maurice Chevalier.
JACK:	Oh, Ethel how can you say that? Look at my lower lip.
SADYE:	Yes, and he's been wearing a straw hat all summer.
JACK:	Never mind, Mary....Ethel, you're just hard to please that's all.... I suppose Olsen looks like Chevalier.
ETHEL:	No but he stays out of Hollywood.
JACK:	Ethel, I'm hurt. You introduce the next number while I look in the mirror and see if you're lying. ETHEL: Now, ladies and gentlemen, my very handsome husband George Olsen will play "Mickey Mouse", sung by Fran Frey.

3. MICKEY MOUSE   ORCHESTRA & FRAN FREY

(OPEN WITH GENERAL NOISE PEOPLE WALKING AROUND RUNNING THRU SCALES, etc.)

JACK:	What's all that noise?
HICKS:	Jack, that's the talent from the Sure-Fire Radio Agency.

JACK:	Oh, the talent - well, well! they don't look it…. Take seats, everybody….
	Ladies and gentlemen, the talent is here, and it looks like a <u>great</u> night. So, take a tip and stay with us…. Now who's first?
SEVERAL VOICES (together):	Me, I'm first. __ ,
	No, I was here first, Mr. Benny.
	I was.
	Hey me!
	I've been waiting ten minutes….
BLANCHE STEWART:	I'm first, Mr. Benny.
JACK:	Take your time take your time - you'll all get your chance…. Now, young lady, I see you're ready…. You look very talented. Will you step to the microphone, please?
BLANCHE (Irish dialect):	Shure and oi will, Mr. Binny.
JACK:	<u>Benny's</u> the name.
BLANCHE:	Yis, Mr. Binny.
JACK:	Well, let's not have any trouble. Just step to the microphone…no, <u>not there</u>…that's Fran Frey's saxophone…This is the Canada Dry program having trouble…right there, Miss the <u>microphone</u>.
BLANCHE:	Oh yis and I big your pardon.
JACK:	What is <u>your</u> specialty?
BLANCHE:	He's a motorman.
JACK:	I don't mean your boy friend <u>what do you do</u>? …. sing, dance or whistle?
BLANCHE:	I moind babies.
JACK:	Well, that's something…. altho I don't think it would register over the air…Now isn't there <u>something</u> you can do? …. What's one of your late hits? For instance, what did you work in lately? BLANCHE: I was in Grand Hotel.
JACK:	Oh, Grand Hotel…what did you do in it?
BLANCHE:	I was the chambermaid.
JACK:	Are you listening, customers? …. Do we give you <u>talent</u>…and these stars come to you weekly…If you are not listening in tonight, you will never hear these artists again …. Now Miss….er…Miss… BLANCHE: Bridget.
JACK:	Oh, <u>Bridget</u> - where do you live?
BLANCHE:	Brooklyn.

JACK: Oh, you're the <u>Brooklyn</u> <u>Bridget</u>. Now let's see some of your talent what are you going to do for us this evening?

BLANCHE: I do imitations...My first one will be that Irish comedian <u>Eddie O' Cantor</u>.

JACK: <u>O'</u> Cantor ...oh yes from Coney Ireland...I beat you to <u>that</u> one. Well, let's hear Eddie <u>O'Cantor</u>.

BLANCHE: (<u>Quack</u> business)

JACK: That's fine can you do Benny <u>O'Rubin</u>?

BLANCHE: No but would you care for S<u>h</u>amus and Mc<u>Andy</u>?

JACK: What part of Ireland are they from?

BLANCHE: Burnt <u>cork</u>.

JACK: I don't think I care for that do you know any Irish crooners?

BLANCHE: Oh shure.

JACK: WHO?

BLANCHE & JACK (together): Rudy O'Vallee...

FRAN FREY (interrupting): Hey, wait a minute, Mr. Benny....what's this? I've been waiting here long enough. Either I'm going to do my specialty or I'm going home.

JACK: Well, I guess you're next, young feller. What's your specialty?

FRAN: I's a contortionist.

JACK: Are you doing anything for it?

FRAN: That isn't a sickness it's <u>talent</u>.

JACK: Oh, I see a contortionist you mean you're double jointed.

FRAN: Yes, I go from one joint to another and <u>here</u> I am.

JACK: All right let's see some of your tricks. By the way, tell us your name.

FRAN: Frank <u>P</u>. Twist.

JACK: What's the <u>P</u>. for?

FRAN: Pretzel.

JACK: I see- and you come from –

JACK & FRAN (together): <u>South Bend</u>.

JACK: I know all those jokes, too...now what is your first trick?

FRAN: Well, I put my feet behind my back.

JACK:	WHY?
FRAN:	Because I get a _kick_ out of it.
JACK:	I see I'd like to help you out with that sometime.
FRAN:	They generally do I will now tie myself into a knot.
JACK:	Okay, Frank…a little atmosphere, George. (LIGHT DRUM ROLL) Now, ladies and gentlemen, let me give you a description of this chump….I mean, artist…his left arm is wrapped around his biceps …his right knee is between his shoulder blades…his feet are under his chin…his head is in his vest pocket…and his watch is in hock…what a figure!…a little applause, boys. (ROUND OF APPLAUSE) Well, what's your _next_ trick?
FRAN:	I can't get out of this one.
JACK:	That's fine boys! carry him out and untangle him….
FRAN:	Hey! get me out of this knot.
JACK:	Is there anyone else?
FRAN:	Get me out of this knot.
HICKS:	These _knots_ come to you thru the courtesy of Canada Dry Ginger Ale now sold at all fountains. JACK: And made-to-order by the glass.
FRAN:	Hey help me out of this…help me out of this…
HICKS:	With the right amount of syrup and everybody's drinking it.
FRAN:	HELP! …. HELP!
JACK:	Don't worry, folks that's just a little static.
GEORGE OLSEN:	And now while Mr. Twist _unpretzels_ himself, I will play "Nightfall" sung by Bobby Borger.

4. NIGHTFALL   ORCHESTRA & BORGER

JACK:	Now on with our talent the cream of radio entertainers what other program gives you these artists? _None_….Well, we can't all be good….Ladies and gentlemen, I am going to introduce to you a great treat…a once-in-a-lifetime event…a man who came here from….a gentleman who has been….well, anyway, I take great pleasure in introducing Mr. Ralph Sunz-fran-sanlyz…young man, what do you do? HARRY CONN: Nothing.
JACK:	Well, that's the best thing we have had yet…At least, you _admit_ it…. Say, how old are you?

HARRY:	22 years.
JACK:	How long have you been doing nothing?
HARRY:	22 years.
JACK:	Doesn't it get tiresome?
HARRY:	No, I take long naps in between times.
JACK:	I think the next nap you take will be the last one.
HARRY:	I don't sleep very much because when I sleep, I dream that I'm working…and when I get up, I'm all tired out.
JACK:	I suppose in the afternoon you <u>rest</u>.
HARRY:	No I generally sleep.
JACK:	Why don't you go to sleep now and dream that you're not here…
HARRY:	No that's too much trouble.
JACK:	Hey, wait a minute your face is very familiar to me…I know you aren't you the fellow who came up here one night and sang about your girl Nellie?
HARRY:	Yes that's what I came up to tell you.
JACK:	Say, will you sing that Nellie song for us again?
HARRY:	I'd like to but I don't go around with Nellie any more.
JACK:	You don't?
HARRY:	No she double-crossed me she got <u>married</u>…But I got a new girl now, and I wrote a song about <u>her</u>. Do you want to hear it?
JACK:	Sure so ahead.
HARRY:	Here's the piano part.
JACK:	Well, at last we've got somebody who can do something…. All right, start it for him, George.
	(PIANO VAMPS)
HARRY:	I got a new girl – Oh, I've got a new girl Kate, Flo or May's not her name… She's very pretty and only half-witty. But Oh! what a swell-looking dame…….
JACK (AD LIB):	<u>Well, what's her name?</u> Her name is Iodine that girlie of mine… Yes, Iodine and for her I pine. She's poison for some guys but okay for me,

	And she soothes my bruises, wherever they be. Her name is Iodine that baby of mine And I could die for my Iodine....
JACK (AD LIB):	Here's hoping......... Her name could be Dinah or Sweet Adeline Or Halitosia but it's Iodine. Oh, Iodine...I I I Iodine, I I I adore Iodine...
HARRY CONN (RECITES):	When the world's against you, and you haven't got a friend And you've lost all hope and you're looking for the end.... You're full of pains and sorrow and you know not where to go. Who kills those pains and sorrows...is it Fanny, Kate or Flo! NO..... (last eight bars of chorus reprise) It's Iodine - I I I Iodine... Not Peroxide, but Sweet Iodine.... (gets hot) Iodine, etc.
OFFICER (BALSWIN):	Mr. Benny, is this the man?
JACK:	Yes, Officer.
HARRY CONN:	(STILL SINGING, " IODINE"...INTO DISTANCE)
JACK:	Ladies and gentlemen, please forget for the moment that this was the Canada Dry Program....
FRAN FREY:	Help! .... help! ...get me out of this knot....
JACK:	And now George Olsen will help us out of this <u>mess</u> by playing - "TIGER RAG."

5. TIGER RAG   ORCHESTRA

JACK:	That was the last number of the forty-first program on the 19th of September. And we want to apologize for our <u>real</u> Guests not appearing this evening, but we did the best we could with the talent that was thrown at us......And now on Wednesday night --
SADYE:	Oh, Jack Jack....
JACK:	What is it, Mary?
SADYE:	Pardon me, Hotcha...Say, Jack, I heard what Ethel said to you before.
JACK:	What was that, Mary?
SADYE:	What you have no romantic appeal to women...<u>I</u> think you have.
JACK:	Well, thanks, Mary...I am glad you feel that way about it.

SADYE:	Gee, I don't know how she could even say that.... I think you're wonderful.
JACK:	Well, that's all that's necessary, Mary.
SADYE:	Gee, you remind me of the Greek Apollo.
JACK:	I'm _not_ a Greek, Mary.
SADYE:	But you _are_ an Apollo.
JACK:	Well, you're mighty sweet to stick up for me like that. Now I _know_ you like me.

---- [Ed. note: page 22 is missing] ---

ANNOUNCER [continuing the closing] …. cents for an extra-large glass. Remember, too, that with the exception of a few localities where freight charge do not permit, you can take back your Canada Dry bottles to the dealer and get a cash refund. So that now when you buy Canada Dry you pay for the contents only. Next Wednesday night at this same time, Jack Benny, Ethel Shutta and George Olsen will again entertain you. This is the National Broadcasting Company.

September 21, 1932

Jack and George are in jail for speeding (another early skit imagined to be away from the studio). Ethel and Mary visit them. Jack tells his "three lobsters" story from his old vaudeville routine. This episode, like others in the Olsen/Shutta period, makes good use of numerous members of the orchestra to play small roles. Subsequently, Jack would need to hire additional help from voice actors.

Septepber 26 1932 MISSING from this volume. The cast proclaims that this is Russian Night, with Cossack dancers and a "Volga Boatman"-themed romantic skit. It will be included in Volume 3.

STATION WJZ   PROGRAM CANADA DRY GINGER ALE, INC.

           AND   DATE MONDAY, SEPTEMBER 21, 1932.

BLUE NETWORK   TIME 9:30 10:00 P.M.

SIGNATURE JOLLY GOOD COMPANY

1. LIBESTRAUM   ORCHESTRA

2. SUCH IS LIFE   ETHEL SHUTTA

3. YOU'RE TELLING ME   FRAN FREY

4. MILLION DOLLER BABY   ETHEL SHUTTA AND FRAN FREY

5. JUST KNOCK AT MY DOOR   GARDNER

SIGNATURE ROCKABYE MOON

CANADA DRY GINGER ALE INC   WEDNESDAY, SEPTEMBAR 21,1932.

SIGNATURE JOLLY GOOD COMPANY

ANNOUNCER: Ladies and gentlemen, another half year of entertainment about Canada Dry the champagne of ginger ales now available by the glass at soda fountains, as well as in bottles for the home. You'll find the new, large size bottle very economical and particularly convenient for home use. Once more we present George Olsen, Ethel Shutta and Jack Benny, the Canada Dry humorist, who will perform for your enjoyment.......Pardon me a moment, ladies and gentlemen. We seem to be in hot water tonight. For some reason or other, neither Jack Benny nor George Olsen have shown up at the studio. As a matter of fact, there's no one here but the orchestra and the janitor, Mr. Kvetch.

SCHLOSSBERG (POLISH DIALECT) Hello, ladies and peoples of the rattio au-dience.... I'm the janitor of the building.... there's nobody here but me tonight. I wish I could help out.... If I could sink, I would sink.

HICKS: Give me that mike, quick.... Special announcement, ladies and gentlemen...I have just received word that Jack Benny and George Olsen were arrested for speeding on the way over hero from the Paradise Theatre, where they are playing. So please stand by while we investigate. Meanwhile, the orchestra will entertain you with the first number, "LIEBESTRAUM". Okay, boys.

1.LIEBESTRAUM   ORCHESTRA

RALPH ASHE: It's no use, Hicks I can't do a thing about getting the boys out. The judge <u>won't</u> listen.

HICKS: But this Canada Dry program <u>must</u> go on.... what shall we do?

[ED.: These next three lines of dialogue were removed…

SCHLOSSBERG: Vy don't you borrow the magic rug from the Lucky Strike program? Maybe you could broadcast from the jail.

HICKS: That's a good idea -- get the magic rug, Kvetch.

SCHLOSSBERG: It's right here – I was dusting it off. –removed]

[ED.: They were replaced by this line and the sound effect]

RALPH: I don't know. We will have to make this a hook-up program – that's all we can do.

(SOUND EFFECT: Siren)

JACK BENNY (IS HEARD SINGING): If I had the wings of a swallow.... I'd fly....

HICKS: There he is, ladies and gentlemen.... And speaking of swallow when you swallow Canada Dry Ginger Ale, you are giving yourself a real treat.

JACK: Oh boy! If I could get out of here for just one minute -- I heard that one, Hicks. I'm tuned in..... This is Jack Benny....broadcasting. From Cell Number one, Tier three, the Tombs Prison.... Jack Benny...."B" as in bail...."E" as in early to bed...."N" as in no freedom.... another "N" as ---

FRAN FREY: Hey you in Cell One shut up!

JACK: Now wait a minute I'm Jack Benny.

FRAN: Oh, you are eh? .... Well, that will also be held against you.

JACK: What was my landlord, ladies and gentlemen.... Boy! are these cells cold.

HICKS: And every fountain cells cold Canada Dry Ginger Ale.

JACK: Say, Hicks get out of this jail!........What are you prisoners all laughing at?......I see, away from your wives, eh?

FRAN: Hey there do I have to tell you to shut up again. You should be cracking rocks instead of jokes.

JACK: This is Jack Benny talking.... ain't I smart?

ROBBY BORGER: Bight this way, ma'am.... here's the guy you want. And make it snappy.

JACK: Hello, Ethel.

ETHEL: Oh, Jack I'm so sorry to see you here. I was in the Studio and they told me about this, and I nearly fainted.... What happened?

JACK: Well, you see we were driving from the theatre to the studio to broadcast.... we were only going seventy-two miles an hour and ......

ETHEL: Well, they can't put you in jail for they, Jack.

JACK: They can't?

ETHEL: No.

JACK: Well, Ethel where do you think I am in Bermuda?......of course we had a slight accident.... I ran into a telegraph pole.

ETHEL: Didn't you blow your horn?

JACK: Yes, Ethel but the pole wouldn't move an inch.

ETHEL: Why didn't you tell the officer that you were Jack Benny of the Canada Dry Program?

JACK:	I did, Ethel and that's why we're here.
ETHEL:	Oh, for Heaven's sake - was <u>George</u> with you?
JACK:	In the next cell, Ethel - <u>Oh, George</u>!
GEORGE OLSEN (SADLY):	Yes, Jack....
JACK:	Ethel is here.
GEORGE:	Hello, Ethel...Gee, I'm glad you're here.... You'll have to bail me out.
ETHEL:	<u>What for</u>? .... (Sings: "Li-de-di-di....li-de) ------
GEORGE:	Now, Ethel you'll have to do something about getting me out of here.
ETHEL:	I told you to wait for me. But <u>no</u>! - you had to go ahead with Jack. If you had listened to me, this never would have happened.
GEORGE:	Well, you certainly pick a fine time to holler at me.
ETHEL:	What a fine-looking leader you are now.... well, the rates here should suit you, anyway.
GEORGE:	<u>Some</u> wife I've got!
ETHEL:	Well, I'll know where you are for the next few months, anyway.
JACK (HUMS):	Li-dee-di-di...this is Jack <u>Single</u> Benny Singing.
ETHEL:	Well, good-bye, boys.... have a good time.
HICKS:	Pardon me, Jack - but we've got to get on with our program. I've arranged it so that you can broadcast from here....so let's get started.
JACK:	All right, Hicks....now the boys in the orchestra will play, "SUCH IS LIFE" from the Studio....George Olsen will direct from <u>his cell</u>.... while Ethel will <u>sing-sing</u>.....De-na<u>morra</u> of our jokes......and it will be Leaven<u>worth</u> your while to listen....<u> What</u> a hook up!
FRAN:	Any more puns like that, and we'll throw you out of here.
JACK:	<u>Yeah</u>? .... I'd like to see you put me out of here, you big stiff.
FRAN:	Yeah! ....one more word out of you---

SEGUE INTO NUMBER....JACK AND FRAN AD LIB.

2. SUCH IS LIFE   ORCHESTRA AND ETHEL SHUTTA

JACK:	Hello, everybody.... this is Number six three five eight talking.... <u>Jack Benny</u> to you. Coming direct from the Grill Room of Tombs Prison...I'm still stuck in this cell, but

don't worry, friends, --I'm not here alone. I have two companions with me <u>also</u> guest stars of the prison.... charming-looking fellows.... Hey, bud! What are <u>you</u> in for?

HARRY CONN: Who <u>me</u>?

JACK: Yeah.

HARRY: Oh, nothing much--I <u>found</u> a limousine standing in the gutter.

JACK: I see.... you didn't happen to find the Empire State Building standing on Fifth Avenue did you?

HARRY: Yeah – but I couldn't carry it.

JACK: I see…. I suppose if you ever found a ten-dollar bill, there'd be a <u>safe</u> around it.

HARRY: No – but I'll remember that…. Say, who is that lug in the next cell?

JACK: George Olsen.

HARRY: Well, tell him to keep those fish hooks out of his pockets……. I keep cutting my hands all the time.

JACK: That was <u>Olsen</u> all right…. Say, how long are you in for, Buddy?

HARRY: Fifty-nine years.

JACK: Oh, just for the <u>week-end</u> – eh? …. Say, how old are you now?

HARRY: Forty-three.

JACK: You'll be a <u>hundred and two</u> when you get out.

HARRY: Yeah – and it'll be a darned good lesson to me.

JACK: You said it! …. we're never too old to learn…Say, who's our friend in the upper berth?

HARRY: You mean the colored gentlemen?

JACK: I don't Know …. Hey, Son! …. Son!

RALPH ASHE: What do you want?

JACK: How long are you in for?

RALPH (COLOURED DIALEECT): Man! I'm in heah from now till three more <u>e</u>-clipses….Ah comes out when de moon passes de sun for do third time…..Don't you fail me, Moon!

JACK: What are you in for?

RALPH : Well, de give me fifteen yeahs fo' robbin' a bank…..den fifteen mo' fo: stoppin' de man dat tired to stop me…..den dey give me twenty – two mo' years for totin' a razor without shavin' creem….and den dey also give me an extra year fo' arson.

JACK: Arson'….oh, you burned down a building.

RALPH: No…..ar<u>son</u> he's only fourteen years old, and he got closely acquainted with a strange pocket book…..so <u>I</u> took the rap.

JACK: Say, who's that fellow in the cell on the left? I'm new around here and I'd like to meet my neighbors.

RALPH: He just threw him in thar fo' talkin' to himself…….He says one thing and keeps repeating it over and over again.

JACK: Poor fellow – I'll talk to him. Maybe he has something on his mind…. Hello, neighbor   what do you say?

HICKS: Canada Dry Ginger Ale, made-to-order by the glass, is now sold at all fountains, with just the right amount of syrup – also good in ice-cream sodas.

JACK: George, have the boys play the next number.

SEGUE INTO-----

3. YOU'RE TELLING ME   ORCHESTRA AND FRAN FREY

GEORGE OLSEN: Jack – say, Jack!. …how long do you think we're going to be stuck in here?

JACK: I don't know, George.

GEORGE: Gee, this is awful.

JACK: Yup – I told you we never know when we're well off……I used to hate to hear Hicks say "a nickel back on the bottle", but I'd give <u>anything</u> just to hear his voice again.

GEORGE: Yes, sir – we're certainly in a <u>pickle</u> now.

HICKS: Remove the "P" from pickle – substitute an "N" – and what have you?... a nickel…. which is exactly the coin you get back on each large Canada Dry Bottle……I thank you.

JACK: Warden! …give Hicks the chair and I'll pay for the juice…. George, I'm going to tell you something. You know, we're not so badly off.

GEORGE: Oh, it's bad enough.

JACK: George, I could tell you a story I heard the other day that would make you glad you're living…. really, it's one of the saddest stories I've ever heard in my life. Just listen to this—there were three lobsters living up in Maine…. a mother lobster – a father lobster….and a baby lobster.

And they were happy and contented in their own simple way --eating, sleeping and leading a healthy out door existence…..when one day the baby lobster was caught and taken away from its parents…..Well, of course, you can imagine the feelings of the mother and father living there for years afterward, yearning for the return of their one and only son….Well, twenty years have passed, and they had given up hopes of ever seeing their baby again. And one day while they were in Rhode Island, visiting some relatives, the father and mother lobster were caught…. but they were satisfied as they were old by this time and the father lobster and rheumatism in all twelve of his legs. Well, anyway, they took the mother and father lobster and threw them in the window of a seafood restaurant, among fifty or sixty other lobsters…. when lo and behold! Right in front of them, they saw a great big giant muscular lobster…. the largest one in the entire window – loafing on a piece of ice. They recognized him immediately as their long-lost son who was taken from them twenty years ago. So, of course, they had a great reunion. Finally, the mother said, "Son! Tell me – how is it in all these twenty years you managed to keep out of hot water – that you weren't eaten?" …and the son replied, "I'll tell you, Ma. I'm the Big lobster that the waiter always shows the customer that the customer never gets." …Isn't that sad, George?

GEORGE: Yes, Jack – that's the <u>worst</u> story I ever heard.

SADYE'S VOICE (IN DISTANCE): Where's Mr. Benny's room…. where's Mr. Benny's room…JACK! …. OH, JACK….

JACK: Oh hello, Mary….how did you get in here?

SADYE: Oh Jack, I found out that you were here, and I rushed right over…. How do you like my new hat?

JACK: Very nice, Mary….did you see anyone about getting me out of here?

SADYE: No – but my father will be back from the next month and he knows the Judge – and I'm sure he'll do something…. How do you like my new hat with this purse – or do you think <u>blue</u> would look better?

JACK: It's awfully nice of you to come over and see me, Mary….did you bring the mail?

SADYE: Yes…and I brought you a little present. It's in this package. Guess what it is.

JACK: I'll bet its <u>cigars</u> or <u>fruit</u>.

SADYE: No, Jack – it's a nice set of books – enough to last till <u>Christmas</u>.

JACK: What makes you think I'm going to get out Christmas?

SADYE: Why, Jack – I think if you stayed any longer, you'd be overdoing it…. Say, is there anything else I can do for you?

JACK: Yes, Mary – get me a good lawyer.

SADYE: Oh, Jack – I know the handsomest lawyer. I think he's swell. You know – he got a divorce for my aunt in Plainfield and she didn't even have to pay her husband alimony.

JACK: Well, for Heaven's sake – go and get him.

SADYE: All, right, Jack –but I've got two tickets for a movie and as soon as it's over. I'll go and get him…. Oh, hello, George. I didn't see you there.

GEORGE(SADLY): Oh hello, Mary.

SADYE:	Was Ethel here? I have to meet her downstairs. We're going to a picture.... Oh, Jack! Do you think this hat would go better with <u>Brown</u> shoes – or <u>black</u>?
JACK:	George! Announce the next number – will you, please?
SADYE:	Good-night, Jack – so long, George.
JACK AND GEORGE (TOGETHER):	Good Bye, Mary.
GEORGE (SADLY):	And now my boys will play, "Million Dollar Baby" – sung by Ethel Shutta.

4. MILLION DOLLAR BABY   ORCHESTRA & ETHEL SHUT-TA

(SOUND EFFECT: SAW AGAINST IRON BAR)

JACK:	This is Jack Benny, trying to get out of jail.
RALPH ASHE (IN DISTANCE):	Where is Mr. Benny?
FRAN:	Right over there – Cell One.
SADYE:	He's right in this cell – and I'm sure you can help him.
FRAN:	Say, young lady – you can't be running in and out of this jail.
SADYE:	This is a lawyer – and he's going to talk to Jack.
FRAN:	All right – go ahead.
SADYE:	Jack! Jack! .....what are you doing with that saw and shotgun?
JACK:	Sh!...Sh!....Mary, I'm trying to get out of here.
RALPH:	Is this Mr. Benny?
SADYE:	Yes – don't you think he's swell?....Jack, won't need that crowbar and chisel now.... <u>He'll</u> get you out.
JACK:	Quiet, Mary....they'll hang me.
RALPH:	Mr. Benny I'm a lawyer – my name's <u>Stir</u> – just got in from <u>Chi</u>.
JACK:	A see – Shy – stir, the lawyer.... well, it looks like I'm going to have trouble with you, too.
RALPH:	Mr. Benny – tell me...what did you do?
JACK:	Well, I –
RALPH:	You didn't do it.
SADYE:	Oh, yes, he did – we have three witnesses.

JACK:	Mary, will you please go home?
SADYE:	But Jack, I'm just trying to help you.
RALPH:	Now, Mr. Benny – the judge will ask you several questions.... for instance, where were you on the night of April 12, 1902 at a quarter to five?
JACK:	Why?
RALPH:	What's it.
JACK:	But supposing he asks me –
RALPH:	You don't remember.
JACK:	Yes – but supposing he questions me about the accident?
RALPH:	Then we'll have to get a habeas corpus.
JACK:	What?
RALPH:	A habeas corpus.
JACK:	What's that?
RALPH:	That's ten dollars extra – and I'm losing money.... But don't worry – I'll get you out of this. I just won my last case.
JACK:	Yeah?
RALPH:	Yes, sir – a fellow was parking in front of a hydrant, and I got him off with ten years.
JACK:	Do me a favor, will you? .... Go over there and defend Olsen.
RALPH:	Over where?
JACK:	There – on the right.
RALPH:	Mr. Olsen, my name's Stir....I'm a lawyer from Chicago.
GEORGE:	How do you, Mr. Stir....are you a good lawyer?
RALPH:	Am I? ......I've got over a hundred clients in Atlanta alone.
GEORGE:	Go back and defend Mr. Benny.
RALPH:	All right, Mr. Olsen – but if any time you're in trouble, send for me.
GEORGE:	I'd rather have aspirin.
RALPH:	Phooey! – what a lawyer he is.... Now, Mr. Benny. I've already talked to the Judge on the way in – and he said he would fine you fellows three dollars apiece and close the case.
JACK:	It's all right with me – I'll pay it.

RALPH:	What? I wouldn't let you pay a cent! ...Let me do the worrying – Why sometimes I go away for three months and worry about a case like this.... I'll take care of this for you and it won't cost you a cent – except my fee.
JACK:	What do you get?
RALPH:	My retainer is seventy-five dollars.
JACK:	How much?
RALPH:	Well – fifteen.
JACK:	I'll give you two dollars....
RALPH:	Okay – do you think it's bad these days?
JACK:	Now do me a favour – here's six dollars.... give it to the judge and get Olsen and me out of here.
RALPH:	No, sir I'll bring this to trial...good bye, gentlemen. I'll be back here next week with some good news – I hope.
JACK:	Well, George, cheer up – we got a good lawyer, anyway.... It looks like a long night, Have you a radio there, George?
GEORGE:	Yes.
JACK:	Tune in and see if you can get anything.
	(SOUND EFFECT: STATIC AND TUNING IN)
HICKS' VOICE HEARD:	......made to order, by the glass, and sold at all fountains – also good with ice cream.
JACK:	See else you can get, George.
HICKS' VOICE:	And now George Olsen's orchestra – without Olsen – will play. "Just Knock at My Door", sung by Hotcha Gardner.

5. JUST KNOCK AT MY DOOR   ORCHESTRA & GARDNER

JACK:	That was the number of the 42nd program on the 21st of September.... are you sorry for us, hmm? And, folks, if we are out of here by Monday night, I hope you will all listen in as we are going to take you to Russia....We will have our Russian Night on Monday.
HOTCHA GARDNER:	Hello, George – oh, hello, Jack – I'm sorry to see you here.
JACK:	That's all right, Hotcha – nice of you to come over.
GARDINER:	I just wanted to ask you, Jack – can I borrow your car tonight? You won't need it.

JACK:	What do you want it for?
GARDINER:	I'm taking Mary home tonight, and I thought it would be a great idea to drive her home.
JACK:	Come here, Hotcha – right up to the bars.
	(SLAP EFECT)
GARDNER:	Ow! my eye....ow!...ow!...
JACK:	It was a great fight, Ma...and now I want to meet Canzoneri.....Good night, folks.

SIGNATURE – ROCKABYE MOON

ANNOUNCER:	Remember, you can enjoy Canada Dry – the champagne of ginger ales – anywhere, anytime, for it is now available two ways – either made to order by the glass at soda fountains or in bottles, as always, for your home. The new big bottle is particularly economical and convenient.
	Remember, too, that with the exception of a few localities, where freight rates do not permit, you pay for the contents only, that is, twenty cents for the big five glass bottle, or twenty-five cents for two regular twelve – ounce bottles. In addition, you make a small deposit on each bottle, but this deposit is refunded when the bottle is returned. Next Monday night at this same time Jack Benny, Ethel Shutta and George Olsen will again entertain you. This is the National Broadcasting Company.

September 28, 1932

Jack reads made-up news headlines, then provides play by play of the Schmeling-Walker fight, and mixes in a bit of baseball discussion. Jack exclaims, "Play, George, Play!" a phrase he would use with subsequent bandleaders in the coming years. The Benny-Livingstone romance plot is heating up - Jack gets upset that band member Hotcha Gardner is romantically involved with Mary. Jack tries to convince George Olsen to fire Hotcha.

STATION WJZ   PROGRAM CANADA DRY GINGER ALE, INC.

AND   DATE WEDNESDAY, SEPTEMBER 28, 1932.

BLUE NETWORK   TIME 9:30 10:00 P.M.

SIGNATURE JOLLY GOOD COMPANY

        1. SONG OF INDIA   ORCHESTRA
        2. SWEETHEART HOUR   MARSHALL
        3. AFTER TWELVE O'CLOCK   ETHEL SHUTTA
        4. SAY IT ISN'T SO   MARSHALL
        5. SHINE ON YOUR SHOES   FRAN FREY

SIGNATURE ROCKABYE MOON

CANADA DRY GINGER ALE INC.   WEDNESDAY, SEPT. 28, 1932.
SIGNATURE JOLLY GOOD COMPANY

ANNOUNCER: Ladies and gentleman, another half hour of entertainment about Canada Dry the champagne of Ginger ales now available by the glass at soda fountains, as well as in bottles for the home. You'll find the new, large size bottle very economical and particularly convenient for home use.

HICKS: Once more, we present George Olsen, Ethel Shutta and Jack Benny, the Canada Dry Humorist, who will again perform for your enjoyment. Tonight, we are dedicating our program to our good friends the National Association of Retail Druggists who are holding their convention in Boston this week. George Olsen opens the program with "SONG OF INDIA."

HICKS: And Now Jack Benny!

JACK: Well, as Hicks says we're dedicating our program tonight to the Retail Druggists who are holding their Convention in Boston this week. I have a good many friends up there - and if you're listening in, boys -- hello, <u>Louis</u> <u>Somberg</u> and <u>Martin Adamo</u>, of Boston...Hi, there! <u>Sam Henry</u>....how's everything in Chicago? <u>John Gould's</u> up there, from Asheville........hello, "<u>Doc</u>" <u>Cousens</u>, where were you on our Rodeo Night?......

I hope you're having as much fun in Boston as we are down here. Say, is <u>Frank East</u> taking good care of you fellows? And are you drinking Canada Dry....hmm?

That was just personal, folks. They're all friends of mine and I wish you could meet them. Are you ready for our program?......Well, hello members of our Club! This is Jack <u>Brisbane</u> Benny, the Earth Galloper...coming to you again with the late news events thru the courtesy of the Uni-<u>Worse-than</u> Ever Service....<u>sees</u> all, <u>knows</u> all and <u>exaggerates</u> everything...We have dispatches from all over the world...all the <u>latest happenings</u> and a few <u>scoops</u> that won't happen until tomorrow.... This is <u>Jack Benny</u> talking, the <u>eye</u> of the world –

OLSEN: He's right, folks - it's <u>I</u> this - <u>I</u> that - and <u>I</u> everything.

JACK: George, get out of the editorial- room...And now for the news, folks - <u>HARTFORD</u>, Conn.... Man finds job.... <u>will recover</u>.... HOLLYWOOD, CALIF. – James Cagney quitting films to practice medicine...Oh, well, from <u>thrills</u> to <u>pills</u>.... <u>HICKSVILLE</u>,

LONG ISLAND - New liner christened with Canada Dry bottle.... No nickel back on <u>that</u> bottle. Too bad, Hicks! Oh, <u>a second dispatch</u> says that ship was sunk but <u>bottle still in shape to get nickel</u> back.... Disregard that, Hicks! <u>BOMBAY</u>, INDIA Gandhi fasts ten days and <u>will start eating</u> on Yom Kippur....<u>STOCKHOLM</u>, SWEDEN - Garbo glad to put feet back on home soil.... Is Sweden <u>big enough</u>, Greta? Oh, well.... <u>MAMARONECK</u>, NEW YORK - <u>Four</u>-cylinder roadster turns over in ditch. Olsen and <u>twelve</u> friends injured. <u>NEW YORK CITY</u> - Two burlesque theatres closed...Dress business picking up again......

<u>BOSTON</u>, MASS - Miss <u>Becky Bean</u> bitten by <u>Boston bull</u>.... Uh-uh, Becky! Stay away from those detectives!......And now the thing you've been waiting for results of today's baseball game....<u>Brooklyn Stars</u>, twelve - <u>Lincoln Giants</u>, six...We haven't got the Yanks and Cubs score yet...<u>PHILADELPHIA</u>, PA. - Eclipse <u>just arrived</u>...No other news.....<u>TIMES SQUARE</u>, N.Y. - Gunman holds up roomful of actors...Gets away with <u>twelve</u> cents and <u>ten pounds</u> of press notices...Well, that's just local....<u>BUTTE</u>, MONTANA - Franklin Roosevelt stops off here and is entertained by <u>five copper</u> kings.

HICKS: And you can get <u>five coppers</u> back on each large Canada Dry bottle.

JACK: I meant to leave that last news item out...Hicks! Is there <u>anything</u> we can do to keep you from butting in on these scenes?

HICKS: I guess not, Jack. I'm here to do my duty. You know, this is <u>business</u> with me. Now if I had to wait <u>for you</u> to give me a chance to say that you get a nickel back on each large Canada Dry bottle, the people would never know that they get a nickel back on the bottle --

JACK: All right, Hicks, all right.

HICKS: I know, Jack - but I'm naturally conscientious - it's the principle of the thing with me...You see, I have a sense of honor that prompts me to –

JACK: All right, Hicks I'm sorry I started it.

HICKS: Oh, Jack, can't you see the position I'm in? You see, I've got a job, and I'm here to protect it.

JACK: I see, Hicks...Play, George, play!

SEGUE INTO NUMBER –

2. SWEETHEART HOUR   ORCHESTRA & DAVE MARSHALL (OLSEN MAKES HIS OWN ANNOUNCEMENT ALSO ABOUT DAVE MARSHALL)

HICKS (AS NUMBER STARTS): But Jack, I don't want you to get me wrong. Don't feel that this is a personal issue. Please understand that it's a matter of <u>business with me</u>.

JACK: All right, Hicks let's go over in the corner and talk about it...Folks, where else do they let you in on these impromptu discussions?

HICKS:	Jack, I want you to realize –
(AFTER NUMBER –)	
JACK:	That was Dave Marshall singing, "SWEETHEART HOUR."
HICKS:	Jack, can't you see the position I'm in? Whenever an opportunity presents itself, I'm supposed to mention Canada Dry by-the-glass --
JACK:	I know, Hicks but not by the microphone.
HICKS:	It is essential that my discourse regarding the commodity be reiterated whenever the occasion thromologates......
JACK:	This is Jack Benny looking for a dictionary...Say, Hicks, that last word got me...thromologates! Are you a college man?
HICKS:	Yes I'm Yale '28...And you?
JACK:	Vanities '31....you remember Dean Earl Carroll...thru these portals pass the most beautiful students in the world! Yes, folks, I had some education.
SADYE:	Jack! Oh, Jack!
JACK:	Yes, what is it, Mary?
SADYE:	Jack, I think you ought to answer some of this fan mail. It keeps on pilling up. Now here's a letter that came by Special Delivery and marked personal. I read it to some of my friends, but none of them could make it out.
JACK:	Thanks. Mary - if a telegram comes for me marked private, pin it on the wall where everybody can read it.
SADYE:	All right, I'll remember that.
JACK:	Paying her a salary is like paying alimony - I mean, you get nothing for something... Well, let's see what the letter says. Hmmm, it's a lady's handwriting....." DEAR JACK BENNY WITH ICE CREAM -- I HAVE BEEN LISTENING TO YOUR PROGRAM STEADILY AS OUR RADIO HAS NO KNOBS AND YOU WERE TUNED IN WHEN WE LOST THEM.....hmmmmm!
	SO YOU SEE I HAVE TO ENJOY YOUR PROGRAM....NOW WHAT I WOULD LIKE TO HAVE IS A PICTURE OF ALL OF YOU – NOT THE ORDINARY PICTURE YOU ONCE SENT ME, BUT A GROUP PICTURE TO BE POSED AS FOLLOWS: YOU FALLING OUT OF AN AEROPLANE WITHOUT A PARACHUTE.... ACCOMPANIED BY FRAN FREY AND LANDING ON GEORGE OLSEN.....YOU KNOW WHAT I MEAN, A SORT OF AVIATION POSE. DON'T BOTHER TO AUTOGRAPH THIS. (SIGNED) MISS FANNY MALL-EY.....
	Of course, folks, this letter is only one of the complimentary kind...we get others panning us.....Oh well, we can't please anybody ...Say, Mary you'd better answer this.
SADYE:	Yes, and I'll certainly enclose a piece of my mind. She can't tell my boy-friend to jump out of an aeroplane.

JACK:	That's awfully sweet of you, Mary but the customer is <u>always</u> right.
SADYE:	I know but they can't insult anybody <u>I like</u>.
JACK:	But, Mary, don't let it annoy you...I appreciate it and all that.
SADYE:	well, far be it from me to get sore at anyone, but I think her remarks are <u>very unswell</u>....When I like a person, I like him...that's all there is to it.
JACK:	I like you, <u>too</u> Mary.
SADYE:	Why the <u>idea</u> of her talking that way about <u>Fran</u> <u>Frey</u> wanting <u>him</u> to fall out of an aeroplane. JACK: I see, Mary you know, she wanted <u>me</u> to fall out, too.
SADYE:	Yes, Jack but <u>you</u> can care of yourself...<u>Fran</u>, the poor sap, would get hurt.
JACK:	Oh, so it's <u>Fran</u> now! I thought you were going home nights <u>with</u> <u>Hotcha</u>.
SADYE:	Yes, but that doesn't mean anything. It's just in fun....And you know what? He asked me <u>to</u> <u>marry</u> him last night.
JACK:	<u>He did</u>?
SADYE:	Oh huh, and I said <u>yes</u>. Wasn't that silly?
JACK:	Why, you're not <u>serious</u>, Mary about marrying Hotcha Gardner!
SADYE:	No, of course not.
JACK:	My advice to you is stay away from Hotcha.
SADYE:	All right, Jack but what do you think I ought to do with <u>this ring</u> he gave me?
JACK:	Better put it back in the popcorn box where he got it.
SADYE:	All right, Jack, if you say so...Gee whiz! A girl can't have a ring or anything....I'll <u>never</u> get to Niagara Falls.
JACK:	May be some day, Mary....Pardon this little interlude, folks.....not that it <u>means</u> anything because after all I don't really care <u>who</u> Mary goes out with........you know, it's none of my business....She's her own boss, and it means nothing to me......You know, I just want to see the kid get along all right that's all......
ETHEL:	Say, Jack I know how you feel.
JACK:	<u>I feel fine</u>, Ethel ....it's just that –
ETHEL:	I know, I know, Jack George once broke up a romance for me. I gave up a guy with brains <u>and</u> money.
JACK:	Why, George's got <u>money</u>.
ETHEL:	Leave <u>George</u> out of it now don't you <u>worry</u> about Mary. It's going to turn out all right.
JACK:	Ethel, I'm <u>not worrying</u> about her. Say, what makes you think I'm worrying?

ETHEL: Then quit biting your nails! And, Jack, you look <u>so pale</u> - <u>so depressed</u>.

HICKS: Well, I'm tired of waiting when you're feeling <u>depressed</u>, drink a glass of Canada Dry Ginger Ale, made-to-order at the fountain –

JACK(HUMS): Hicks, I'll be glad when you're dead, you rascal you Play, George.

SEGUE INTO NUMBER –

3. AFTER TWELVE O'CLOCK   ORCHESTRA & ETHEL SHUT-
   TA (OLSEN MAKES OWN ANNOUNCEMENT)

JACK: And, now, ladies and gentlemen, for the <u>last</u> time on the air a description of the Mickey Schmelling-Max Walker Fight....er, the Schmelling-Maxie - Mickey the Mouse....er, the Walker-Seabury Fight...in other words, the <u>Schmelling</u>-<u>Walker</u> Fight held in <u>No Man's Land</u>, Long Island......First of all, to end the suspense, I want to tell you that <u>Schmelling won</u>, But it was robbery <u>highway robbery</u>...How they could give the decision <u>to</u> <u>Schmelling</u> after the terrible beating Walker took is beyond me.... Oh well, you know <u>politics</u>......It just gets my goat not because I <u>bet</u> on Walker....it's the principle of the thing. Oh, you heard <u>different</u> eh? Well, I was right on the rim of the Bowl, and saw everything.... Well, I'll admit that the <u>first eight</u> rounds went to Schmelling yes! But how about the ninth tenth eleventh and twelfth rounds, after the crowd left? It was <u>all Walker</u> up to the <u>twenty-sixth</u>.... of September....which was <u>all Schmelling's</u>. How about it?......

Now personally, I think Walker is a much nicer fellow a gentleman a scholar...which entitles him to <u>at least a draw</u>.....but last night he just happened to be <u>the fall guy</u>, and this being the <u>Fall</u> Season, he took advantage of it....Immediately after the next number, I will give you a day by day...er, a <u>round by round</u> description of the Fight. And to ease the tension of this hair-raising battle, Olsen will play, "Say It Isn't So", sung by Dave Marshall.

4. SAY IT ISN'T SO   ORCHESTRA & MARSHALL

JACK: And now, ladies and gentlemen, the <u>hot</u> news while it's still <u>lukewarm</u>.

Once again, the Madison Square Bowl was filled...this time <u>with milk</u> for the Milk Fund a very worthy cause. But to keep even, this is the Canada Dry Ginger Ale program...Before the fight got under way, all the champs and we-champs were introduced. <u>Dempsey</u> stepped into the ring, shook hands with Schmelling, Walker and Kearns. However, he couldn't find an opening, so he left the ring....Then <u>Carnera</u> three fine fellers....entered the ring, and you couldn't see Walker, Schmelling or the Empire State Building....<u>Carnera</u> then took out a handkerchief and out fell <u>Jimmy McLarnih</u>. But McLarnih is a game boy and looked Carnera <u>straight in the knee</u>..... <u>Jack Sharkey</u> then stepped into the ring, looked around and was <u>glad</u> he was unemployed for the evening.....Of course, I had a great seat, only a ten-minute bus ride from the ring....But then I didn't want to miss the third battle of the Century this year...Now here's just what happened as I saw it......

(SOUND EFFECT: GONG RINGS)

Round one! ... Walker and Schmelling met in the center of the ring. Walker looked terribly surprised as he didn't know that Schmelling was in town.... Walker then got up from the floor....and Schmelling looked confident. Walker looked at Schmelling... Schmelling looked at Dempsey...Dempsey looked at Carnera, and the audience looked for better seats.... What a fight!......Walker then jabbed two lefts to Schmelling's jaw, and for some reason or other, fell down with a black eye.... It was a surprise to everyone including Walker....Then Maxie countered with a stiff right that knocked Game Tunney off a soap-box in Maine....Maine got up...er, Walker got up at the count of six and met Schmelling again. They embraced affectionately, and Walker was having his face lifted at the gong.

(SOUND EFFECT: GONG RINGS)

Walker's round third down seven to go and Schmelling's ball......

Nothing happened in the second round, so I'll tell you a funny story. A Scotchman an Irishman and a Hebrew were walking down the street and passed a delicatessen store, so they –

(SOUND EFFECT: GONG RINGS)

Round three four and five! ..... Schmelling loaned these three rounds to Walker at six percent interest....which was paid back later. Walker forgot that Schmelling had a right hand, but found it out while strolling thru the Park one day......

(SOUND EFFECT: GONG RINGS)

The next two rounds were nip and tuck Schmelling nipped and Walker tucked.....

(SOUND EFFECT: GONG RINGS)

Round Eight...Walker gets up from the floor again and makes a mad rush at Schmelling....Schmelling steps back and crosses with a right that made Sharkey Dempsey and Carnera call a Peace Conference....At this point, Schmelling receives a cable from Von Hindenburg, reading: " Mox where were you in 1917 when we needed you?" ....Schmelling stops to read the cable. Walker sees an opening and falls to the floor...They are fighting again! The floor leads a long right to Walker's jaw... Schmelling takes advantage of this and answers Von Hindenburg's cable as the gong rings.... In this round the floor had the shade the best of it.

(SOUND EFFECT: GONG RINGS)

Round nine! The bell rings.... Kearns walks to the door.... answers the bell, and tells Schmelling that Walker has retired for the evening.... What a fight! What a night! and eleven dollars to get in what a bite! And now, ladies and gentlemen, for the surprise of the evening. We have here in the Studio in person the two stars of this great bout......May I present Herr Max Schmelling , the winner!

CROWD (YELLS):	Hooray! Schmelling!....The Winner!
	(ROUND OF APPLAUSE)
SCHMELLING (HARRY CONN):	I'm glad I won the tusell...it was lots of fun, and glorious exercise.
JACK:	And now the loser...Mickey Walker.
ORCHESTRA CROWD:	HOORAY! MICKEY WALKER!
	(ROUND OF APPLAUSE)
WALKER (GERMAN):	Ich bin sehr frau das ich hab gewohnen...Und muter, ich vil kam gleich su-hauser in twelve days...Auf wiedersehn!....
JACK:	Thanks, Mickey - hey, why don't you fellers get those dialects right?
WALKER:	Yeah? Well, why don't you tell us who was fighting?
JACK:	Fourth inning Yanks and Cubs...Babe Ruth walks to the plate with three men on base. Ruffen pitches the ball –
	(SOUND EFFECT: SMACK) What's that? oh-oh, there goes Walker down again... what a game! Play, George!

SEGUE INTO NUMBER –

5. SHINE MAKES OWN SHOES   ORCHESTRA & FRAN FREY
    (OLSEN MAKES OWN ANNOUNCEMENT)

JACK:	That was the last number of the forty-fourth program on the 28th of September – Say, George, George....
GEORGE OLSEN:	What is it, Jack?
JACK:	Come here a minute, I want to talk to you.
GEORGE:	Yes, Jack.
JACK:	Say, how many men have you got in your orchestra?
GEORGE:	Thirty- one - why, Jack?
JACK:	Oh nothing, George. But I was thinking that thirty men would be enough.
GEORGE:	Thirty? Why, I need every man I've got.
JACK:	Well, tell me what kind of a musician is Hotcha Gardner?
GEORGE:	He's very good say, Jack, what are you driving at?
JACK:	Oh nothing, George - but sometimes he sounds a little out of tune besides, he doesn't seem to be interested in his work.

GEORGE: I think he's fine.

JACK: Well, I was thinking you might want to cut down on expenses I don't mean to <u>fire</u> him.

GEORGE: Oh, yeah?

JACK: That I mean, he's worked pretty hard and I thought if you'd give him a little vacation say, <u>until</u> <u>next July</u>, Of course, I don't want to butt into your business, George.

GEORGE: Why, Hotcha Gardner's the <u>backbone</u> of the orchestra.

JACK: I'll get you another bone and say, George, it would be a personal favor to if you gave him the air. And any time I can do something for you you know me, George.

GEORGE: I'm sorry, Jack I'd like to help you but I like Hotcha very much.

JACK: All right, George, I get it...that guy Olsen wouldn't do you a favor if it was your last request.... good-night, folks. See you Monday.

SIGNATURE ROCKABYE MOON

ANNOUNCER   Remember, you can enjoy Canada Dry the champagne of ginger ales anywhere anytime, for it is now available two ways-either made to order by the glass at soda fountains or in bottles, as always, for your home. The new big bottle is particularly economical and convenient. Remember, too, that with the exception of a few localities, where freight rates do not permit, you pay for the contents only, that is, twenty cents for the big five glass bottle, or twenty-five cents for two regular twelve-ounce bottles-In addition, you make a small deposit on each bottle, but this deposit is refunded when the bottle is returned. Next Monday night at this same time Jack Benny, Ethel Shutta and George Olsen will again entertain you. This is the National Broadcasting Company.

October 3, 1932

Its World Series night. Jack calls play-by-play of a baseball game between the Gingeralians and the New York Yanks. He interviews silent screen vamp Theda Bara (an interesting precursor to indications that the Jack Benny character was laughably old, as Bara had been retired from films since 1920). Jack is the star athlete of the baseball match, and hits a home run (claiming that a sip of Canada Dry had inspired him). Jack allows Theda take him home in her car, making Mary so jealous that she cries and breaks off her relationship with Hotcha.

[ED.]: the cover page is missing from this script]

CANADA DRY GINGER ALE INC. MONDAY, OCTOBER 3, 1932.
SIGNATURE -- JOLLY GOOD COMPANY

ANNOUNCER: Ladies and gentleman, another half hour of entertainment about Canada Dry the champagne of Ginger ales now available by the glass at soda fountains, as well as in bottles for the home. You'll find the new, large size bottle very economical and particularly convenient for home use.   Once more we present George Olsen, Ethel Shutta and Jack Benny, the Canada Dry Humorist, who will again perform for your enjoyment. George Olsen opens the program with "TO BE OR NOT TO BE COLLEGIATE," Fran Frey singing.

HICKS: And now Jack Benny.

JACK BENNY: Hello, you faithful followers of this what-chu-ma-call-it .... we had to cancel our regular program tonight on account of our challenge to the New York Yankees being accepted.... You didn't hear about it eh? Well, to cap the climax of our series of productions on outdoor sports, this is <u>WORLD SERIES</u> Night in this studio. We have already brought to you prizefights, bullfights, fights between George and Ethel.... but <u>tonight</u> right here in this studio on our own Baseball Diamond - we bring to you the World Series Game between the <u>Canada Dry</u> Gingeralians and that famous <u>dental</u> team....the New York <u>Yanks</u>.....who, as you know, play up near <u>Yankers</u>, New York...All right, I grant you that the Yankees beat the Cubs, but they cannot claim anything like they beat our team......and we haven't lost or played a game this season....

Both teams are now in the field, practicing for this stupid...er, I mean - <u>stupendous</u> series.

First, I'm going to introduce to you some of the real Yankee stars. Let me introduce to you <u>Senor Gomez</u>...Say something, Senor.

BALDWIN(SPANISH): Estoy muy felicitas que a estaraqui esta noche.

JACK : Grathias, Senyor...And now <u>another</u> good old Yankeo <u>Tony Lazzeri!</u>

LAZZERI (ITALIAN):(RATTLES OFF SPEECH IN ITALIAN)

JACK: Thanks. Tony -- <u>what</u> Yankees! ...Lazzeri, by the way, got his early training as the <u>sand lots</u> of California.

HICKS: And remember you get <u>five sands</u> back on each large Canada Dry bottle.

JACK:	Well, that was my fault, folks…And now may I present our own <u>Babe Ruth</u>…Come here, Babe. SADYE: What is it, Jack?
JACK:	Not you, Mary <u>Babe Ruth</u>.
SADYE:	Oh, she's not here yet.
JACK:	And now while the Yanks are warming up, George and the Canada Dry tear will play, "IT WAS ONLY A SUMMER NIGHT'S DREAM", sung by Dave Marshall.

2. IT WAS ONLY A SUMMER NIGHT'S DREAM   ORCHESTRA & MARSHALL

(SOUND EFFECT:	BAT AND GLOVE SMACKS WHICH CONTINUE THRUOUT FOLLOWING DIALOGUE: -
JACK:	The boys are now limbering up batting them out to the fielders and catching on the sidelines …. That was a nice one, Joe!……….That was Joe Thump, folks hitting them out. Joe has <u>only one</u> <u>eye</u> but played in the Three "I" League all last season…. which is a pretty good record. During the whole season, he made only <u>one</u> error, but a <u>divorce</u> will fix that …. From now on, he will just <u>hit-and-run</u>…. Atta boy, Joe! Well, the pitchers are now warming up and throwin' em in. (SOUND EFFECT: LOUD GLOVE SMACK) That was a <u>pip</u> Grass! And there's <u>Pennock</u> over there - throwing a few to Dickey. It looks as tho <u>Pennock</u> will pitch tonight….
HICKS :	And don't forget you get <u>five Pennocks</u> back on each large Canada Dry bottle.
JACK:	Hicks! Get out of the pitcher's box …. Well, folks, it certainly looks like a big <u>afternoon tonight</u> at this ball park…and it's just dark enough for us to beat the Yankees… And what a mob in the stands …. <u>seventy thousand</u> people - <u>or less</u> …. yelling for action …. Hear that mob! <u>Hear that mob</u>!
THREE VOICES:	Walla walla- walla- walla- walla.
JACK:	That's enough, mob. Don't overdo it.
FRAN:	Get your popcorn and peanuts here made-to-order by the glass.
JACK(WHISPERS):	Canada Dry.
FRAN:	Canada Dry Ginger Ale made-to-order --
JACK:	Say, who hires these actors? Stand by, folks, as there are several celebrities entering the grandstand. Ah! who's that? Why, none other than <u>John McGraw</u>….which proves it was a false report about <u>the Shooting of John McGraw</u>….And here comes that famous sports writer whose descriptions of sport events bring <u>tears to your eyes</u>…. Damon R. <u>Onion</u>….He's entering now with that Japanese <u>food</u> expert…. Grantland <u>Rice</u>….And, if Hicks was quick enough, he's said, "it's also good with <u>rice</u>-cream…."
HICKS:	Gee, I'm sorry I forgot that.

JACK:	Well, well, well among the seventy thousand <u>baseball bugs</u>, I see Bugs Baer...and Hal <u>Roach</u> .... <u>Baer</u>, by the way, was a former <u>Cub</u>....which is all I can get out of that joke... How are you, Bugs?
RALPH:	Fine, Jack- how are you?
JACK:	Ah! who is this distinguished, white-haired gentleman walking into the press-box? None other than the Czar of Baseball....<u>Judge Landis</u>. What do you say, Judge?
RALPH ASHE:	<u>Ten days!</u>
JACK (LAUGHS):	Same old judge trying to Landis in jail.... I ought to get thirty days for that one .... Oh well, I call 'em as I see 'em...Ah! Here comes that famous movie star, <u>Theda Bara</u>....who was brought here to <u>vampire</u> the game.... I went back six years for that one...Say something, Theda.
ETHEL:	A rag, a bone and a Hank <u>O'Day</u>....even as I owe rent.
JACK:	Well, let's see if you know your baseball, Theda...now what is <u>a strike</u>?
ETHEL:	A strike is when men want more wages.
JACK:	What a game <u>this</u> is going to be...Tell me, what is <u>a base on balls</u>?
ETHEL:	Ham and eggs <u>with the ham up</u>.
JACK:	Theda, I'm afraid we're going to lose this game...what is <u>a foul</u>?
JACK AND ETHEL(TOGETHER):	<u>A chicken</u>.
JACK:	This is Jack Benny beating her to the answer...Are you sure you're in the right <u>park</u>, Theda?
ETHEL:	What park! Isn't this the <u>Fox Studio</u>?
JACK:	No, ma'am...try the next counter...This is men's ribbons and petticoats...Well, folks, the excitement is about to start. You will shortly witness the baseball game of the <u>century</u>.
HICKS:	And remember, folks, you get <u>five cent</u>-uries back---
JACK:	Hicks, don't swing on those high ones...wait until they cross the plate...And now, ladies and gentlemen, the lineup for today's game is as follows: New York Yankees...<u>Pennock</u> pitching.... <u>Dickey</u> catching...<u>Gehrig</u> on first...and <u>Walker</u> –on the Mediterranean.... <u>Combs</u> – in left field.... <u>Brush</u> – in center.... <u>Lazzeri</u>, the Barber on short....and <u>Ruth</u> is next...all ready to play for the <u>Shampoo-ship</u> of the World. Now the lineup for the Canada Dry Gingerralians - <u>Hicks</u> catching.... <u>Dizzy Vance Olsen</u> pitching.... <u>Fran</u> Frey first base...<u>Hotcha Gardner</u>. second base...<u>Ethel Shutta</u> alto......and <u>Lawrence Tibbitt</u> baritone.... <u>Jack Benny</u> left <u>field</u> and <u>microphone</u>...<u>Bob Rice</u> center <u>field</u>....and <u>Happy Landing</u> Roosevelt <u>Field</u>....How can we miss with a team like that? And now while the <u>infield</u> is being cleared, George Olsen and his orchestra will play that beautiful number dedicated to Babe Ruth, (SINGS) "Hmmmm, here's four balls and take a walk".... after which our game will start.... Kvetch! dust off the diamond.

3. I LOVE YOU LIZZICATO						ORCHESTRA AND ETHEL SHUTTA

JACK: Hello, folks this is Jack Benny again, announcing and playing left field at the same time. What a man!

SADYE: Jack! oh, Jack! someone wants you on the telephone.

JACK: Mary, you mustn't run out on the field.

SADYE: No, it's right in the next room.

JACK: Well, the game is about to start, folks –

SADYE: But, Jack - you're want ---

JACK: Scram! Canada Dry is in the field, and the Yanks are at bat. (CROWD MUMBLES)

PLAY BALL! Combs is at bat...Olsen, pitching...George is now winding up. There goes the first ball...There she goes like a bullet –

(SOUND EFFECT: GLOVE SMACK) right over the plate waist-high.

RALPH ASHE (in distance): Ball one!

JACK: That was a strike. The ball is now returned to pitcher. He winds up. There it goes again...three feet over batter's head...what a wild pitch.

ASHE (in distance): Strike!

JACK: That was a ball! .... Olsen has a grim look on his face .... and after yesterday's game Grimm doesn't look so good, either...are you grimming at these jokes? Ooh, there goes the ball again right over the plate.

(SOUND EFFECT: BAT SMACK) (CROWD CHEERS)

Combs caught that one at the end of his bat and hit a beautiful single right between second and third...Can you imagine that? We forgot to put in a shortstop. Oh well! .... Combs is safe on first...One on - no outs - and Sewell at bat.

SADYE: I think he's Sewell...wasn't that good, Jack?

JACK: Mary, go lose yourself in the bleachers...Sewell stands up to the plate swings and oh-oh......oh-oh....

(SOUND EFFECT: BAT SMACK) (CROWD CHEERS)

He hit a fast liner which Olsen stops with his shins...preventing a home run...Good boy, Sewell! Combs on second...Sewell on first, and Olsen on crutches...Good boy, Sewell! PLAY BALL! Ah! .... who is this coming to the plate? That famous new Yankee, Bing Cross-etti...Until last year Crossetti was a plumber and played with several leaks...Combs takes a long lead off of second as Olsen is winding up....and is now on third...Olsen is still winding up and Combs scores.

	(CROWD CHEERS)
	<u>One</u> run for the Yankees! Score now <u>one to nothing</u>…Sewell on third and Crossetti at bat…While Olsen is winding up, the ball slips out of his hand and goes over for a strike.
RALPH ASHE (in distance):	Ball one!
JACK:	Ball returned to pitcher…There she goes again…What's this?
	(SOUND EFFECT: BAT SMACK)
	(SHORT CHEER)
	<u>A long fly</u> to left field…ball coming right <u>my way</u>…pardon me a moment, folks (slight pause)
ORCHESTRA (on signal from Benny)	Booooo!
JACK:	There are now <u>two on base</u> and <u>no</u> outs…that was a long <u>fly</u>, folks. And I caught it on the second bounce…<u>Here it is</u>! Say something, Fly….bzzzzzzzzz….
ASHE (in another voice):	Hey, throw the ball throw the ball!
JACK:	Pardon me, folks…There is no one on base and the score is <u>three to nothing</u>…. Olsen now has nothing to worry about and can wind up again. People are still coming in ah! who is that walking across the field? It's the <u>Four Marx</u> Brothers. (LOUD CHEERING AND APPLAUSE)
	<u>Babe Ruth</u> walks to the plate. Olsen sees Ruth stops winding packs grip and looks over time tables…He sees no cheap cruises, so he throws the ball. Oh-oh! (SOUND EFFECT: GLOVE SMACK) Ruth swings and misses! Hicks, who is still catching, catches cold from the breeze….
HICKS (sneezes):	Kerchoo!
JACK:	Gesundheit! Ruth is <u>plenty</u> mad…. Olsen realizing this calls in <u>two more</u> pitchers… Olsen, Bush and Maloney now pitching for Canada Dry. They are winding up again. there go the balls and (SOUND EFFECT: GLOVE SMACK) two of them are balls. and Ruth <u>misses</u> the good one…. <u>Two balls</u> and <u>two strikes</u>!……<u>Six</u> pitchers are now pitching to Ruth. They are all in a huddle. They wind up again and there <u>go the balls</u>. (SOUND EFFECT: BAT SMACK) (CROWD CHEERS) Ruth picked out a <u>good one</u>, and it's a long, clean hit <u>ANOTHER HOME RUN</u>….scoring the <u>Four Marx</u> Brothers…The score is now <u>eight</u> to <u>nothing</u> …. favor the Marx Brothers …. Now let's see where the ball went. Ah! here's the news: baseball picked up by <u>Norwegian fishermen near Iceland</u>….what a hit! Oh well, <u>we</u> haven't been up yet… Gehrig now at bat…Olsen sees Gehrig…winds up again, and pitches a fast ball to <u>second base</u>…. which Gehrig can't reach. That was a nice one. <u>ONE STRIKE</u>! Gehrig now batting <u>at second base</u>. Olsen sees this throws another fast one crosses plate and <u>again</u> Gehrig misses…<u>Strike</u> <u>two</u>…. Yanks now have a batter <u>at each base</u>….and Gehrig is batting from left field as he doesn't know where Olsen is going to throw the ball…Olsen winds up again throws a fast curve to right field, outsmarting Gehrig and retiring the side…<u>Roosevelt</u> to <u>Hoover</u>…to <u>Garner</u>…. (CROWD CHEERS) Gehrig

now chasing Olsen with bat...and <u>Canada Dry</u> up.... Play something, George while <u>we</u> go to bat.

SEGUE INTO NUMBER –

4. WALKING IN THE MOONLIGHT   SHUTTA & FREY
                    (OLSEN MAKES HIS OWN ANNOUNCEMENT)

JACK: And now <u>our</u> team is coming to bat.

(ORCHESTRA PLAYS FEW BARS OF " JOLLY GOOD COMPANY" IN MARCH TEMPO)

      All right, folks <u>Canada Dry</u> now batting...and the Yanks are in the field... Score still <u>eight</u> to <u>nothing</u>, but they had the Four Marx Brothers...Wait!.........<u>we</u> have the whole cast from Grand Hotel, and are we downhearted, boys?

ORCHESTRA (all together):   <u>Yes</u>!

JACK: Oh, you can't take it eh?........There you are, folks, our snappy, peppy little team...... Well, we're not doing any worse than the Cubs!.........Pennock now pitching---Hotcha <u>Gardner</u> at bat.... Pennock winds up but he looks much better than Olsen.......Oh-oh, <u>there goes the first ball</u>!

ASHE (in distance):   Strike one!

JACK: Hotcha didn't even see it.

SADYE: Gee, <u>I</u> didn't even see it, Jack.

JACK: All right, Mary you didn't pay to get in........The ball is returned to Pennock, who looks worried.... but <u>not</u> about this game......

      Pennock feels confident closes his eyes and throws <u>another</u> ball, and (SOUND EFFECT: <u>LOUD THUMP</u>)

HOTCHA GARDNER: Ow! Ow!

JACK: Hotcha is hit by a pitched ball.... good work, Pennock! Hotcha <u>carried</u> to first base... <u>One on</u> - <u>no outs</u> and Olsen walks to the plate. He finds nothing on plate....so he walks to first, sees Hotcha and walks to second.... There are now <u>two men on base - no outs</u> and the <u>coaches</u> are now dancing up and down the side lines. You know, <u>coach dancers</u>...get what I <u>Minsky</u>? Watch yourself, Hotcha......Fran Frey now at bat. Here comes a fast one. (SOUND EFFECT: <u>DULL THUD</u>) What's that? Fran gets his head in the way, and ball bounces off head into deep left. <u>What a head! scoring</u> <u>Olsen</u> and Frey safe on third - Hotcha <u>still</u> on first.

      (CROWD CHEERS)

      One run no errors and <u>two hit</u>........<u>Schmelling</u> now at bat. Boy! what confidence... <u>Pennock</u> winds up and pitches first ball....and <u>there she goes</u>. (SOUND EFFECT: <u>TERRIFIC BAT SMACK</u> CROWD CHEERS) Schmelling swings at ball hits a long liner, and <u>Walker</u> goes down again.... <u>scoring Frey</u> - Schmelling on second and Hotcha <u>still</u> on first.... What a game! What a game! two on base...one out and <u>Jack Benny</u> at bat... (ORCHESTRA LAUGHS) ...Pardon me a moment, folks...Hicks, take the mike!

HICKS: Jack Benny walks to the plate with a smile on his face. Never felt better in his life - Associated Press....Pennock looks worried for the first time.... <u>There he goes</u> winding up. Here comes the ball. (SOUND EFFECT: <u>BAT SMACK</u>) (CROWD CHEERS LOUDER THAN BEFORE)

HICKS: <u>What's this</u>?.......Look at that ball go. There she goes over the fence and out of the park...A HOME RUN! scoring Schmelling, Sharkey and Conzoneri! .... Hotcha Gardner <u>still</u> on first.... Here comes Jack Benny, back to the Microphone. Atta boy, Jack...<u>great work</u>!

JACK (RETURNS TO "MIKE" PANTING): hello, folks they <u>laughed</u> when I walked up to the plate. Little did they know that I had a drink of Canada Dry Ginger Ale made-to-order by the glass.

(SOUND EFFECT: PEAL OF THUNDER)

Uh-uh-- looks like rain. you better play fast, fellers.

(<u>THUNDER</u> AGAIN)

(<u>TALKS FAST</u>) Bob Rice now at plate...pitcher throws ball...strike <u>one</u>! strike <u>two</u>! <u>ball</u> one! <u>ball</u> two!

(MORE THUNDER RAIN EFFECT STARTS HERE AND CONTINUES)

Oh, boy! is it coming down now.... what's that? game <u>called on account of rain</u>? Well, here are your rain checks, folks.... This game will be continued on October third, 1933 - - <u>rain or shine</u>.......Play George...Can you imagine! It started to rain <u>just</u> when we were ahead? Oh boy! <u>what</u> breaks.

5. MARGY   ORCHESTRA & GARDNER (OLSEN MAKES HIS OWN ANNOUNCEMENT)

(AFTER NUMBER – START <u>RAIN</u> <u>EFFECT</u> AGAIN

JACK: that was the last number of the <u>forty-fifth</u> program on the third of October...and Hotcha is still on first...Say Hotcha, come here a minute will you?

GARDNER: Yes, Jack.

JACK: I want to ask you something - when we were hitting the ball knocking out homers and three- baggers, why didn't you get off first and <u>run home</u>?

GARDNER: I couldn't do that I promised to take <u>Mary</u> home. I wouldn't disappoint <u>her</u> for the world. JACK: I see.

ETHEL (character of Theda Bara): Well, good-night, Mr. Benny.

JACK:	Oh, Miss Bara.
ETHEL:	Yes Oh, I want to tell you how much I enjoyed the game tonight...particularly <u>your</u> playing.
JACK:	Thanks very much...I'm awfully glad you came up.
ETHEL:	I have my car outside can I take you any place?
JACK:	Thank you - yes, I'm going to the <u>Friars' Club</u>.
ETHEL:	Oh, that won't be out of my way. Besides, I have plenty of time this evening.
JACK:	That's mighty sweet of you...Well, goodnight, George...Goodnight, folks.
	(SOUND EFFECT: <u>AUTOMOBILE</u> HORN)
SADYE:	Jack Oh, Jack!<u> Why, he's gone</u>!
GARDNER:	What's the matter, Mary?
SADYE:	Oh, you're talking up all of my time, and I don't get a chance to go out with Jack at all...See what happened? Take back these peanuts you bought at the ball game....and I <u>never</u> want to see you again. So there!
GARDNER:	Well, gee whiz...what are you bawling me out for? What did I do?
SADYE:	Aw, keep quiet! Anyway, I think Jack's got some nerve going home with somebody else.... Goodnight, everybody. (STARTS TO CRY) (SIGNATURE Rockabye Moon)
ANNOUNCER:	The next time you stop at a soda fountain for a refreshing drink, ask for a glass of Canada Dry, the Champagne of Ginger Ales, it will be made-to-order for you and costs only five cents for a regular glass or ten cents for an extra-large glass. Remember, too, that with the exception of a few localities where freight charges do not permit, you can take back your Canada Dry bottles to the dealer and get a cash refund. So that now when you buy Canada Dry you pay for the contents only. Next Wednesday night at this same time, Jack Benny, Ethel Shutta and George Olsen will again entertain you. This is the National Broadcasting Company.

October 5, 1932

Jack has an unusual discussion with "Jake" his alter ego (this kind of ego switch won't happen again until Jack is hit in the head by cans from his pantry and becomes generous in the October 2, 1949 episode). Jack tries to persuade George to break up the Hotcha-Mary romance. Jack provides voice over of a film travelogue trip through China. Also in an unusual twist, Jack reads a poem about Fall that is like one of Mary's early morose Harry Conn creations.

STATION WJZ　　　　　　　PROGRAM CANADA DRY GINGER ALE, INC.

　　　AND　　　　　　　　DATE WEDNESDAY, OCTOBER 5, 1932.

BLUE NETWORK　　　　　　TIME 9:30 10:00 P.M.

SIGNATURE JOLLY GOOD COMPANY

1. WHAT A SWEET SENSATION　　　FRAN FREY
2. HARLEM MOON　　　　　　　　ETHEL SHUTTA
3. THREE KISSES　　　　　　　　MARSHALL
4. HUM A TUNE　　　　　　　　　ETHEL SHUTTA
5. BUGLE CALL RAG

SIGNATURE ROCKABYE MOON

　　　CANADA DRY GINGER ALE INC.　　　　　WEDNESDAY, OCTOBER 5, 1932.
　　　SIGNATURE JOLLY GOOD COMPANY

ANNOUNCER	Ladies and gentleman, another half hour of entertainment about Canada Dry the champagne of Ginger ales now available by the glass at soda fountains, as well as in bottles for the home. You'll find the new, large size bottle very economical and particularly convenient for home use. Once more, we present George Olsen, Ethel Shutta and Jack Benny, the Canada Dry Humorist, who will again perform for your enjoyment. George Olsen opens the program with "WHAT A SWEET SENSATION," Fran Frey singing.
JACK:	Hello, you lucky listeners...this is Jack Benny talking remember? No, it isn't your radio I've got a bad cold.
JAKE:	Oh yeah? Well, <u>what of it</u>? [Ed. Laura Leibowitz and I assume this is Jack speaking in a different voice]
JACK:	Oh, nothing just thought I'd warn you that's all.
JAKE:	Well, what's new, Jack?
JACK:	Nothing new.... everything's the same...the landlord <u>still</u> wants his rent (dirty Laugh) ....my grocer isn't talking to me...and I got a little <u>fan mail</u> from my tailor this morning.... Oh well, you can't please everybody, but things are going along about the same.
JAKE:	<u>Say, Jack how's Mary</u>?
JACK:	Oh, she's all right. Of course, I don't pay any attention to her she's just a friend, you know...means nothing to me.... I mean, she's cute and all that.... But you know that guy <u>Hotcha Gardner</u>....
JAKE:	Say, Jack.
JACK:	Yes?
JAKE:	How was Olsen's opening at the New Yorker the other night?
JACK:	Gee, I'm glad you changed the subject.... <u>It was great</u>. One of the nicest crowds I've ever seen. After all, I was Olsen's <u>guest</u> - so what can I say?

JAKE:	Oh, you were Olsen's guest, Jack! does that mean <u>Olsen</u> took care of the check?
JACK:	No, not exactly - I wouldn't say that he didn't <u>mean</u> to take care of it…He just happened to get <u>busy</u> at the moment the check came…<u>but I was his guest</u>. It's a nice day - isn't it?
JAKE:	Jack, do you mean to tell me that Olsen <u>invited</u> you up there and then didn't take care of the check?
JACK:	Oh, forget it…<u>Say</u>, what do you think of those Yanks taking four straight---eh?
JAKE:	Yes but I can't understand how a person could invite you out as <u>his guest</u> - and then <u>not</u> take care of everything.
JACK:	All right, don't keep harping on it let's forget the whole thing.
JAKE:	Well, Jack – all I can say is that Olsen certainly is <u>a cheap guy</u>.
JACK:	Now wait just a minute – don't start talking about my <u>pal</u>. George is <u>all right</u>.
JAKE:	Oh, if you're going to let him make a chump out of you—
JACK:	<u>Nobody</u> is going to make a chump out me – and <u>one more word</u> out of you ….
JAKE:	Oh, yeah?
JACK:	<u>Yeah</u>!
ORCHSTRA BOYS:	Yeah!
JACK:	Say, you fellers keep out of this – nobody is going to pan Olsen to us…. Say, what's <u>your</u> name?
JAKE:	Jack Benny.
JACK:	Well, so's mine – and I'm just as tough as you are.
ETHEL (WHISPERS):	Say, Jack…. Jack! What's <u>the matter </u>with you?
JACK:	Nothing, Ethel…. I was panning Olsen and I'm not going to let myself go with it …. I <u>hate</u> Olsen – but I <u>like</u> him.
ETHEL:	Say, Jack – you've been standing here for three minutes, talking to yourself.
JACK:	I might as well, Ethel…I can't talk to anybody else. If I talk to <u>Mary</u>, it's Hotcha…if I talk to <u>George</u>, he's never got it…and if I talk to <u>Hicks</u>, it's always the nickel back on the Canada Dry bottle.
ETHEL:	Well, you can talk to me.
JACK:	You're right. You're about the only one I can talk to…at least you make me feel good.
ETHEL:	Thanks, Jack - I'm sorry you're not feeling well tonight.
JACK:	Oh, I'm all right. I've just got a slight cold.

ETHEL: But you don't look good. You look awfully pale and thin.

JACK: I don't know - I <u>weigh</u> the same.

ETHEL: Well, I never saw you looking so bad. Gee, I hope it's nothing serious...Let me see your tongue. JACK: Baaaah!

ETHEL: You have a terrible <u>coat</u> on your tongue.

JACK: It's last year's...I haven't been shopping lately.

ETHEL: Jack, you're a sight!

JACK: Ethel, introduce the next number will you?

ETHEL(QUICKLY): Where are you going?

JACK: I'm going over to the cemetery and take a nap.

ETHEL: (INTRODUCE NUMBER)

2. HUM A TUNE　　　　　　　　　　　　　　　　ORCHESTRA AND ETHEL SHUTTA

(SECOND ROUTINE)

JACK: Well, folks, I feel a lot better now...Oh, George!

GEORGE: Yes, Jack.

JACK: George, I hope you didn't take that seriously last week - when I asked you to fire Hotcha Gardner. You know, I didn't mean that.

GEORGE: Aw, I know you didn't.

JACK: He's a nice kid - handsome, too. But, you know, he should really go to Hollywood or <u>even</u> <u>further</u>.... George, I want to ask a little favor of you.

GEORGE: What do you want me to do now?

JACK: Just tell Mary a few things that will steer her away from Hotcha - you know how to do it, George. Get what I mean?

GEORGE: All right, Jack I'll try.

JACK: Thanks - I'll kind-a stay in the background so she won't think I said anything... There's Mary now. Talk to her.

GEORGE(LAUGHINGLY): Oh, Mary.

SADYE: Yes, Mr. Olsen.

GEORGE: How are you?

SADYE:	I'm fine how are you?
GEORGE:	I'm all right. Mary - say, you certainly are a sweet little girl.
SADYE(LAUGHS):	Aw now, Mr. Olsen.
GEORGE:	You have beautiful eyes.
JACK(WHISPERS):	George, get to the point.
GEORGE:	Mary, you like Hotcha pretty well - don't you?
SADYE:	Oh, sometimes - but I don't know…. he doesn't say anything clever like Jack.
GEORGE:	Why Mary, Hotcha is a <u>very intelligent</u> boy - he's a college graduate.
SADYE:	He doesn't show it.
GEORGE:	Why Mary! …and <u>another</u> thing, he was lots of money.
SADYE:	Oh, when I marry it won't be for money…. Money isn't everything…<u>how much has he got</u>?
GEORGE:	<u>Plenty</u>….not that I want to influence you, Mary but Hotcha's <u>a swell guy</u> and <u>crazy about you</u>.
SADYE:	GEE! I didn't want it to be serious…you know, we're just friends. He buys me peanuts - here, do you want one?
GEORGE:	Thanks-- now, Mary, why don't you give Hotcha another chance?
SADYE:	Oh, well -- --
GEORGE:	Give him another chance. He's a swell guy, and you won't regret it.
SADYE:	All right, Mr. Olsen - thanks very much for your interest……Do you want another peanut?
GEORGE:	No, thanks - so long, Mary.
SADYE:	Good-bye.
GEORGE:	Oh, Jack!
JACK:	Well, did you fix it, George?
GEORGE:	<u>Did I</u>!
JACK:	Thanks, pal - and now, ladies and gentleman, the next number will be "Three Kisses", played by George Olsen and his boys, and sung by Dave Marshall.

3. THREE KISSES　　　　　　　　　　　　　　　　　　　ORCHESTRA & MARSHALL

(THIRD ROUTINE)

JACK: Ladies and gentlemen, I owe an apology to the latest member of our group, Dave Marshall. He has been with us now for two weeks, and I overlooked introducing him. So now I want to formally present our new vocalist. Mr. Marshall....Come here, Dave.

DAVE MARSHALL: Pardon me, Mary.

SADYE: Certainly, Dave.

JACK: Hmm, I'm going to have trouble with him, too.... Ladies and gentlemen, this is Dave Marshall....say hello to the folks, Dave.

MARSHALL: Hello, folks I'm very glad to meet you, and I hope that –

JACK: A really nice fellow with a trained voice. He's good-looking, young and <u>six feet</u> tall.... and the microphone stands only <u>four feet nine</u>, so you can imagine what he has to go thru.... Mr. Marshall is a California boy and comes to us direct from <u>Hollywood</u>.... where he was with the M.G.M. Studio and made fifty is that right, Dave?

MARSHALL: Seventy.

JACK: Pardon me seventy <u>screen tests</u>......They were all successful, and <u>here he is</u> with Olsen's MGM Band....

MARSHALL: Thank you, Mr. Benny.

JACK: You're welcome...Mr. Marshall is really <u>a Crosby</u>....<u>a cross-be</u>-tween a baritone and a tenor.... okay, Dave!......

Well, folks, we have another little surprise for you tonight - a very novel offering. We have here and for tonight's program only an exclusive <u>film travelogue</u> which we will run off in this studio on our own picture screen. It is away from the usual <u>hokum</u> that you find on <u>most</u> programs...<u>our</u> purpose, as you all know, is strictly an <u>educational</u> one...and if a hokum <u>should</u> sneak in, remember that this is the <u>Canada Dry Ginger Ale</u> program. The picture we have tonight is," Traveling Thru China".... which I will describe to you as we go along. While we are preparing for this novelty, George Olsen and his boys will play, "Under the Harlem Moon", sung by Ethel Shutta.

4. UNDER THE HARLEM MOON　　　　　　　　　　　　ORCHESTRA & ETHEL SHUTTA

(FOURTH ROUTINE)

JACK: And now for our picture...turn out the light, boy...A little atmospheric music, George. (ORCHESTRA STARTS CHINESE MUSIC HERE)

China, as you know, is a large country in Asia noted for its famous singers <u>Sing-Hi</u> - Sing-<u>Lee</u> - and Sing-<u>Lo</u>... It has a population of four hundred million people darned clever these Chinese!

(SOUND EFFECT: WINDING OF FILM REEL)

The picture is about to begin, so follow closely.... We start here at the mouth of the Yank-Tsee River not far from Shanghai - and <u>what</u> a gorgeous sight it is - with its quaint fishing smacks and picturesque mountains in the background. (CHINESE MUSIC VERY PIANNISSIMO)

On the left of the Yank-Tsee River, you see the <u>Yank- Tsee</u> Stadium...where the Yank-Tsee Team beat the <u>Shi-High Cubs</u>...As we move along, we find ourselves in the fascinating city of Shanghai, and we follow the white line into Chow <u>Main Street</u>... which is just like our Broadway only <u>fewer Chinese restaurants</u>.... Thousands of coolies are in the streets, pushing Canada Dry <u>rick-shaws</u>....and what a <u>coolie</u> drink it is...I'm glad Hicks isn't here....

Now we pass thru the <u>Reno</u> District of Shanghai where they all make <u>soo</u>-ey.... We are now leaving Shanghai, still sailing down the Yank-Tsee....and arrive at last in the beautiful Shanghai, still sailing down the Yank-Tsee....and arrive at last in the beautiful harbor of <u>Tsing-Tsing</u>. There in the distance you see the grim, grey walls of <u>Tsing-Tsing Prison</u>....Are you <u>lits-tsing-tsing</u>?. As we direct our gaze upward to the celestial heavens, we see the bright, full moon that gave our American songwriters the inspiration to write <u>China Harvest Moon</u>....Oh, you heard that eh? Well, we can't stop the trip....

It is now morning, and the first rays of sunlight bring us into the Oriental city of Peking, now called <u>Peiping</u>....the birthplace of <u>Sam Fat Winchell</u>....who learned his <u>peeking</u> in <u>Peiping</u>...From Peiping, we go to <u>sleeping</u>...and arrive early the next morning, in the busy industrial center of <u>Canton</u>, named after that popular Chinese actor, <u>Eddie Canton</u>....

FRAN FREY: It's <u>Cantor</u>, Mr. Benny.

JACK: No, you're thinking of Canter, Ohio....<u>scram</u>.... Canton is noted for its superb <u>climate</u>.... <u>silk</u> <u>trees</u>....and <u>Canton-Dry</u> Ginger Ale...

HICKS: And don't forget you get <u>five yen</u> back on each <u>Canton Dry</u> Bottle.

JACK :   We will now leave Canton <u>and Hicks</u>....and proceed down the Yank-Tsee, which branches into the Miss-iss-<u>slippi</u>.....

(SOUND EFFECT: BOAT WHISTLE AND WATER EFFECT)

Ah! what city is this we are approaching?

(SOUND EFFECT: AUTO HORN)

It is that great automobile center <u>Honk Honk</u>! This is a very fascinating district, and it was here that <u>Confucius</u> was first <u>confused</u>...Anyway, that's what I've got written down here...As we walk slowly up the narrow little streets, we come to a quaint <u>coffee shoppe</u>......where we stop off for <u>One Long Dunk</u>....Strangely enough, Honk Honk is noted for its <u>lack of dough-nuts</u>...Oh well, lacks-doughnut.... I mean, <u>lackaday</u>.

	We leave Honk Honk by aeroplane –
(SOUND EFFECT:	WATER EFFECT)
JACK (REPEATS):	Aeroplane...
PROP MAN:	Ah!
(SOUND EFFECT:	HORSES HOOFS)
JACK:	And again, follow the white line...arriving at the Capital of China - <u>Washee Dee Cee</u>...where we meet <u>the Plesident</u>, <u>Herb Hoov Vee</u>....This is, indeed, one of the most beautiful cities in all China only surpassed by <u>Ko-Ko-Mo</u> and <u>Kan-Kak-Kee</u>....and is famous for its <u>iron mines</u> you know, <u>iron mine</u> shirts and I'll iron yours.... oh well, let's travel on...
	While traveling up the Main Street, we pass the costly <u>Oriental</u> Theatre...in the <u>Loopee</u>....Section of <u>China-cago</u>...are you listening, Balaban and <u>Katzee</u>?.....

(ORCHESTRA STARTS CHINESE MUSIC HERE)

    We now come to the end of a perfect day –

    (SOUND EFFECT: BOAT WHISTLE AND WATER EFFECT)

    and board our little steamer, which will carry us far away from this strange, fascinating country of China...And as we sail away, we hear the almond-eyed Orientals singing their native melody---

ETHEL & FRAN (SING):	Listen to the German Band, The music's grand, etc.
JACK:	Ah! beautiful China...holding the key to the mysteries of the Far East...We shall never forget you, China! And next week, ladies and gentlemen, we will take you to far-away <u>India</u>...And now, I feel sure you will all enjoy meeting <u>the pilot</u> who made it possible for us to take this hazardous journey thru the interior of China. I will now introduce to you that well-known Chinese aviator <u>One Long Hop</u>....Say something, <u>One</u>.
FRAN FREY :	Wong Gow Hi Tee Gow <u>Fooey</u>.
JACK :	<u>Fooey</u> on you!
FRAN:	<u>Fooey on you, too</u>.
JACK:	Hmm. I'm going to have trouble with you...Play, George!
SEGUE INTO---	

5. BUGLE CALL RAG   ORCHESTRA

                      (OLSEN MAKES HIS OWN ANNOUNCEMENT)

                              (CLOSING ROUTINE)

JACK: That was the last number of the forty-sixth program on the fifth of October. Did you enjoy our little trip? And next week we are going to bring you our Special Fall program. After all, everyone sings the praises of Spring and Summer. But how many of us ever think of Fall? Well, we do! And just before leaving tonight, I'd like to read a little poem which I wrote about Fall.

When the summer days are over
And grass absconds the lawns,
And the chillness intercedes it – THEN
You know that we have Fall......
Falling leaves tell you the story
That 'tis summertime no more.
So away with Bathing suits and –
KNOW YE THEN - that it is Fall.
Moonlit meadows --

HOTCHA GARDNER: Good-night, Jack.

JACK: Good-night, Hotcha...Moonlit meadows come a-creeping
Down the valleys and thru the hills.
And the bare trees of the forest –

FRAN FREY: So long, Jack.

JACK: Good-night, Fran...Seem to tell you it is Fall.
Cows have ceased to pasture yonder,
Yellow skies –

MARY: Good-night, Jack.

JACK: Good-night, Mary when will I see you?

MARY: In the Fall.

JACK: Yellow skies and Hotch Gardner -

And the river wends its way ward....

(SIGNATURE MUCIS ROCKABYE MOON" STARTS HERE)

[Ed. Closing announcement is missing.]

October 10, 1932

Mary opens the show, as Jack is late. H is having a problem with his new suit. The skit is "Grind Hotel" which parodies MGM's then-current all-star film hit "Grand Hotel." This is one of the first times Jack says "Music, George, Curtain…." Jack will repeat this phrase for 20 years on the radio program when they perform movie or play skits. Jack plays the romantic role of the Baron (John Barrymore in the film) sneaking in to the famous ballerina's room to steal her pearls but instead make love to her (Ethel plays Garbo's part). Jack will continue "Grand Hotel" parodies for more than a year, and he and Conn loved to feature the character Kringelein, played in the film by Lionel Barrymore. Kringelein is a poor accountant who has worked faithfully for a corrupt boss for years. Now he is dying and has gained access to a large fortune, and although he croaks out "I only have two minutes to live!" wants to party and make the most of it. Benny and Conn worked this character into the program often in subsequent months, perhaps as a kind of bitterly ironic rejoinder to the Depression's deprivations.

STATION WJZ   PROGRAM CANADA DRY GINGER ALE, INC.

    AND   DATE MONDAY, OCTOBER 10, 1932.

BLUE NETWORK   TIME 9:30 10:00 P.M.

A. SIGNATURE JOLLY GOOD COMPANY

1. GET YOURSELF A CUP OF SUNSHINE
2. MY SILVER ROSE   ETHEL SHUTTA
3. WE'RE ALONE   MARSHALL
4. MEANEST GAL IN TOWN   ETHEL SHUTTA
5. SWEET MUCHACHA   GARDNER

Z. SIGNATURE ROCKABYE MOON

    CANADA DRY GINGER ALE, INC.   MONDAY, OCTOBER 10, 1932.
    SIGNATURE JOLLY GOOD COMPANY

ANNOUNCER: Ladies and gentlemen, another half hour of entertainment about Canada Dry the champagne of Ginger ales now available by the glass at soda fountains, as well as in bottles for the home. You'll find the new, large size bottle very economical and particularly convenient for home use.   Once more, we present George Olsen, Ethel Shutta and Jack Benny, the Canada Dry Humorist, who will again perform for your enjoyment. George Olsen opens the program with "HELP YOURSELF TO A CUP OF SUNSHINE".

HICKS: And now I will turn the program over to Jack Benny.

SADYE: Hello, darling public.... this is Jack Benny's secretary talking. Remember, hmm?.... Mary Livingston of Plainfield? .... <u>Livingston</u>...."L" as in 'leven...."I" as in your head..."V" as in Vo-de-o-do......"I" as in <u>me</u>..."N" as in <u>you</u>, and so forth. Mr. Benny may be a little late tonight, and asked me to be mistress of ceremonies until he gets here.... And does what <u>he</u> does. So here goes: first of all, George Olsen has been doing business with one bank for <u>fifteen</u> years and hasn't met the <u>paying</u> teller yet. Get it, hmm? You see, he only puts money <u>in</u> the bank but never takes---

OLSEN: They get it they get it, Mary. You don't have to explain.

SADYE: I know, Mr. Olsen, but <u>I</u> don't get it.... I'm just reading what Jack wrote here on this paper.... Well, it looks like a big night, and I feel very witty.... I SAID I FEEL VERY WITTY....Where's Mr. Hicks?

HICKS: Here I am, what is it, Mary?

SADYE: I said <u>witty</u>....and you didn't say anything about nickel back on the bottle.

HICKS: Well, <u>witty</u> doesn't suggest nickel, Mary.

SADYE: Oh, are you dumb! ...<u>Witty</u> rhymes with <u>jitney</u>, doesn't it?.......and <u>jitney</u> is a nickel. Do you get it, Hicks or am I wasting my time?

HICKS: Did Jack write that last line about <u>witty</u> rhyming with jitney?

SADYE: No I made it up myself. Don't you think it's <u>swell</u>?

JACK'S VOICE (IN DISTANCE): Hello....hello...everybody...hello, Mary...Hello, George. How are you getting along, Mary?

SADYE:	Fine, Jack. You didn't have to hurry. I'm getting along just swell, but (WHISPERS)... <u>Olsen</u> and <u>Hicks</u> are very dumb.... They don't understand my jokes.
JACK:	I see, Mary....Well, thanks very much. Now go out and get ten cents worth of <u>kilocycles</u> and don't drop them.
SADYE:	All right, Jack .... If you need me, I'll be sitting over there <u>with Hotcha</u>.
JACK:	Hmm...well, ladies and gentlemen, <u>this</u> starts the Canada Dry Program for tonight. I'm sorry I was a big late, but blame it on my tailor. He kept me waiting. You see, we have an agreement like that...he keeps me waiting for the suit and I keep him waiting for the dough… Well, anyway….
ETHEL:	Hello, Jack!
JACK:	Oh, Hello Ethel - Now tonight, folks, we are bringing you our special Fall program as I promised you last --
ETHEL:	Say, Jack, that's a good-looking suit you have on.
JACK:	Thanks, Ethel you know, it has always been the aim of this program to keep in season and we are not going to dissa --
ETHEL:	Is that a <u>new</u> suit, Jack?
JACK:	Yes, I just bought it...I got a great trade-in on my old one. This is the latest model…. you know, free walking…. spare trousers……just an all-around suit.
ETHEL:	All round suit?
JACK:	Yes, it goes <u>all-around</u> the family...Now, folks, as we promised you tonight……
ETHEL:	I like the way it's cut, Jack -- it's a nice style for you.
JACK:	Oh, just a <u>good business</u> suit.
ETHEL:	It isn't cut like a business suit.
JACK:	Well, <u>business</u> isn't what it used to be -- Say, Ethel, go over there and sit with Hotcha.
ETHEL:	Why, Mary is sitting with him.
JACK:	You're telling me! ...And now, folks, to get back to our Fall Program. Here it is the second week in October, and it doesn't seem possible. Now first, what is the meaning of <u>October</u>? It is taken from the Latin word, "Oct" meaning eight which means that October is the eighth month of the year.
DAVE MARSHALL:	Jack, it's the tenth month of the year.
JACK:	Well, anyway, this is Fall...and who am I to change the calendar? Now what does <u>Fall</u> mean? It means that summer is over and <u>winter draws</u> on.... How time flies! Only eight more months to pick out your summer vacation spot....and time waits for nobody….
HICKS:	And don't forget you get <u>half a dime</u> back on the large Canada Dry bottle.

JACK:	<u>Time</u> waits for no one and neither does Hicks
HOTCHA GARDNER:	I got to play the next number, Mary -- see you later.
JACK:	And neither does Hotcha.
START NUMBER HERE –	
JACK:	and neither does Olsen.

2. MY SILVER ROSE   ORCHESTRA AND ETHEL
            (GEORGE OLSEN MAKES OWN ANNOUNCEMENT)

                    (SECOND ROUTINE)

JACK:	Well, ladies and gentlemen, I think we have gone just about long enough without a contest. During the past summer we have accumulated many first second and third prizes...some grew here...some were thrown through the window- and we even <u>bought</u> a few. <u>But you will have to win</u> <u>them</u>.... Right now we are going to give you a special <u>Fall</u> test something <u>very</u> <u>novel</u> and passed by the Board of <u>Censors</u>.
JACK AND FOUR VOICES:	And you get <u>five censors</u> back on each Canada Dry Bottle.
HICKS (STARTS TO CRY):	That's no fair that was <u>my</u> line.
JACK:	All right, Hicks don't cry. Wipe the tears off your beard <u>and scram</u>! .... And now, folks to get back to our contest. We are in a very altruistic mood this evening and are going to give away <u>fifty-thousand</u> iron men....I repeat, fifty thousand...count it yourself...<u>five oh comma</u>....<u>Oh oh oh period</u>....<u>oh oh</u>......Oh boy!....the last two oh's being donated by Olsen...Yes, folks, we are giving away fifty thousand <u>plasters</u>....fifty thousand bucks..... fifty thousand <u>anything</u> you can think of <u>except dollars</u>......and there are no strings attached to this contest as even <u>strings</u> cost money. And we will play <u>no favorites</u> as they are all losing in Jamaica.

Now, what is this contest all about? I'll tell you. It is a <u>color test</u> which even color-blind people can play. <u>Again</u> you will have to take names of celebrities - your favorite <u>radio</u> <u>picture</u> and <u>stage</u> stars. Then you take several different colored pieces of silk say, about ten <u>yards in length</u>.... Now we will give you the <u>first</u> names of the stars then you must send us the pieces of colored silk representing their <u>last</u> names. For instance, if I give you these three names Mitzie Alice and Joe naturally, you would send us <u>green</u> <u>white</u> and <u>brown</u>.... you see? <u>Mitzi Green</u> <u>Alice White</u> and <u>Joe Brown</u>...Simple, isn't it?......then when we receive the green-white-and brown pieces of silk that you send us, we take the material and have shirts and neckties made for Olsen, Fran Frey and myself. And the shirt that <u>wears the</u> <u>longest</u> is the winner, and the prize will be awarded to the sender. NOW <u>IS THAT CLEAR</u>?

If there is the slightest doubt in your mind, let me explain this again. Take three names like <u>Zane</u> <u>Primo</u> and <u>Zazu</u>....and the colors you would immediately think of are <u>Zane Grey</u> <u>Primo Canary</u> and <u>Zazu</u>....<u>Peach</u>.... Now, on the other hand, if you |

prefer <u>radio</u> stars, and we should give you their last names like Colombo .... Vallee.... and Crosby....<u>what colors</u> would you immediately think of? Why, naturally, you would think of <u>Rose Columbo</u> - <u>Reddy Valee</u> and <u>Pink Crosby</u>......Fascinating, isn't it?......

Now to make it still clearer - not that you care, but we have to get our jokes in - suppose you prefer famous <u>songwriters</u>. For example if we give you these three <u>first</u> names - Lew - Buddy - and Ray - naturally, the three colors you think of would be Brown- <u>De Silva</u> - and <u>Henderson</u>.... (PAUSE)

DAVE MARSHALL: What color is <u>Henderson</u>?

JACK: Henderson <u>is white</u>...and a fine fellow...Are you laughing, Ray?

All right, folks now for the one <u>you</u> have to work out yourself. I am going to reverse it this time and give <u>you</u>...the colors, and <u>you will have to fill in the names of the celebrities</u>. Now take the three colors <u>radish</u>...<u>olive</u>...and <u>celery</u>...This is your problem... Get right to work, folks as our prizes are perishable and are decaying right now.... George, put some ice on those prizes. Oh, I almost forgot to tell you - you must take a piece of paper - write your answers clearly across a fountain pen...and <u>send us the blotter</u> - And now George Olsen who is <u>eating one of the prizes</u> will play, "We're Alone", sung by Dave Marshall.

3. WE'RE ALONE   ORCHESTRA & MARSHALL

(THIRD ROUTINE)

JACK: That was Dave Marshall singing, "We're Alone".... well, here we are still in the middle of the Fall season. Baseball is over...the summer resorts are closed...and all you hear now is football, with the <u>Quarter backs</u> the <u>half backs</u> and <u>nickel backs</u>......Our own Canada Dry football team is training hard and will, no doubt, within a few weeks be in shape to beat the Notre Dame, Princeton and the Army and Navy....<u>Store</u> teams. Fall also brings us <u>the new plays</u>...You remember the hits of last year... "<u>The Cat and the Interlude</u>" ....and that stock market play, "Of Thee I <u>Sink</u>!".....and the colored show about the amateur clergymen....."Green Pastors"?....Well, there are several new ones opening up this Fall, and we do not intend to be left at the post...so right here tonight in our Canada Dry Studio Theatre, we will offer our own play, "<u>Grind Hotel</u>"...written by that famous playwright, <u>Vicki Salve</u>... Reports have reached us that <u>another</u> hotel drama with a similar title has been playing around the country for the past two or three years....Oh well, people will steal ideas.....There is nothing we can do about it, So tonight, for the first time on the air, we will present our new play, "Grind Hotel". The scene takes place in a <u>Roumanian</u> hotel....in <u>Belfast</u>....Ireland.... run on the <u>American</u> plan.... which is just an old <u>Spanish</u> custom. Now, while the hotel is being cleaned up and the maids change the linen, George Olsen and <u>his Grind Hotelians</u>......will earn their room and board, by playing, "Meanest Gal in Town", sung by Ethel Shutta.

October 10, 1932

4. MEANEST GAL IN TOWN   ORCHESTRA & ETHEL

(FOURTH ROUTINE)

JACK: And now for our play.... Music, George....Curtain! (ORCHESTRA PLAYS FEW BARS OF CURTAIN MUSIC. (SOUND EFFECT: SQUEAKY CURTAIN THEN TELEPHONE BELLS BUZZERS, VOICES IN DISTANCE, ETC)

ETHEL: Hello...Grind Hotel...no, he isn't here...yes, sir, I'll tell him....

DOROTHY ROSS: Hello...Grind Hotel...Yes, Madame, all right...

HOTCHA: Hello, Fraulein Mary.

SADYE: Vie gates, Hotcha? ...Are you a bellhop here?

HOTCHA: Yah Yah.

ETHEL: Hello...Grind Hotel...yes madame at once. (Rings hand bell) Boy! Take a corkscrew up to 808. JACK: Wait, I'll take it up myself.... (aside) They're eating oysters up there and it will give me a chance to get the pearls...I need money who don't? .... Hey Hans! .... I'm going up to Ethel-co-vitch's room.... Music, George! (ORCHESTRA PLAYS A FEW BARS OF MYSTERY MUSIC). The scene now changes to Room 808....

FRAN: Come, come, Ethel-co-vitch we leave for the theatre at once. It is growing late, and the house is completely sold out.

ETHEL (the dancer): No,no,no -- no,no,no....I cannot dance tonight. I have a sore throat.

FRAN: You have a sore throat! .... Well, surely you can tonsil a little.

ETHEL: Go! Go! I want to be alone.

FRAN: All right then you're through I never want to see you again.... auf weidersehn (DOOR SLAMS) ETHEL: Ah, Gretchen I'm so tired tonight...so sick of it all... Why must I dance.... when it is love that I need. (HEAVY KNOCK AT DOOR) Who is there?

JACK'S VOICE: It's me the Baron.

ETHEL: Baron who?

JACK: Baron von two three...

ETHEL: Four five six.

JACK: Seven eight-nine.

ETHEL: Come in, Baron.... (DOOR OPENS- FOOTSTEPS) I want to be alone.

JACK: No wise cracks now.

JACK: Ah, Ethel-co-vitch, you are divine...more beautiful than ever...but look! it is eight o'clock...how is it you are not at the theatre?

ETHEL:	Bah! Theatre...
JACK:	Are you still doing that dance in the show?
ETHEL :	Yes, it ees the sensacheon.
JACK:	What? the Mayor hasn't stopped it yet? .... But tell me, my sweet, do you really love me?
ETHEL (in colored dialect):	Jah, Baron you knows I do...and do you love me, honey?
JACK :	Do I?....Do I?....Come here, kiss me...(SMACK-SMACK-SMACK)
	Ah, <u>Ethel</u>-co-vitch, how you can <u>kitch</u>......Darling, this is the first time I have ever been on love...never before have I felt this way about any woman...
SADYE:	I might as well go back to Plainfield...I'm no good here.
JACK:	Mary! .... get off the set. (KNOCK AT DOOR)
ETHEL:	Who is there?
OLSEN:	It's me, String-a-line.... I have two minutes more to live, and I have come to say good-bye.
ETHEL:	Good-bye, String-a-line.
JACK:	Good Luck! (DOOR SLAMS)
JACK:	Tell me, how long are you going to stay in Berlin, <u>Ethel</u>-co-vitch?
ETHEL:	Tomorrow night I leave for Vienna. And <u>you</u> will go with me.
JACK:	Well, it looks like I will have to loaf in Vienna.
HICKS:	Pardon me – did you see a bottle of Canada Dry Ginger Ale lying around here?
JACK:	No, Hicksala and close that door gently on your way out...Was this Hicks up here before?
ETHEL:	I don't remember.
JACK:	You're lying what is this guy Hicksala to you?
ETHEL:	Nothing I swear it.
JACK:	Then forgive me, darling it is only because I am broke and love you so much that I am jealous.
ETHEL:	Ah, you silly little boy...you know I love you and you only.
JACK:	Yes, you belong to me... (KNOCK AT DOOR)
JACK:	Who is there?
OLSEN:	It's me String-a-line...I have <u>one more</u> minute to live, and I just came to say good-bye.

ETHEL:	Good-bye, String-a-line.
JACK:	Good luck! (DOOR SLAMS)
	Where were we, <u>Ethel</u>-co-vitch?...Oh yes.... Ah, Stringaline...er, Ethel-co-vitch. when I gaze into your sad, pale, face, I want to make you so, so happy.... Here's your pocket book.
ETHEL:	Thanks, Baron and here's your watch.
JACK:	Ah, but I do love you...tell me, Ethel-co-vitch, whose little blue eyes are those?
ETHEL:	Yours, Baron.
JACK:	Whose little pug nose is that?
ETHEL:	Yours, Baron.
JACK:	Whose little red lips are those?
ETHEL:	Yours, Baron.
HICKS:	Say, when you come to a Canada Dry bottle, <u>its mine</u>!

(ORCHESTRA PLAYS FEW BARS OF CURTAIN MUSIC)

SADYE:	Hello, Grind Hotel...
ETHEL:	Hello yes ma'am. I'll send it right up.
DOROTHY ROSS:	Hello, Grind Hotel...yes.... no...
JACK:	Grind Hotel, people come and people go, but Canada Dry goes on forever....
	(ROUND OF APPLAUSE)
	Operator! Operator!
SADYE:	Yes....Grind Hotel....
JACK:	Wake up Olsen in 1612 and tell him to play the next number.

(SEGUE INTO NEXT NUMBER)

5. SWEET MUCHACHA   ORCHESTRA & GARDNER

JACK:	That was the last number of the 47th program on the 10th of October. Be sure to listen in Wednesday night as we will bring you more surprises, more fun and more problems.... Come early and reserve your radios...Well, I have to leave you now.
OLSEN (as String-a-line):	Good-night, Mr. Benny.
JACK:	Good-night, String-a-line...are you <u>still</u> living?

OLSEN:	Yes, I have five more seconds to go, and I'm going to make a real holiday of it and go to Paris.
JACK:	well, have a good time.
SADYE:	Good-night, Jack.
JACK:	Good-night, Mary if you want to wait, I'll take you home.
SADYE:	I'm sorry, I can't. I'm going to Paris with String-a-line...
JACK:	Well, here's to a happy five seconds...
ETHEL:	Where are you going with that gun, Jack?
JACK:	I'm going to look for the guy who wrote this play.... Good-night, folks.
ANNOUNCER:	The next time you stop at a soda fountain for a refreshing drink, ask for a glass of Canada Dry, the champagne of ginger ales it will be made-to-order for you and costs only five cents for a regular glass or ten cents for an extra-large glass. Remember too, that with the exception of a few localities where freight charges do not permit, you can take back your Canada Dry bottles to the dealer and get a cash refund. So that now when you buy Canada Dry you pay for the contents only. Next Wednesday night at this same time, Jack Benny, Ethel Shutta and George Olsen will again entertain you. This is the National Broadcasting Company.

October 12, 1932

Jack as "The Earth Galloper" provides commentary on celebrity gossip. The show commemorates Columbus Day. Jack interviews Queen Isabella. Prince the trained dog gets another routine. Jack announces that he is going to take train to Chicago to visit his father.

STATION WJZ   PROGRAM CANADA DRY GINGER ALE, INC.

AND   DATE WEDNESDAY, OCTOBER 12, 1932.

BLUE NETWORK   TIME 9:30 10:00 P.M.

A. SIGNATURE JOLLY GOOD COMPANY

1. I BEG YOUR PARDON MADEMOISELLE   FRAN FREY
2. WHEN MOTHER PLAYED THE ORGAN   ETHEL SHUTTA
3. YOU'LL GET BY   ETHEL SHUTTA & FRAN FREY
4. HOW DEEP IS THE OCEAN   MARSHALL
5. GERMAN BAND   ETHEL SHUTTA

Z. SIGNATURE: - ROCKABYE MOON

CANADA DRY GINGER ALE, INC.   WEDNESDAY, OCTOBER 12, 1932.
SIGNATURE JOLLY GOOD COMPANY

ANNOUNCER: Ladies and gentlemen, another half hour of entertainment about Canada Dry the champagne of Ginger-ales now available by the glass at soda fountains, as well as in bottles for the home. You'll find the new, large size bottle very economical and particularly convenient for home use. Once more, we present George Olsen, Ethel Shutta and Jack Benny, the Canada Dry Humorist, who will again perform for your enjoyment. George Olsen opens the program with "I BEG YOUR PARDON MADEMOISELLE". Sung by Fran Frey.

HICKS: And now Jack Benny.

JACK: Hello, steady customers. This is Jack <u>Gibbons</u> Benny....the Earth Galloper - coming to you again with the late news events thru the courtesy of the <u>Keyhole</u> News Syndicate...<u>sees</u> nothing...<u>knows</u> nothing...and <u>prints</u> everything.... Now here are late news flashes by wire telephone cable and <u>stool</u> <u>pigeon</u>......

HANNIBAL, MISSOURI - Conditions improving here. Mississippi running on <u>full time</u>.

ATHENS: Insull located here. When asked what he was doing here, he said: "As long as I'm put <u>on the pan</u>, I might as well be <u>in Greece</u>."

NEW YORK CITY - Subways flooded. People now getting submarine rides for a nickel......<u>Stay out of this</u>, <u>Hicks</u>!

<u>UPPERCUT</u>, New YORK - Schmelling says he will fight Max <u>Baer</u>...for one hundred thousand dollars...<u>or with clothes on</u>.... for fifty thousand.

HOLLYWOOD, CALIFORNIA --John Barrymore <u>killed</u>....by Wallace Beery in <u>GRAND HOTEL</u>....He's feeling fine now and will be killed in another picture shortly.... Ah, you missed <u>that one</u>, Winchell!

WALLA WALLA, WASHINGTON - Things so bad here, we have to cut everything in half. From now on town will be known <u>as Walla</u>....Well, walla-we-care--eh, George?

NEW YORL CITY - <u>FOUR P.M.</u> - Ethel Shutta, famous radio star, receives large bouquet of flowers from her husband.

BROOKLYN - THREE P.M. - Famous orchestra leader caught stealing flowers from cemetery.... Why, George Olsen!

LUNCH WAGON, OHIO - Circus midget commits suicide in restaurant by jumping off of three-decker-sandwich.

Now for the sport events - Cubs wintering at Bear Mountain....Reds wintering in Russia...Robins flying South.......YANKEE STADIUM, New York - Good old Yankees returning to their homes Gomez to Cuba......Lazari and Crossetti to Italy....Gehrig to Germany....and Sewell to Sewell City, Iowa.... (Starts humming, "Yankee Doodle") Are you listening, Benny Rubin? Ah! we Yankees.... some day I'd like to go back to Romania and see what the folks are doing...

And now for the football news -- SING SING, NEW YORK - Prison team opens football season and will play all games at home this year.... In first game three men found running for touchdown without ball....and were caught out of bounds.......

CLEVELAND, OHIO - It is rumored that the Nickel Plate Railroad will merge.

HICKS: And don't forget, folks, if you merge Canada Dry Ginger Ale with ice cream, you will have a great drink.

JACK: Hicks, you're getting away with merger.

HICKS: Oh, you talk too merge, Jack

JACK: All right, Hicks you're one up, but wait till Monday, ...And now George Olsen will merger the next number but it will be sung very sweetly by Ethel Shutta.

ETHEL: Merge obliged, Jack.

JACK: You're welcome, Ethel.

SEGUE INTO NUMBER –

2. WHEN MOTHER PLAYED THE ORGAN   ORCHESTRA & ETHEL

(SECOND ROUTINE)

JACK: Well, ladies and gentlemen, as you all know this is Columbus Day, and as usual, we are prepared. We are going to honor Christopher Columbus tonight and not wait until Thanksgiving or Christmas to pay tribute to this brave adventurer - the man who discovered this great country of ours which was like finding a .... needle in a haystack .... a clam in clam chowder.... or a golf ball on a public course......Imagine finding a little piece of land like North America. He must have been tipped off. Somebody told him....... Well, anyway, he found it. But did he keep it? No! Can you imagine if Columbus had kept just a small part of it like from here to Los Angeles.... what he'd be worth today?

OLSEN: Jack. what did you do with your two lots?

JACK: I can't get rid of them, George....I wish Columbus had kept them......Just think - it is four hundred and forty years since Columbus <u>discovered America</u> - and it seems like only yesterday - doesn't it, folks? My, how time flies!....Words cannot express my amazement at how <u>Chris crossed</u> the <u>crest</u> of the waves what <u>crust</u>!......making that trip in three hundred and forty-six-days....seven hours...and three-fifths seconds, clipping two-fifths of a second off of <u>Jimmy Walker's last trip</u>....you will have to admit that was going some. <u>What a boat</u> that little Santa Maria was.......with Columbus at the <u>wheel</u>.... Gar Wood at the Helm....and the <u>helm</u> with the crew.... I mean, the <u>crew at the helm</u> with Gar Wood.

Now how many of you older people listening in tonight can recall when Columbus first landed <u>at Pier Six</u>, and was met by the Indians? How they marched him up Broadway then known as <u>Wigwam Avenue</u>....with <u>Big Chief Mulrooney</u> and <u>Mayor Running Walker</u>...leading the parade. The City Hall was then only a tent....and the Empire State Building, <u>a tent-cent stage</u>.

Now history doesn't tell you this, but this manuscript does....Columbus really came here, <u>looking for prosperity</u>, and the Indians told him it was around <u>Heap Big Corner</u> but in those days there were no corners, so Chris kept on running around in circles, round and round, until he made a beaten path which is known today as - you said it!....<u>COLUMBUS CIRCLE</u>. Now four hundred and forty years ago, Columbus said the earth was <u>flat</u>. We didn't believe him then but we found out......Well, anyway, Columbus <u>discovered</u> us. We're here, and the State of Ohio paid him a great tribute when they named that beautiful city after him known as <u>Toledo</u> --

GEORGE OLSEN (WHISPERS): Not Toledo.

JACK: Akron.

OLSEN: You mean <u>Columbus</u>.

JACK: Well, they're all listening in, George.

GEORGE: Say, Jack, I've been listening to you and I don't think you know what you're talking about. In the first place, Columbus landed <u>in the West Indies</u>.

JACK: I know, George. They only <u>stopped</u> in the West Indies for a couple of <u>nights</u>....to celebrate their arrival...And, boy! <u>what nights</u> they were.

OLSEN: And that's what started the <u>Nights of Columbus</u>.

JACK: That was George Olsen speaking, folks.... I give him <u>all the old jokes</u>.

OLSEN: Go ahead, Jack. Tell us <u>more</u> about American history.

JACK: Well, once a Ponce de Leon time, there was a man called Ponce who went to Florida with his brother, <u>Toopaira Ponce</u>.

OLSEN: You're right, Jack. He went there, searching for the <u>fountain of youth</u>.

HICKS: And at every <u>fountain youth</u> can get Canada Dry Ginger Ale, made-to-order by the glass.

JACK: Also, a nickel deposit <u>a-ponce-de</u> large bottle.

HICKS: Jack, I agree with George. I don't think you're very familiar with American History. Don't you know that New York was bought by the Dutch settlers from the Indians for one large bottle of Canada Dry Ginger Ale?

JACK: I grant you that, Hicks considering that it's time to boost our product, but not from a historical standpoint.... But pray tell me, Hicks, did the Indians get a nickel back on the bottle?

HICKS: Yes, Jack the Indians got a nickel back.

JACK: Then that is why, ladies and gentlemen, there is an Indians on the back of every nickel....and I think it was a great honor to have a picture of Columbus on every five-dollar bill in this country –

HICKS: That's Lincoln's picture.

JACK: What am I talking about? I mean Lincoln....Play something, George before Hicks makes any more mistakes.

SEGUE INTO NUMBER –

3. YOU'LL GET BY   ORCHESTRA AND ETHEL AND FRAN

(THIRD ROUTINE)

JACK: That was "You'll Get by", sung by Ethel and Fran....Well, folks, to keep up the spirit of this holiday, we have a few guest stars up here this evening, who are directly connected with the expedition made famous by Christopher Columbus. Now what distinguished person do you think we have up here tonight as our guest......who so graciously consented to appear here. You guessed it!......it is the little lady who pawned her jewels, thus making it possible for Columbus to make this trip to India, landing in America........None other than Her Majesty, Queen Isabella...who discovered our studio while looking for an American Plan hotel......It gives me great pleasure now to introduce to you the Queen of Spades....er, of Spain.

(ROUND OF APPLAUSE ORCHESTRA PLAYS FEW MEASURES OF POMP MUSIC)

JACK: Greetings, your Majesty! Say something, Queenie.

BLANCHE STEWART: One no trump.

JACK: Oh, you're a bridge queen.

BLANCHE: Yes, I came over the Queens boro Bridge.

JACK: Hmmm....well, it looks as tho the Queen might be crowned tonight.... Is it true that you gave Columbus the necessary funds to make that historic trip?

BLANCHE: No he took the dough and beat it.

JACK: I see.... did you report it yet?

BLANCHE: No, I just sold the castle got a fresh bankroll and blew Spain.

JACK: Is that so?......Well, what happened to the King?

BLANCHE: Oh, he's the Fish on the Amos 'N Andy program.

JACK: (Oh, Kingfish?) .... But on the level, Queenie you were a little crazy about Columbus weren't you?

BLANCHE: Yes but I got over it.... I got a new feller now.

JACK: Oh, you have? What's his name? (slight pause) Come on, now what's his name?

BLANCHE (BASHFULLY): Cincinnatus.

JACK: Oh, you went from Columbus to Cincinnatus! That's quite a trip isn't it?

BLANCHE: Yes, but I took a sleeper.

JACK: Hmmm, I see. Very interesting.... But getting back to nobility are you acquainted with the Prince of Wales?

BLANCHE: Oh yes, we used to go horseback-falling together.

JACK: Then you're familiar with all my friends.... are you listening, Newport? Tell me, Queenie, do you happen to know the Duchess of Cleanser?

BLANCHE: Sure I used to cleanse her apartment every Saturday.

JACK: Never mind, Newport it's a social error, a foh-pah...and a pah-foh........You know, Queenie I'm afraid to ask you this next one. But speaking socially, do you happen to know Cholly Knickerbocker? JACK & BLANCHE (TOGETHER): No but I know his brother, Golf Pants.

JACK: I was afraid of that well Queen Isabella, that's very democratic of you coming up here this evening, and I assure you it was a real treat for us of the Middle Class, to meet such a charming member of the Royal Family....Now don't hurry away, Queenie.

BLANCHE(WHISPERS): Then stop pushing me. I'll go.

JACK: Good-night, Queenie.

BLANCHE: Good-night.... Come on, Prince.... (DOG IMITATION) Woof-woof-woof......

JACK: What royalty! And what other program brings you no-ability.... Next Monday night we will bring you King Levinsky....and His Highness. October the 17th.......And now George Olsen and his Royal Four Flushers will play, "How Deep Is the Ocean," sung by Dave Marshall - while I see the Queen to her carriage - Her baby has been crying for ten minutes.

4. HOW DEEP IS THE OCEAN   ORCHESTRA & MARSHALL

(FOURTH ROUTINE)

JACK: That was Dave Marshall singing, "How Deep is the Ocean." Well, the Queen has gone......And now, ladies and gentleman, as much as it is against the policy of this program <u>to brag</u>, we have a gentleman up here this evening who fits in perfectly with this Columbus Day Program. He is <u>also</u> a great discoverer. Columbus <u>discovered</u> America Franklin <u>discovered</u> electricity Peary <u>discovered</u> the North Pole - and Mary <u>discovered</u> Hotcha...But as I started to say, we have with us this evening a gentleman who first <u>discovered</u> that it was <u>possible</u> to eat an oyster.... the very first man mind you <u>ever</u> to eat an oyster. What heroism! what bravery! what courage! And now I take great pleasure in presenting to you the Honorable and Daring .... <u>J. FISH-HOUSE CLAM</u>.... (ROUND OF APPLAUSE)

<u>Take it, Clam</u>!

HARRY CONN: Hello, folks. I am very happy to be here on this great holiday program. I am here tonight to speak of <u>seafood</u> as I didn't <u>see food</u> in three days.

JACK (AD LIB): These guest stars have better jokes than I have. Oh well......Tell us about <u>your great discovery</u>, Mr. Clam.

HARRY: Well, I shall never forget the first time I met an oyster. I can still see the expression <u>on her face</u> JACK: How do you know it was <u>a she</u>?

HARRY: All right <u>his</u> face....and I was --

JACK: Just a moment was he <u>laughing</u> or <u>crying</u>?

HARRY: Neither just frightened.

JACK: I see a frightened oyster.... Well, we can always learn something. Go ahead.

HARRY: Well, there he lay in bed and --

JACK: <u>What bed</u>?

HARRY (YELLS): Oyster bed.

JACK: Well, don't yell.... I don't want to have any trouble with you. After all, <u>you were there</u>.

HARRY: Well, anyway, there he was in his <u>pajamas</u>, reading a paper.

JACK: Wait a minute you say the oyster was in his pajamas?

HARRY: <u>Just the coat</u> he was on <u>the half</u> shell.

JACK: Pardon me a moment have you any other place to go?

HARRY: NO.

JACK: Well, there are times in our lives when we <u>have</u> to take it.

HARRY:	Say, do you want to hear this story or pay me off now? (PAUSE) OUCH!........Well, I hated to get the oyster out of bed but business is business. I was looking for a pearl, so I --
JACK:	Wait a minute - how did you discover that an oyster was good to eat?
HARRY:	That's what I'm coming to.... I found his <u>weakness</u>. When he saw me coming, he got mad so I pulled out a bottle of tabasco sauce and horseradish -- and <u>threw</u> <u>it</u> in his face.
JACK:	And what did the oyster do?
HARRY:	What would you do if I threw horseradish in <u>your</u> face?
JACK:	I'd get mad and jump right down your throat.
HARRY:	That's just what <u>this</u> oyster did.... And do you think it was bad? <u>NO</u>! ..... And I've been eating oysters ever since.
JACK:	That's a very good story.... I'm glad you came up.
HARRY:	How would you like to hear a song I wrote about an oyster?
JACK:	No, but I guess I'll have to.... Do you want <u>music</u> with it?
HARRY:	No just a little ketchup.
JACK:	I'm not a mind-reader...but I <u>know</u> what's going to happen to you.... Go ahead and sing your oyster song.
HARRY (coughs then sings -):	I <u>oyster</u> to love her but it's all over .... All over (STOPS SUDDENLY)
(SOUND EFFECT:	LOUD THUMP)
JACK(PANTING):	It was the kid's last oyster! .... And now Sharkey, you've got to listen to me..... Play something, George while we sweep out the celebrities.

SEGUE INTO NUMBER –

5. GERMAN BAND   ORCHESTRA & ETHEL SHUTTA

(CLOSING ROUTINE)

JACK:	That was the last number of the forty-eighth program on the 12th of October. Well, folks, sorry to leave you now, but I have to rush away to make a train for Chicago. I'm going to spend a couple of days with my folks, but I'll be back Monday.
ETHEL:	Well, so long Jack. I hope you have a nice trip.
JACK:	Thanks, Ethel. See you Monday....Good-bye. George.

GEORGE:	S'long, Jack.
JACK:	Good-bye, Mary.
MARY:	Good-bye, Jack. Gee, I hate to see you go.
JACK:	Oh, I'll be back in a few days.
MARY:	Say, Jack, are you going to bring me a little present when you come back?
JACK:	Sure, Mary what would you like?
MARY:	Oh, anything just so it's a little present from you.
JACK:	All right, Mary......well, good-bye.
MARY:	Good-bye, Jack....<u>Come on, Hotcha</u>....Did you bring your car tonight?
HOTCHA:	No, Mary I left it in the garage.
HARRY:	Good-night, Hotcha....<u>Come on, Dave</u>.
DAVE:	Okay, Mary.

ANNOUNCER: Remember, you can enjoy Canada Dry the champagne of ginger ales anywhere, anytime, for it is now available two ways either made-to-order by the glass at soda fountains or in bottles, as always, for your home. The new big bottle is particularly economical and convenient. Remember, too, that with the exception of a few localities, where freight rates do not permit, you pay for the contents only, that is, twenty cents for the big five-glass bottle, or twenty-five cents for two regular twelve-ounce bottles. In addition, you make a small deposit on each bottle, but this deposit is refunded when the bottle is returned. Next Monday night at this same time Jack Benny, Ethel Shutta and George Olsen will again entertain you. This is the National Broadcasting Company.

October 17, 1932

First part of the Big Romance between Jack and Mary. Announcer notes that the show is tuning into the train station to join Mary as she picks up Jack from the train, as he is late to the opening of the broadcast. They flirt romantically in the cab and sigh about their love for each other. Once back in the studio they reprise the "Grind Hotel" skit, with Jack as a confident romantic performer asking Ethel to put more romance in her acting, when he as Baron again makes love to her. The film scene morphs from the "Grand Hotel" narrative into their other favorite of the extra lovers having to hide. Ethel the ballerina hiding men under her bed when others enter. Jack provides voice-over of a film travelogue of India.

STATION WJZ PROGRAM CANADA DRY GINGER ALE, INC.

AND DATE WEDNESDAY, OCTOBER 17, 1932.

BLUE NETWORK TIME 9:30 10:00 P.M.

SIGNATURE JOLLY GOOD COMPANY

1. ALL-AMERICAN GIRL FRAN FREY
2. COP ON THE BEAT ETHEL SHUTTA
3. FIT AS A FIDDLE FRAN FREY
4. THANKSGIVING GARDNER
5. SO TO BED ETHEL SHUTTA

Z. SIGNATURE ROCKABYE MOON

CANADA DRY GINGER ALE INC. WEDNESDAY, OCTOBER 17, 1932.
SIGNATURE JOLLY GOOD COMPANY

ANNOUNCER: Ladies and gentleman, another half hour of entertainment about Canada Dry the champagne of ginger ales now available by the glass at soda fountains as well as in bottles for the home. You'll find the new, large size bottle very economical and particularly convenient for home use.   Once more we present George Olsen, Ethel Shutta and Jack Benny, the Canada Dry Humorist, who will again perform for your enjoyment. George Olsen opens the program with "ALL AMERICAN GIRL". Fran Frey singing.

HICKS: And now Jack Benny.

GEORGE OLSEN: Say, Hicks I think we'll have to play another number. You know Jack's train is due from Chicago about this time, and we'll have to give him a chance to get over here from the Station.

HICKS: I have a better idea. Let's tune in to the Depot and catch Jack as he arrives. Tom! Take the boys to the Grand-Penn Station.

VOICE: Okay.

(SOUND EFFECT: STATIC TAXI HORNS BRAKES SCREECHING EXHAUST NOISE PEOPLE CALLING "PORTER" AD LIB GREETING, ETC.)

[ED.: These next several lines were crossed out in pencil....]

FRAN FREY (AS CONDUCTOR): Train now arriving on Track seven from Chicago. (MORE TAXI HORNS AD LIBBING OF PEOPLE, ETC.)

FRAN (IN DISTANCE): Train leaving for Albany Rochester Buffalo on Track Five....All aboard! WOMAN'S VOICE: Good-bye, John. Take care of yourself.........Good-bye, dear. (SOUND EFFECT: TRAIN PULLING IN BELL- EXHAUST FROM STEAM ENGINE)

FRAN: Step aside and let the passengers thru, please. (MORE AD LIBBING OF PASSEN-GERS)

[ED.: script picks up here, it's unclear if the lines before the crash were performed]

HOTCHA (AS COLORED PORTER): Right this way, Boss. I'll get you a cab.

JACK BENNY:	All right, Porter. Leave my grip here.
HOTCHA:	Yas, suh. (SOUND EFFECT: TERRIFIC GLASS CRASH)
JACK:	Hey, I told you to be careful with that grip.
HOTCHA:	Sorry, boss.... Say, ain't you Jack Benny?
JACK:	Oh, you know me, eh?......Well, here you are, Porter.
HOTCHA:	Thank you, Boss....wait a minute. This is a nickel you gave me.
JACK:	Well?
HOTCHA:	Mr. Benny, I toted this heavy grip for you, and I didn't bring you no large Canada Dry Bottle. JACK: You should be glad that I'm not Olsen.
HOTCHA:	Yes, suh. (LAUGHS)
MARY:	You wait here, Dave. I want to see what time the train gets in.
BALDWIN:	All right, Mary.
JACK:	Oh, hello Mary.
MARY:	Hello, Jack.
JACK:	Gee, it's nice of you to come down to the station to meet <u>me</u>.
MARY:	Oh, I-er....er...er...gee, Jack, you're looking <u>swell</u>.
JACK:	And you're looking fine, Mary....Come on, let's grab a cab and rush over to the Studio.
MARY:	I can't, Jack. You see <u>Hotcha</u> gets in from Albany in ten minutes.... Ain't you glad I came down? JACK: Huh-hmm....
MARY:	And wasn't it swell of Dave to come with me to meet Hotcha?
JACK:	I t sure was.
MARY:	You know, Jack, it's certainly a surprise to see you...I thought you got in <u>last night</u>.
JACK:	I'm glad you even knew I was gone.... Hey, Taxi! .... Taxi! ... (SOUND EFFECT: SOREECHING OF BRAKES HORNS) You better come back with me to the studio, Mary. I might need you on the program.
MARY:	Oh, all right, then. Dave can wait for Hotcha....So long, Dave.
BALDWIN:	Good-bye, Mary.
JACK:	Get in, Mary. (TAXI DOOR SLAMS HORN) NBO Studio....and <u>step on it</u>! I'm late.
TAXI DRIVER:	OKAY. (MOTOR START AND HORN)

(DURING THE FOLLOWING SCENE, HUM OF MOTOR CAN BE HEARD FAINTLY)

JACK:	Well, Mary anything new while I was away?
MARY:	Oh, nothing much, Jack. I answered the mail your tailor was over and wanted his money, and I told him you were in South America....Wasn't that swell?
JACK:	I mean around the studio.... What's new? How's Fran Frey?
MARY:	Oh, fine. He took me to dinner last night. You see, Hotcha was out of town, and I –
JACK:	I see. You must have had a lot of trouble.
MARY:	Oh, I forgot.... George Olsen gave a party last Friday, and we were all there, and we had lots of fun.
JACK:	At the New Yorker?
MARY:	No, the <u>Automat</u>....We all brought our own nickels. You see, I was with Hicks, and he had some nickels he got back on the large Canada Dry bottles and we—
JACK:	Oh, you had dinner with Hicks, too? You didn't dine with Herbert Hoover any place, did you?
MARY:	No, Jack, Was he in town? I wish I had known it.
JACK:	Say, Mary, I want to ask you something. Why do you keep running around with Hotcha?
MARY:	Oh, I don't know. He's different...He never takes me any place nor buys me anything.... just different, that's all.
JACK:	Well, I can do that, too, Mary. You know I like you a whole lot, and I've tried to show it.
MARY:	I know, Jack. I think you're just too good for me. You see, you're a Big City Feller and I'm just a Small-Town Girl.
JACK:	Well, what of it?
MARY:	And look at the different in our ages. When you'll be fifty, I'll only be thirty-eight. And when you're an <u>old man of ninety</u>, I'll still be a <u>young girl of seventy-eight</u>.
JACK:	I know when I'm a hundred and forty, you'll still be running around with Hotcha... Well, anyway, Mary, I'm stuck on you.... Now what do you say? Do you like me?
MARY:	Of course, I do.
JACK:	(SIGHS) Mary!
MARY:	(SIGHS) Jack!
FRAN (TAXI DRIVER):	NBC Studio- here you are! (TAXI DOOR SLAMS)
JACK AND MARY:	(AD LIB FADING INTO DISTANCE)

SEGUE INTO NUMBER –

2. THE COP ON THE BEAT　　　　　　　　　　　　　ORCHESTRA & ETHEL SHUT-TA (OLSEN MAKES HIS OWN ANNOUNCEMENT)

(SECOND ROUTINE)

JACK AND MARY: (AD LIB AD THEY ENTER)

JACK: Hello, paid-up members. This is Jack Benny back from the Middle West...and <u>what</u> a time I had.

OLSEN: Did you enjoy your visit, Jack?

JACK: Did I? …. Yes, sir. I had a great time. After all, there's no place like home. You see, George, I live in a small town called Lake Forest, Illinois...which is about thirty miles out of Chicago. And when I got off the train, there was the Mayor the Chief of Police the Postmaster the Fire Chief the Board of Aldermen and the Chamber of Commerce...and let me tell you, George <u>he's</u> one fine fellow......

OLSEN: How did you find your father, Jack?

JACK: I didn't have any trouble. You see, I know him pretty well and he hasn't changed much...And do you know, George he <u>certainly likes you</u>. Why, he bawled me out the other night for saying that you pinched a penny so hard that you <u>put a permanent wave in Lincoln's beard</u>.

GEORGE: Well, hooray for your Dad. He knows what he's talking about.

JACK: You bet he does! …. He said it was a nickel you pinched...and you made <u>hamburger</u> out of the buffalo.

GEORGE: I knew that was coming. I'll bet it took you all day on the train to figure that out... And by the way, Jack I paid a laundry bill for you while you were gone.

JACK: Thanks, George. I'll give you the money later.

GEORGE: That's <u>three</u> bundles you owe me for.

JACK: Well, Chicago certainly is a wonderful place. I met a fellow who owed me some money and he--- ETHEL: Hello, Jack. Did you have a nice time?

JACK: Oh hello, Ethel. Say, I want to tell you something and I know you'll be tickled to hear it.

ETHEL: What is it, Jack?

JACK: Well, while I was visiting back home, I heard some wonderful comment on your work - and <u>particularly</u> the way you played that Garbo part last week in "Grind Hotel."

ETHEL: Thanks, Jack. I'm <u>awfully</u> glad to hear it.

JACK: You know, Ethel, nobody believed it was you. I had a hard time convincing them that <u>Garbo</u> was still in Sweden.

ETHEL(LAUGHS): Aw, you're kidding.

JACK: Of course, Ethel, that was their opinion.... Personally, I thought that er. er...well, that you played the part all right, but...oh. you know....

ETHEL: That's all right, Jack. You can tell me. I appreciate honest criticism.

JACK: Not that I want to tell you how to act, Ethel, but in our love scene .... you remember, when I played the Baron...you could have put a lot more fire in it. Your response should have been much stronger to my love-making.

ETHEL: Well, I thought I did pretty good with what I had to work on....

JACK: I get it...You see, Ethel, when I come over to you and hold you close...like this---

ETHEL: Oh, Jack! You're smothering me. (GASPS FOR BREATH)

JACK: THAT'S the way this should be played...Isn't that right, George?

GEORGE (VERY SLOWLY): Well, I think it would be better if you held her like---

ETHEL (QUICKLY): You stay out of this, George...Continue, Jack!

JACK: I'm sorry, George but the play's the thing! Now, Ethel, you must put more feeling into it. You see- on the screen, people can see your expression but over the air, they only know what they hear.... You know a sigh once in a while....

ETHEL: I get the idea.

JACK: Now, Ethel let's take that love scene over again from our play. "Grind Hotel". You remember the scene? You're the wealthy Russian dancer who wants love...and I'm the Baron who has it and wants to get paid for it? ...Now first, close your eyes and think of me as John Barrymore. What can you lose?

ETHEL (DRAMATICALLY): All right, Mr. Bennymore.

JACK: Let's not have any trouble...Now us take that scene again where you refuse --

OLSEN: Jack, would you mind rehearsing over there in the corner? I've got to play the next number.

JACK: All right, George. Now look here, Ethel...you refuse to go --

(BOTH EXIT AD LIBBING)

SEGUE INTO NUMBER --

3. FIT AS A FIDDLE ORCHESTRA AND FRAN FREY
(OLSEN MAKES HIS OWN ANNOUNCEMENT)
(THIRD ROUTINE)

JACK: Ready, Ethel? Let's take that scene over again where you refuse to go to the theatre. You're in your one-room suite in "Grind Hotel". Remember? Your manager has just left you, and I, the Baron, come up looking for the pearls. Have you got it, Ethel?

ETHEL:	Uh-huh.
JACK:	Then let's run thru it. I just want to show you how much better you could have done in this scene...A little music, George.

(ORCHESTRA PLAYS FEW MEASURES OF "DANUBE")

ETHEL (SING-SONG FASHION):	Hello...Grind Hotel...I want to be alone......
JACK:	Wait a minute, Ethel...You've got the wrong scene. That was <u>last week</u>.... this is <u>upstairs</u>.... It's just before I knock at the door. Have you got the same room, Ethel?
ETHEL:	Yes.
JACK:	All right, George. Music again, please.

(ORCHESTRA PLAYS FEW MEASURES OF "DANUBE")

	Funny here I am, playing a love scene with George's wife and he's got to play the music. You ought to see his face right now.... Go ahead, Ethel.
ETHEL (A LA GARBO):	No, No, No, No, No, I will not go to the theatre tonight...I want to be alone.

(INTO SONG GETTING HOTTER) All alone...I'm just all alone...and there's no one here but me....boop-boop-a-doop. (HEAVY KNOCK AT DOOR DOOR SLAM) Who is it?

JACK:	It's the Baron.
ETHEL:	Which Baron?
JACK:	From Wilkes <u>Barron</u>, Pennsylvania.
ETHEL:	Ah! Come in, Baron.
[ED:	this line is crossed out. SADYE: Good-morning, it's six o'clock...you have two more hours to sleep.]
[ED.	I am unsure how they transitioned from the room down the lobby here]
ETHEL:	Hello......Grind Hotel....
JACK:	Grind Hotel <u>what a grind</u>! .... people come and people go...you can fool all of the people when they come...but not when they go.... <u>What a joint!</u>
ETHEL:	Hello, yes, this is Tuesday....you want a call for <u>Friday</u>? Okay....
SADYE:	Hello yes, sir, I'll tell the Clerk....Say, Clerk! the man in 1214 says he can't find the <u>bed</u> in his room. He's sitting on a bench up there waiting.
JACK:	<u>What bench</u>? .... tell him <u>that's</u> the bed.
ETHEL:	Hello, Grind Hotel...yes ma'am...Say, Clerk, the lady in 415 says there's a mouse running around her room.
JACK:	Oh yeah? ...Tell her that he'll have to come down and register...Good evening, Herr Prince-a-ling-ling. Glad to see you here again.

MARSHALL:	Tank you.
ETHEL:	Hello...yes, sir right away.... (rings hand-bell) Boy! the man in nine eleven wants five bottles of Canada Dry Ginger Ale.
HICKS:	And don't forget.... he gets a quarter back on the five bottles.
JACK:	Hicks, get out of Grind Hotel.
SADYE:	Hello...yes sir. I'll tell him...Clerk! the man in 2020 says the <u>bed sheet</u> is missing from his bed. JACK: Let's see...who had that room last night? Wait a minute...hmmm, just as I thought, <u>Mahatma</u> <u>Ghandi</u>...he walked out with the sheet again.

(FOOTSTEPS APPROACHING) How do you do, sir? .... What can I do for you?

OLSEN:	Say Clerk I want you to give me a nice room. I'm a poor man...with pockets full of money...(coughs)...and the doctor warned me that I have only <u>six minutes</u> to live.... Just think! only six minutes...I want to live that short time like the big shots in Grind Hotel...My name is String-a-line....
JACK:	You say you only have <u>six minutes</u> to live? .... Well then, I'm afraid you'll have to pay <u>in advance</u>. I have something very nice on the twenty-eighth floor. It will take you three minutes to get there so you will <u>still have three minutes left</u>.
OLSEN:	Have you anything about two minutes from here?
JACK:	Wait a minute, I'll see...Hare you are, sir.... a room on the eighth floor.
OLSEN:	Is it a nice room?
JACK:	This will kill you....
OLSEN:	Thank you...(coughs) thank you.... I still have <u>five</u> minutes to go....and I'm going <u>to live</u>! (Dramatic laugh)
JACK:	That laugh sounds <u>very negative</u>.
MARSHALL:	Want a taxi, Mister?
JACK:	No get him a hearse.
ETHEL:	Grind Hotel....hello...Grind Hotel....
JACK:	Grind Hotel...people <u>check</u> in and people <u>check</u> out...and all the <u>checks</u> are bad... <u>what a dump</u>! SADYE (as stenographer Flam-Flam): Pardon me, sir is Mr. <u>Gravy</u> in from <u>Hamburg</u>?
JACK:	No but we have Mr. <u>Mustard</u> here from <u>Frankfort</u>...what can I do for you?
SADYE:	I'm Fraulein Flem-Flem... from Flushing...and I'm his stenografter...I'll wait over here until he gets here.
[ED.:	I am unclear how they switched back to Garbo's room]
JACK:	I <u>am</u> in.

ETHEL:	Then out, out I want to be alone.
JACK:	Ah, Ethelcovitch!
ETHEL:	What were you doing in that closet?
JACK:	Playing moth-ball with the moths...Ah! Don't send me away. <u>Again,</u> I come to tell you of my love....and steal a few pearls on the side killing <u>two birds</u> with <u>one</u> hotel...
ETHEL:	Well, it's about time you came. Sit down by me, Baron closer...closer...I want to be alone.
JACK:	Ah, Ethelcovitch, I do love you. This is the first time I have ever really been in love. Ever since I met you in "Grind Hotel" last week, I cannot sleep I cannot eat - I cannot—

(HEAVY KNOCKING AT DOOR)

(WHISPERS) Who is that?

ETHEL:	I don't know...Get under the bed <u>quick</u>! ...I want to be alone.
JACK(WHISPERS):	All right, but don't forget I'm under the bed...BRYANT 9247.

(KNOCK AT DOOR)

ETHEL:	Come in who is it? I want to be alone.
OLSEN:	It's me, Stringaline... (COUGHS) (DOOR SLAMS)

I still have three minutes to live...and I want to live them with you.

JACK (AWAY FROM MIKE): Ain't that guy dead yet? I sent him flowers last week.

ETHEL:	Sit down by my side, Stringie...I want to be alone.
OLSEN(COUGHS):	Ah, Ethelcovitch - at last my happiness is complete just being here by your side. JACK (AWAY FROM MIKE): He only has three minutes to live and still he won't live right.... (KNOCK AT DOOR)

OLSEN (WHISPERS): Who is that?

ETHEL:	Quick! Hide under the bed...I want to be alone.
OLSEN:	All right, then. I'll wait for you.
JACK:	Hello, Stringie.
OLSEN:	Hello, Baron.
JACK:	You're looking fine.
OLSEN(COUGHS):	well, considering that I have only - (KNOCK AT DOOR GETS LOUDER)
ETHEL:	Come in - who is it? (DOOR SLAMS)
FRAN:	It's me...Price-a-ling.

ETHEL: Ah, Price-a-ling... I'm so happy to see you...Sit down by me.

ETHEL & JACK(TOGETHER): I want to be alone...

FRAN: Ah, Ethelcovitch, ever since I met you in "Grind Hotel" last week, I cannot Sleep I cannot eat I cannot (HEAVY KNOCK AT DOOR)

JACK: Come under the bed, Price-a-ling... I want to be alone..."Grind Hotel".... people come and people go...and they're all under this bed. (KNOCKING GETS LOUDER)

ETHEL: Come in who is it? I want to be alone. (DOOR SLAM)

HICKS: It's me, Hick-a-line...Ah, Ethelcovitch, pardon me a moment...Ladies and gentleman, Canada Dry Ginger Ale, made-to-order by the glass. can now be bought at all fountains and it's also good in ice cream sodas.

ETHEL(ROMANTICALLY): Ah, my Hicks-a-line...say it again.

HICKS: It can also be bought by the bottle and you'll find it a most satisfying drink –

(HEAVY KNOCK ON DOOR)

JACK OLSEN FRAN (TOGETHER): Under the bed, Hick-a-line...

ETHEL: Who is there? .... I want to be alone. (DOOR SLAM) (GENERAL CONFUSION FOOTSTEPS) Ah, Hotcha-kaline.

HOTCHA: Ah, Ethelco-vitch! (DOOR SLAM)

ETHEL: Ah, Harry.

HARRY: Ah, Ethelco-vitch! (DOOR SLAM)

ETHEL: Ah, Reggie.

REGGIE: Ah, Ethelco-vitch! (DOOR SLAM)

ETHEL: Ah, Tommy.

TOMMY: Ah, Ethelco-vitch! (MORE VOICES AD LIB)

ETHEL: Come in, everybody...I want to be alone.

ENTIRE ORCHESTRA (SING- CONTINUING IN BACK GROUND RIGHT THRU ETHEL'S NEXT SPEECH)

> "For she's a jolly good fellow,
> For she's a jolly good fellow,
> For she's a jolly good fellow,
> Dum dum-dee-dum-da da-da.

ETHEL: I want to be alone I want to be alone.... Ah! ten people here...twenty...thirty...forty...fifty...AT LAST I AM ALONE!......

JACK: Grind Hotel....People come and people come...but they don't go.... And I'm still under the bed. (ORCHESTRA PLAYS FEW MEASURES OF "DANUBE"

| JACK: | And now Olsen, the House Detective, and his men will play, "THANKSGIVING", sung by Hotcha Gardner. |

4.THANKSGIVING   OLSEN'S ORCHESTRA AND GARDNER

(FOURTH ROUTUNE)

| JACK: | While lying under the bed, I just happened to remember that we have another film travelog for you this evening. You remember two weeks ago we took you on a <u>journey thru China</u>? Well, tonight we're going to take you on a most interesting and educational trip <u>thru India</u>....exotic mysterious slumbering India! …. So on with the film. |

(SOUND EFFECT: UNWINDING OF FILM)

A little atmosphere, George...and our journey begins.

(ORCHESTRA PLAYS FEW MEASURES OF "SONG OF INDIA")

In our travel thru India, we start right here at the <u>foot</u> of the Indian Ocean which leads us into the <u>mouth</u> of the Arabian Sea.....around the nose of Durante....into the <u>heart</u> of Bombay...We make this long trip on the ocean <u>by rail</u>....that is, we <u>travel</u> by boat but spend most of the time <u>by the rail</u>....watching the restless sea. Ah, what memories! We fellow the white line until we arrive at the beautiful. ancient, <u>mysterious</u> city of Bombay Bombay with its crooked streets.... large temples and <u>narrow</u> foreheads...Here we see thousands of natives sitting on the streets, leisurely idling their time away. As like other cities <u>Bombay</u> is also on the <u>ombay</u>.... We <u>then</u> duck down an alley to get away from the mooching natives...and follow the white line into the business district … the busy marketplace …. and the picture you see here is not unlike that piece of tapestry that hangs on your dining room wall which you bought for forty-nine cents...

(YAWNS) Tiring of Bombay. <u>We hail an elephant</u>...step in and continue our journey into the interior. We find this ride <u>rather uncomfortable</u> as an elephant has <u>no wheels</u>...and you can certainly feel it. <u>However</u>, we mosey along by subway...er, I mean "El" that is <u>e</u>lephant...and we come to one of the largest buildings in all India. It is a <u>confectionary</u> establishment where they make the world-famous <u>Mahatma Candy</u>....We do not wait here, but continue on our trip thru the night, stopping only at a service station to <u>refuel</u>.... the elephant with five quarts of peanuts...

And <u>dawn</u> finds us for no reason at all...entering the magic city of Delhi....We arrive in Delhi tired and hungry so we stop in a Delhi-cattessan store...and after the first bite of food, we <u>know</u> why Ghandi stopped eating....

Well, there's nothing doing in Delhi, so we take it on the Iam....<u>once again</u> following the white line which is now getting a bit dirty...and wend our way eastward thru Terra <u>Hutta</u> to Calcutta...The trip now becomes more interesting and s we jog along the narrow streets of Cal<u>cutta</u>, we see an old native in the <u>gutta</u>....picking up a <u>butta</u>... which was, no doubt, a two-for-a <u>quotta</u>... How weird he looks in his tattered white robe.... barber-proof beard...and turban. shall we stop to talk to him a moment? …. Let's do! …"Hi-ho, my good man, Are we on the right road to <u>Kash-mir</u>?

HICKS: Yes...and you get <u>five cents</u> <u>Cash</u>-mir.... back on each large Canada Dry bottle.

JACK: We <u>leave</u> Calcutta, and follow <u>the black line</u> which leads us to the Castle of the Maharajah. Here we see the royal family in their jewel-bedecked costumes, sitting in their garden- just their own little <u>family</u> group....The <u>Ma</u>harajah, The <u>Pa</u>-harajah... and Little <u>Roger</u>...Wolf Kahn...playing his <u>saxa-fajah</u>....

The royal bodyguard now spies us...and we are chased along the white line...and are run ragged into the Bay of Bengal. <u>And morning</u> <u>finds</u> <u>us</u> on the little Island if Ceylon with the rear of our trousers slightly torn and a little bump or two on our heads. What a close shave!

We are now willing to drop the whole thing and board our little steamer which carries us away from this <u>strange</u>, <u>brooding</u> island of Ceylon....And as we sail away, we see the natives on shore, waving at us with <u>clenched</u> <u>fists</u> in their own strange fashion...And as we sail on from Ceylon...I mean So Lon....er...Sool On....we can hear their voices faintly in the distance, singing their <u>love song</u> to us.

ETHEL HOTCHA FRAN (SINGING): I'll be glad when you're dead, you rascal you...

I'll be glad when you're dead, you rascal you... etc. (UNDER NEXT LINE)

JACK: And believe me, we just left India in time.... Ah, <u>beautiful India</u>, holding the key to the mysteries of the Orient...... We are now heading for that sun-kissed country... <u>Iceland</u>...with its <u>hot sun</u> and <u>burning</u> <u>desserts</u>.... which we will bring to you on our next travelog. And now George Olsen who has been yawning for the past ten minutes- will play "And so to Bed" sung by Ethel Shutta.

5. AND SO TO BED   ORCHESTRA & ETHEL

(CONTINUING INTO SIGNATURE MUSIC "ROCKABYE MOON")

(CLOSING ROUTINE)

(WHILE ETHEL HUMS SECOND CHORUS) –

JACK: That was the last number of the forty-ninth program on the 17th of October. I must leave you now until Wednesday night.... HOME, JAMES! Good night, folks.

ANNOUNCER: The next time you stop at a soda fountain for a refreshing drink, ask for a glass of Canada Dry, the champagne of ginger ales it will be made-to-order for you and costa only five cents for a regular glass or ten cents for an extra-large glass. Remember too, that with the exception of a few localities where freight charges do not permit, you can take back your Canada Dry bottles to the dealer and get a cash refund. So that now when you Buy Canada Dry you pay for the contents only. Next Wednesday night at this same time, Jack Benny, Ethel Shutta and George Olsen will again entertain you. This is the National Broadcasting Company.

October 19, 1932

Second part of the big romantic plot. Mary is jealous of Ethel's love scenes with Jack. Jack tries to confess his love for Mary, but Hicks obnoxiously interrupts their intimate conversation with Canada Dry spiels. Mary slaps Jack. Jack, in a daze, calls play-by-play on a fantasy prize fight between "Battling Herbert Hoover and Fighting Franklin Roosevelt," (which is a joy to read but must have been a tough job to perform the complicated, punning dialogue clearly and correctly.) For all that they are in love, Mary tells Jack at the end that Hicks is going to escort her home.

STATION WJZ   PROGRAM CANADA DRY GINGER ALE, INC.

    AND   DATE WEDNESDAY, OCTOBER 19, 1932.

BLUE NETWORK   TIME 9:30 10:00 P.M.

SIGNATURE JOLLY GOOD COMPANY

       1. YOU'RE TELLING ME   ORCHESTRA & FRAN FREY
       2. NOW THAT I'VE LEARNED   ETHEL SHUTTA
       3. LET'S PUT OUT THE LIGHTS   GRACE AND CHARLEY HERBERT
       4. WHAT'S THE MATTER NO ICE TODAY ETHEL SHUTTA
       5. KNOCK AT MY DOOR   GARDNER

SIGNATURE ROCKABYE MOON

    CANADA DRY GINGER ALE, INC.   WEDNESDAY, OCTOBER 19, 1932.
    SIGNATURE JOLLY GOOD COMPANY

ANNOUNCER: Ladies and gentleman, another half hour of entertainment about Canada Dry the champagne of ginger ales now available by the glass at soda fountains, as well as in bottles for the home. You'll find the new, large size bottle very economical and particularly convenient for home use. Once more, we present George Olsen, Ethel Shutta and Jack Benny, the Canada Dry Humorist, who will again perform for your enjoyment. George Olsen opens the program with "YOU'RE TELLING ME". Fran Frey singing.

HICKS: Who is it?

JACK: It's me.

HICKS: Come in.

JACK: Hello, if I'm not too personal. Remember me…. hmmm? No not the ice man… not the milk man…not the laundry man…Give up? This is Jack Benny, the <u>laugh man</u>, coming to your home with today's supply of fresh jokes…Oh, you don't want any, eh? …. Well, here's one I heard this morning that I <u>know</u> you're going to like. There were two Irishmen walking down the street, and one says to the other--

HARRY CONN: Pardon me- are <u>you</u> Mr. Benny?

JACK: Yes, I'm Jack Benny.

HARRY: That's fine. I represent the Death Valley Life Insurance Company, and I'd like to sell you one of our policies. Now let me show you the----

JACK: What's the name of your company?

HARRY: The <u>Death Valley Life</u> Insurance Company.

JACK: I see. That's a fine name for an insurance company.

HARRY: We know what we're doing. You're the one who's going to die…now let me show you the benefits derived from a---

JACK: I don't want any insurance.

HARRY: Now why don't you try one of our policies? You never can tell <u>when</u> you're going.

JACK: No- but I can tell when <u>you're</u> going...and you can bet on it.

HARRY: Now don't be foolish, Mr. Benny. You look like a smart feller. Now supposing you were walking down the street and a <u>five-ton safe</u> fell on you. Where would you be without one of our policies?

JACK: Under the safe.... But, of course, your policy would make it a pleasure. In the first place, I don't walk under safes....and in the second place----

HARRY: All right, then.... suppose you're out <u>hunting in Africa</u>, and a ferocious lion tore your limb from limb. Now wouldn't it feel nice if we came up and <u>paid you</u> before the last limb was gone? .... It's liable to <u>happen</u>.

JACK: It's liable <u>to happen to you</u> without being in Africa...Well, anyway, I never go hunting. I take long hikes.

HARRY: There are other benefits in this policy. Suppose while <u>on a hike</u>, you cross a railroad track and lose - say, <u>a couple of legs</u>?

JACK: A couple of them.... I suppose I'd walk right in to your office and collect?

HARRY: No but we <u>certainly</u> help you look for them.

JACK: That's nice. That's very sweet of your company. I furnish <u>the leg</u> and <u>you</u> furnish the <u>lantern</u>.... Now suppose I were to break my arms trying to open a Pullman window what then?

HARRY: Now let's see...let's see.... (RATTLES PAPER) Page four.... oh, here it is! .... <u>The Pullman Company</u> gets seven dollars a week till you're well.

JACK: I see. And if I fall from an aeroplane, the aeroplane gets twelve dollars a week?

HARRY: No- but we have a man meet you in mid-air <u>with the money</u>, and when you land you will be a rich man.

JACK: I see.... Suppose a fellow jumped in the river, <u>a fish</u> representing your company would meet him with the money.

HARRY: Read these testimonials...Now there's what some of our satisfied customers say about our policy.

JACK(READING): Let me see.... <u>Evergreen Cemetery</u>...That's cheerful...."It was a pleasure to pass out with one of your policies...having a nice time. Wish you were here."

HARRY: We have hundreds like that. Now who will I make this policy out do?

JACK: I'm sorry, young fellow, but I <u>have</u> some insurance.

HARRY: Yeah? <u>What company</u>?

JACK: Ex-czema Life.

HARRY: Well, if it's in good condition, we'll allow you something on a trade-in.

JACK:	I'm very busy right now - come back a little later and we'll talk it over.
HARRY:	Sure. When would you like to see me?
JACK:	Let's see- what are you doing on November 8th, 1945?
HARRY:	Well nothing. That suits me fine. Remember the date, now! <u>Bearer</u> is my name.
JACK:	Bearer….what's the first name?
HARRY:	Paul.
JACK:	PAUL BEARER….selling <u>life insurance</u>. Hmmm, that's nice…. Well, so long!
HARRY:	S'long, Mr. Benny….and if you ever <u>need a lift</u>, I'll be glad to help you out.
JACK:	I get it…Paul Bearer…and he wants <u>to give me a lift</u>…. Well, this is starting out to be a <u>very</u> pleasant evening…. Hello, folks this is Jack <u>alone again</u>. And I want to tell you that story I heard this morning. There were two Irishman walking down—
FRAN FREY:	Well, well, <u>Mr. Benny</u>, I believe.
JACK:	<u>Don't believe it</u>…. Go away…. Anyway, there two men walking---
FRAN FREY:	Just a minute what is life to a man like you without one of our cars?
JACK:	I don't want a car. So, these two fellows---
FRAN:	Now let me show you our latest model. Here is a gasoline chewer that can't be beat…. Listen to the smooth performance of this motor….(SOUND EFFECT: MOTOR KNOCK AND SPUTTER CARRY OVER FOLLOWING DIALOGUE) Now get the <u>velvet movement</u> of this clutch--- (SOUND EFFECT: SOREECHING CARRY OVER FOLLOWING DIALOGUE) And get this noiseless horn - (SOUND EFFECT: TERRIFIC HORN) JACK : You're right there's so much noise that you can't hear a thing….(LOUDER) There were two Irishman walking down the street, and one says to the other….Oh, never mind!...Play, George…Come here, Mr. Salesman.

SEGUE INTO NUMBER

2. NOW THAT I'VE LEARNED　　　　　　　　　　　　　　　　　　　ORCHESTRA & ETHEL
　　(GEORGE OLSEN MAKES HIS OWN ANNOUNCEMENT)

　　　　　　　　　　　　　　SECOND ROUTINE

JACK:	This is Jack Benny again…with a brand-new car and some more life insurance… Well, those were our <u>pest stars</u> for the evening. And speaking of pests - say, George, I think it's a shame the way that guy Hicks keeps butting in on our plays and sketches. Last Monday night, right in the middle of that love scene I did with Ethel, Hicks butts in and tells us that Canada Dry Ginger Ale is good with ice cream.

OLSEN:	Well it's a <u>fact</u>, Jack isn't it?
JACK:	Yes, George, but we don't want <u>facts</u> on this program. Keep Hicks out of here.
GEORGE:	Say, Jack, Hicks knows that you're sore at him and he's broadcasting tonight from another room. And he says he'll only speak when no one else is talking.
JACK:	That's much better. Not That I dislike Hicks, but you know everybody in his place.
ETHEL:	Say, Jack.
JACK:	Oh hello, Ethel what's new?
ETHEL:	Mary is over in the corner and she feels terrible. I tried to cheer her up, but she won't even <u>talk</u> <u>to me.</u>
JACK:	I wonder what's the trouble. Oh, Mary! …. Ethel, you call her over.
ETHEL:	No, you'd better get her, Jack. She's been looking <u>daggers at me</u>. I don't know why.
JACK:	Mary, come here!
MARY(POUTING):	Yes, Jack.
JACK:	Now what's the matter, Mary? What happened?
MARY:	Oh, It's no use. I've tried and tried and tried to do the right thing. But I might as well go back to Plainfield and forget everything.
JACK:	I don't understand, Mary.
MARY:	No <u>men never do</u>…. Well, you certainly fooled me. After what you said to me in the taxi Monday about liking me and everything….and then you go and play <u>a love scene</u> with Ethel….and a <u>hot</u> <u>one</u>!
JACK:	Oh, we were just acting…you know, just playing parts.
MARY:	Yeah…but you didn't have to get your hair all mussed up and everything…You told me in the taxi that you thought the world of me.
JACK:	Yes, and I <u>meant</u> every word of it.
MARY:	And then you play a love scene <u>with her</u> - and they weren't <u>stage kisses</u>. either….<u> Oh, Heaven help us poor working girls! </u>….
JACK:	Oh, you've been reading Laura Jean Libbey…Now be sensible, Mary. Come over are and sit down on this bench. I want to talk to you.
MARY:	All right, Jack <u>if you say so</u>.
JACK:	Mary, ever since the day you came to this Studio, I've been crazy about you.
MARY:	(SIGHS) <u>Really</u>, Jack?
JACK:	Yes, Mary….I'm wild about you and when I look into your eyes, I can see that –

HICKS:	(THAT) Canada Dry Ginger Ale is good in ice cream sodas.
MARY:	Oh, is that what my eyes show! I'm thru with you!
JACK (IN AN UNDERTONE):	It's that Hicks in the next room...I'll kill him!.......
	(WITH TENDERNESS) Mary, listen. It's all a mistake...I tell you. I'm simply crazy about you.
MARY(SIGHS):	Oh, Jack!
JACK:	Mary, when I look at your ruby lips, they remind me that –
HICKS:	(THAT) You get a nickel back on each large Canada Dry bottle.
MARY:	Oh yeah? My lips are not like a bottle.... Oh, I'm disgusted with you.
JACK:	Mary! Mary! Listen... I tell you I love you...I love you...I love you.... Are you listening, Gable? .... You're the only girl in the whole world for me. I knew that from the very first time I saw you, Mary.
MARY:	And I think You're....er....er....er....
JACK:	Swell!
Mary:	Yes, Swell.
JACK :	And when I hold your little hand in mine, it reminds me of something fragile...like a delicate piece of China...and when I gaze into your lovely eyes, I think of the blue skies above...your cheeks are like the summer roses...and when you smile, your pretty rosebud mouth reminds me that---
HICKS:	(THAT) every fountain now sells Canada Dry Ginger Ale made-to-order by the glass.
MARY:	Oh, how dare you! .... I've got a good mind to slap your face.

(SLAP FOLLOWED BY SOUND EFFECT OF BENCH OVERTURNING)

JACK (FROM THE FLOOR RISING):	Now, Mary you don't understand. Please listen to me.
HICKS:	This sparkling beverage is a delicious refreshing – thor-oly satisfying drink, and you -
JACK:	You've got to listen to me, Mary....Let me –
MARY (VERY INDIGKANT):	I never want be see you again as long as I live.... GOOD-BYE!
HICKS:	And it's a good buy at all fountains and everybody's drinking it.
JACK:	Play, George...Give me that club...What room is that guy Hicks in?

SEGUE INTO NUMBER-

3. LET'S PUT OUT THE LIGHTS   ORCHESTRA AND GRACE & CHARLEY HERBERT (OLSEN MAKES HIS OWN ANNOUNCEMENT)

(THIRD ROUTINE)

JACK: That was "Let's Put Out the Lights", sung by Grace and Charley Herbert. And now for the Big Fight. The papers have been full of it for weeks, and the boys have trained faithfully...The arena is quickly filling up...the betting is brisk...and both sides have plenty of backers. Both contestants won all their fights, and this match looks like a <u>natural</u>.... Everybody that's <u>anybody</u> is here, and the few that couldn't get here sent telegrams. Here's one from Jack Sharkey—

"THEY ARE BOTH GOOD MEN MAY THE BESY MAN WIN. WOULD LIKE TO MEET THE WINNER IN 1936"....

Here's a cable from Max Schmelling. It reads – "THE FIGHT COULD REALLY BE MINE BUT AM STILL A GERMAN CITIZEN."

Here's one from Mickey Walker – "THEY ARE BOTH TOO BIG AND SMART FOR ME."

What a fight this is going to be.... People are now going to their seats in droves.

OLSEN: Say, Ethel, what's the matter with Jack?

ETHEL: I don't know, George. He's acting very queer. He hasn't been the same since Mary slapped him. JACK: What a fight this is going to be. I'm certainly glad I'm here.

OLSEN: Ask him <u>what</u> fight.... I think the poor feller is crazy.

ETHEL: Oh, <u>you</u> ask him.

OLSEN: Er...er...say Jack, <u>what fight</u> are you talking about?

JACK: Don't you read the papers? .... Why, <u>the fight</u> between <u>Battling</u> <u>Herbert Hoover</u> and <u>Fighting</u> <u>Franklin Roosevelt</u>....Say, George, I'm surprised at a man like you not being up on the latest news. Oh well, just a small-town guy.... Now, folks, let me give you the lowdown on this fight. <u>Hoover</u> has trained faithfully <u>at Washington</u>.... skipping the rope...<u>balancing the budget</u>...and DOING <u>Some roadwork</u> in Iowa and Cleveland...<u>Roosevelt</u> has trained in <u>Albany</u>, and has done <u>his</u> roadwork in eighteen different states...They are both sharp in their boxing having sparred with Kid <u>Miner</u> and Joe <u>Farmer</u>...

We haven't seen a fight like <u>in four years</u>.... The last one was when <u>Two-Tem Coolidge</u> retired....and <u>Hoover</u> outpointed Al Smith for the <u>Championship</u>...... The semi-final is now going on between Young <u>Garner</u> of Texas and Kid <u>Curtis</u> of Nebraska...<u>Win or lose</u>, they will be forgotten after the next four years. If you don't think so, <u>name</u> four ex vice-presidents- quick! .... Oh, you can't, eh! I thought so.......

While the contestants for the Main Event are getting ready, George Olsen---- formerly <u>Secretary of Bass</u> <u>Drums in Sweden</u> - will play, "What's the matter No Ice Today, " sung by Ethel Shutta.

October 19, 1932

4. WHAT'S THE MATTER NO ICE TODAY   ORCHESTRA & ETHEL

(FOURTH ROUTINE)

JACK: All right, folks, the semi-finals are over...and it was a <u>draw</u>...And now for the <u>main</u> event of the evening... In the left corner, we have <u>Battling Hoover</u> of <u>White House, D.C.</u> –

(ROUND OF APPLAUE CHEERS)

Battling Hoover...one hundred and <u>fifty-three pounds</u>....in the pink of condition and rarin' to go...Over here <u>on the right</u>, we have <u>Fighting Roosevelt</u> of <u>His House</u>, New York---

(ROUND OF APPLAUSE CHEERS)

Roosevelt....on hundred and [alty? – ED.] eighty-two pounds and a half.... all muscles and bones....and Roose-NEVER-<u>velt</u> <u>better</u> in his life.... There are plenty of celebrities here this evening, and now they are introducing <u>Interstate Commerce</u>, one fine fellow...

The contestants are now receiving last-minute instructions from both their parties in their respective corners....Over in Herbert's corner is <u>Ogden Mills</u>...Over in Franklin's corner is <u>Big Jim Farley</u>...The referee is <u>John Q. Public</u>....and he is looking over the bandages and inspecting the gloves as he is in <u>favor of</u> <u>disarmament</u>.....Everything is okay now, and the Peace Conference...I mean <u>the fight</u>...is about to start. (GONG)

They both meet in the center of the ring. <u>Hoover</u> steps in with a light <u>Rhode Island</u>.....And <u>Roosevelt</u> counters with a hard <u>Smash-achusetts</u> to the Jaw...<u>Herbert</u> comes back and flings a <u>Michigan</u> at Franklin...who blocks with <u>Oregon</u>...They are now both throwing <u>Iowas</u> at each other...and so far it is a <u>pretty</u> EVEN FIGHT.... There they go, dancing around, taking their time....but looking for an opening. Ah! <u>Franklin</u> now comes in and hooks a light <u>Delaware</u> to the head.... <u>Herb</u> now counters with a <u>Nebraska</u>....and <u>Frank</u> drops one knee to the Kansas....I mean, <u>canvas</u>.

SMALL CROWD (BALDWIN, THOMAS, HICKS, ETC.): Oooooh! …. Get up, Frankie...get up.

JACK: Frankie <u>Texas</u> time...and is up again from the <u>Floor-ida</u>.....you can't stick me!..... brushing off his <u>Pants-sylvania</u>.....

(GONG)

And the bell sends them both to their corners, looking stronger than ever.

(ROUND OF APPLAUSE AND CHEERS)

They are now getting rubbed down….and <u>Mills</u> just carried the <u>water budget to</u> hoover….to <u>Cool-idge</u> him off…. <u>Roosevelt</u>, in his corner, recognizes me as he knows my brother Al... get it, <u>Al Benny</u>? …. Oh boy, am I thinking tonight! ….Take it, Hicks.

HICKS:	Thanks, Jack.......This fight does not come to you thru the courtesy of Canada Dry Ginger Ale, made-to-order by the glass. It is Jack Benny's own idea and I think---

(GONG RING)

JACK:	<u>Second round</u>...Ah, there they go again...to the center of the ring...<u>what</u> fighters!...they seem to be stalling a little now.... dancing around and nothing happening. The Referee, <u>John Q. Public</u> is yelling for action------<u>Herbie</u> just tried a hard right, but couldn't <u>Connect-icut</u>....uh-uh, Jackie- describe the fight as you see it....<u>Frankie</u> hits him with one- two- three-four-five-six-seven-eight-nine-<u>Ten-nessee</u>....but <u>Herb</u> looks great in his <u>New Jersey</u>....and they <u>Mish-again</u> in the center of the ring...It is a <u>tariff-ic</u> fight get it?....<u>Herb</u> now hits Frank <u>in-Diana</u>....<u>Frankie</u> counters and hits <u>him-in-Nesota</u> right next to <u>Dakota</u>....and it's pretty even......

(CROWD CHEERS)

The crowd is now cheering.... which gives me a chance to turn the page of this script.... Oh-oh, what's up? ....<u> Frankie</u> lunges out with a hard right, but <u>Missis-sip-pi</u>....and catches a <u>beaut</u>.... but he can take it! (MORE CHEERS)

What a <u>Man-tana</u>!....But <u>Herb</u> is in better shape than ever, as no one thought he <u>Kentucky</u> punch like that....I play no favorites!.....They both laugh as they <u>Merrily-land</u> on each other...that's the best I can do, with that one, <u>Baltimore</u>......

As I run out of jokes, I find the fight is coming to a close, and --- (GONG) as the gong rings...

(CROWD CHEERS AND APPLAUDS)

The crowd goes wild and climbs into the ring, looking for Prosperity around both corners. What a fight.... what an even match! Take it, Hicks.

HICKS:	This fight will be continued on November 8th...and may the best man win! Watch this program for the official results with a nickel back on each large Canada Dry bottle.
JACK:	And now George Olsen whose favorite president is <u>Andrew Jackson</u> because he's on the twenty-dollar bill will play, "KNOCK AT MY DOOR", sung by Hotcha Gardner.

5. KNOCK AT MY DOOR   ORCHESTRA & GARDNER

JACK:	That was the last number of the fiftieth program on the 19th of October. And on next Monday night we are going to bring to you—
MARY:	Jack I'm sorry I slapped your face. I found out it was Hicks...You'll forgive me won't you, Jack?
JACK:	Yes, Mary.

MARY:	All right good-night, Jack...Come on, Hicksie.
JACK:	Mary, why are you going home with Hicks?
MARY:	Well, he just got two nickels back on the Canada Dry bottles and that's the carfare.... Good-night, Jack.
JACK:	Well, everything happens to me...Guess I'll go home now.
FRAN (HEAVY VOICE):	Are you thru, Mr. Benny?
JACK:	Yes.
FRAN:	Well, I represent the Water Bottom Realty Company......
JACK:	No-no.
FRAN:	And I'd like to sell you a couple of lots. Now if you'll just let me drive you over---
JACK:	No, no.
FRAN:	Just feel the dirt on these lots - now you're under no obligations whatsoever how many do you want, Mr. Benny?
JACK & FRAN:	(AD LIB UNTIL FADE OUT)
ANNOUNCER:	Remember, you can enjoy Canada Dry the champagne of ginger ales any- where, anytime, for it is now available two ways either made-to-order by the glass at soda fountains or in bottles, as always, for your home. The new big bottle is particularly economical and convenient. Remember, too, that with the exception of a few localities, where freight rates do not permit, you pay for the contents only, that is, twenty cents for the big five-glass bottle, or twenty-five cents for two regular twelve-ounce bottles. In addition, you make a small deposit on each bottle, but this deposit is refunded when the bottle is returned. Next Monday night at this same time Jack Benny, Ethel Shutta and George Olsen will again entertain you. This is the National Broadcasting Company.

October 24, 1932

Jack is running for dog catcher. Mary admits that she is romantically inclined towards Jack and was making him jealous by flirting with Hotcha Gardner. The episode's skit is a courtroom drama, "Who killed Mr. X," a generic theme they will return to in the future, although they will remake it to feature Captain O'Benny and incompetent policemen instead of lawyers. Mary asks is it true that Jack is heading to New Orleans to broadcast for Canada Dry, and Mary asks if she can come along - but they don't say why they are leaving. NBC would not allow Canada Dry to announce the change of program network and broadcast nights and hours, so radio listeners might have been confused in the coming weeks.

STATION WJZ   PROGRAM CANADA DRY GINGER ALE, INC.

AND   DATE MONDAY , OCTOBER 24, 1932.

BLUE NETWORK   TIME 9:30 10:00 P.M.

SIGNATURE JOLLY GOOD COMPANY   ORCHESTRA, ETHEL
           SHUTTA & FRAN FREY

    1. AINTCHA KINDA SORRY NOW   ORCHESTRA & FRAN FREY
    2. IS I IN LOVE, I IS   ORCHESTRA & ETHEL SHUTTA
    3. PLAY, FIDDLE, PLAY   ORCHESTRA & DAVE MARSHALL
    4. ANGEL CAKE LADY & GINGERBREAD MAN   ORCHESTRA & ETHEL SHUTTA
    5. SCAT SONG   HESTRA & HOTCHA GARDNER

SIGNATURE ROCKABYE MOON

ANNOUNCER: Ladies and gentleman, another half hour of entertainment about Canada Dry the champagne of Ginger ales now available by the glass at soda fountains as well as in bottles for the home. You'll find the new, large size bottle very economical and particularly convenient for home use. Once more we present George Olsen, Ethel Shutta and Jack Benny, the Canada Dry Humorist, who will perform for your enjoyment. George Olsen opens the program with "AIN'T YOU KINDA SORRY NOW?" Fran Frey singing.

HICKS: As chairman of this political rally, I now wish to introduce to you that representative of humanity.... a patriot...a social uplifter.... <u>for</u> the people...<u>for</u> the people....and I might even say, <u>for</u> the people.... the honorable Jack Benny.

(LOUD APPLAUSE AND CHEERS)

JACK: Fellow citizens......taxpayers......brother voters.... sisters...uncles...and <u>one aunt</u> in Poughkeepsie...<u>and</u> ladies and gentleman. As you all know, I am running for the dignified office of <u>Dog Catcher</u> in this municipality......

(MORE APPLAUSE AND CHEERS)

I thank you.... <u>To begin with</u>, it is the platform of my party to abolish waste....er, that is - to eliminate what we call er....er......Well, by that I mean...er, as Coolidge once said, "Umph!"....

(MORE APPLAUSE)

This coming election reminds me of....as Thomas Jefferson once said....to his valet " Hawkins! my white trousers the weather is warmer today." <u>And</u>, ladies and gentlemen, the same situation confronts us here and now. You have all heard my opponent over the networks call me " a liar a crook and a lowlife!"

(TERRIFIC APPLAUSE)

Not here, boys.... <u>Nobody</u> can call me a lowlife and get away with it!... Now fellow citizens, what is my platform? What am I going to do?

[Ed. penciled in] JEWISH FELLER: Woof! Woof! [Ed. edited out, "FOUR VOICES"]

JACK:	You said it! .... But I'm not guessing, folks. I've spoken to the principal dogs in this city, and what they want is <u>honest employment</u>!

(ONLY SLIGHT APPLAUSE)

	Why, only yesterday one of our better class <u>canines</u> a rich uncle of Rin-Tin-Tin, by the name of <u>Rin-Gold-Gold</u>....told me of a trip he recently made thru the <u>Panama Kennel</u>.....where he studied dog conditions in Central America, and he tells me that there is a grave possibility of their going <u>off the bone standard</u> ....
HICKS:	And we make no <u>bones</u> about the fact that you get a nickel back on each large Canada Dry bottle.
JACK:	That is quite true.... but do you realize what <u>going off the bone standard</u> means? It means that the bone will be reduced to three and a-half dog biscuits.... Now what can be done about this? Nothing! ...And you can depend on us to do it.

(APPLAUSE)

JACK :	I thank you...(ASIDE) Stop chewing the leg of my pants....Now take the bonus question, for example.....I am not only in favor of giving the dogs their bone-us.....but meat-us on that bone-us.....so they can eat-us....so help-us.......Now have you given a thought to Helen Kane with her Boop-poop-a-Poo-dle?......Why should the poodle ride in a limousine while a ki-yoodle has to walk?....How about that, Olsen?
OLSEN(ANGRILY):	Aw, shut up--- [ED.: changed from "I don't know!"]
JACK:	It is the fault of the present administration, of which my opponent is the head. But here he is tonight and in fairness to him may I now introduce the present Dog Catcher....the strictly dishonorable J. Barkingham Mutt.......

(SLIGHT APPLAUSE A FEW MINGLED BOOS)

BENNY BAKER:	(CLEARS HIS THROAT) Hmm....you have just heard some lies from my----
JACK:	Now, if I am elected, I will personally see that each Mexican Hairless Dog has a good toupee and one scalp treatment a week, and --
BAKER:	(CLEARS THROAT) Hmmm...you have been listening to a lot of bunk on the part of my suave, oily, glib opponent---
JACK:	And furthermore, I will see that each German Dachs-hund receives an extra pair of legs so that he won't sag in the middle.
BAKER:	I want to go on record as saying that---
JACK:	And I will also see that every Pa-meranian gets a Ma-meranian....and that each setter will be given a seat to set on.... I THANK YOU......(TERRIFIC APPLAUSE - CHEERS) And now you will hear from Mr. Mutt.
BENNY BAKER:	Ladies and gentlemen.... (CLEARS THROAT) Hmmm...I advocate that---
JACK:	Play, George.

SEGUE INTO NUMBER –

2. IS I IN LOVE, I IS....   ORCHESTRA & ETHEL
              SHUTTA

BENNY BAKER: (CONTINUES UNDER MUSIC) I've got about as much chance in this election as a Chinaman has of becoming Mayor of Tokyo.

JACK: Come here, Mutt......(AD LIB)—

SECOND ROUTINE

JACK: Hello, this is Jack Benny again the Dog Catcher....Mary! .... Oh Mary!

MARY: Yes, Jack.

JACK: Come here I want to talk to you a minute.... Now Mary, I want to tell you something for your own good. Promise not to be sensitive about it.

MARY: I won't --what is it, Jack?

JACK: Well, Mary as secretary to Jack Benny, you haven't been doing so lately. I don't know whether you're getting lazy or what it is.... But I notice that the mail has been piling up.

MARY: I don't see how two postcards can pile up.

JACK: Let me talk, Mary.... And this week's phone bill shows a hundred and ten calls to Hotcha Gardner... How do you explain that?

MARY: Well, the phone calls to Hotcha were just to call him up and tell him I don't want to see him anymore.

JACK: That's fine a hundred and ten calls in one week just to tell him you don't want to see him.

MARY: When I don't like anybody, I believe in calling them up and telling them so.

JACK: You certainly do.... I'm Glad you don't hate anybody in California....Mary, you've got to be a little more careful.

MARY: All right, Jack - Oh Jack, I heard you say you were going to New Orleans in a few days to broadcast the Canada Dry program. Is that true?

JACK: Yes- that'll give you plenty of time with Hotcha here.

MARY: Oh, Hotcha huh.... I'd rather go to New Orleans with you.

JACK: Which do you like better Hotcha or New Orleans?

MARY: I think New Orleans is just swell.... Anyway, Jack, I was gust going out with Hotcha to make you jealous, Wasn't I, Hotcha?

JACK: All right, Mary you can go to New Orleans with us.

MARY: Oh thanks, Jack....Gee, that's where Tulane University is located isn't it?

JACK: Yes Mary – why?

MARY: Well, a friend of mine goes there his name is Frank, and he's the swellest feller you ever met --

JACK: And now George Olsen and his gang of swellest fellers will play, "Play, Fiddle, Play", sung by Dave Marshall.

2. PLAY, FIDDLE, PLAY   ORCHESTRA & MARSHALL

(AS MUSIC STARTS, THEY ARE STILL TALKING---

JACK: Now listen, Mary if you're going to start around with anyone in New Orleans, you'd better stay here.... (AD LIB AS THEY WALK AWAY FROM MIKE)

    (THIRD ROUTINE)

OPEN WITH SOUND EFFECTS: Five pistol shots –

ETHEL: (LETS OUT A TERRIFIC, PIERCING SCREAM)

FRAN: (GIVES ONE OF HIS GOOFY LAUGHS) (SLIGHT PAUSE) Nobody is to leave this studio until dismissed!

JACK: Don't get excited, folks. That was just our way of announcing our big murder mystery. A crime was committed on the Rue de Lancey...at eight o'clock last night. The headless victim, Mr. X, was found lying on the pavement, with his head nearby singing - " I AIN'T GOT NOBODY"......Oh, you heard that, eh? Well, this is our mystery.......

Anyway, there were no witnesses, and the only clues discovered so far are a felt hat, which was found in Kansas City last week.......two Russians running down the street in Moscow....and an old banjo in a pawnshop window in Seattle, Washington...... The crime is apparently a recent one as the smoke has not yet cleared away....in Pittsburgh.... Now here is the mystery. Two bullets were taken from this man's right shoulder but no shots were heard. Now the question is who stabbed that man with those two bullets - or did he hang himself? If so, who gave him the poison? ..... Did he jump in the river? If so, what happened to the river? .... He could not have been shot by a taxi as he was found lying in the street...... Was its suicide? No the man was very ill and had lost his last cent in the stock market......so it could not have been suicide.... Was it premeditated murder? Well, everybody hated him, and there were members of the underworld looking for him for muscling in on their territory.... So, you see the murder could not have been planned.......And so our mystery begins. Who killed Mr. X?...... Several suspects have been brought in by detectives, and the trial will commence immediately after the next number, which will be played by Coroner Olsen....and sung by the Ninth Guest in the Thirteenth Chair.......What a mystery!

ETHEL:	Jack, what are we going to do for actors?
JACK:	Hmmmm....another mystery.

SEGUE INTO THE NUMBER-

4. ANGEL CAKE LADY AND THE GINGERBREAD MAN   ETHEL & ORCHESTRA (GEORGE OLSEN MAKES HIS OWN ANNOUNCEMENT)

(FOURTH ROUTINE)

(CROWD MUMBLES

DAVE MARSHALL (CLERK):   (SOUND EFFECT: RAPS GAVEL)

Everybody rise. Here comes the judge!

(SOUND EFFECT: PEOPLE RAISING SEATS SHUFFLING AROUND CROWD MUMBLES THREE MORE GAVEL RAPS)

Order in the Court!

MARY: I'll have a Canada Dry Ginger Ale mage-to-order, by the glass.

JACK: Mary, we heard that.

(SOUND EFFECT: RAPS GAVEL)

MARSHALL: Quiet!

JUDGE OLSEN: We will proceed with the case of Mr. X....Officer Dugan, bring in Four-Gun Blake.

HOTCHA GARDNER (as Dugan):   Six-Gun Blake.

OLSEN: We're not going to argue over a couple of guns. Bring in the prisoner

(FOOTSTEPS SHUFFLING IN)

FRAN (as tough guy): Hurry up, youse guys. I gotta guy on de spot and I don't wanna keep him waitin.

JACK: That's service!

MARSHALL (MUMBLES THRU):   Do you swear to tell truth...the truth...the whole truth...so help you?
     FRAN: So, help you!

JACK: So, help all of us.

OLSEN: Prosecutor, examine the prisoner.

JACK: Where were you on the night of October 23d at eight o'clock?

BLAKE(FRAN): Well, I ran into a guy I didn't like - chased him tree blocks and bumped him off.

JACK: Oh, you won't talk, eh?

FRAN: I told you I killed de guy.

JACK: Oh, you did. Well, you've also killed this mystery.... We're not supposed to find out the murderer until later.... Anyway how did you know it was eight o'clock?

FRAN: I heard de tree little chimes so I added <u>five</u> - and it made eight.

JACK: Do you expect the Court to believe that?

FRAN: Not if you want a mystery, I don't.... But I croaked de guy - and it's the <u>twelfth one</u> this month. JACK: Judge, I can't do a thing with this man.

OLSEN: Throw him out - bring in the next <u>suspect</u>.

(APPROACHING FOOTSTEPS)

MARSHALL: Do you swear to tell the truth...the truth...the whole truth so help you?

BENNY BAKER: Mother taught me never to swear.

JACK: Sit down what's your name?

BAKER: Two Popgun Clarence...but they call me <u>the Rat</u>.

JACK: The Rat?

BAKER: Yes, and the funny part of it is I don't like cheese a bit. (LAUGHES)

JACK: What's your occupation?

BAKER: I whip cream on wedding cakes.

JACK: Well, you must be all tired out...we won't keep you long - now tell the court where <u>were</u> you on the night of October 23d at eight o'clock?

BAKER: Now let me see after lunch we went to a matinee then we stopped in at the Ritz for tea.... then it was a quarter of eight. I Believe when I left my friends and ran into an old enemy of mine. So, I just <u>ups</u> to him and <u>plugs</u> him.

JACK: Look at this photograph. Is <u>this</u> the man?

BAKER: Yes, that's him. But what a <u>terrible</u> picture.

JACK: You can go now.

BAKER: Oh, you.re going to let me get away <u>with murder</u>, eh? .... Well, that's the last time I'll ever kill anyone in <u>this</u> neighborhood.

OLSEN: Dugan, bring that young lady up on the stand.

MARSHALL: Do you swear to tell—

ETHEL (VERY BREEZILY): You said it, Big Boy.

JACK: What's your name?

ETHEL:	<u>Minnie Skee</u>----I'm an actress.... (HUMS FEW BARS OF "HARLEM MOON")
JACK:	Just answer the questions don't demonstrate.... Tell the Court where were you on the night of October 23d at eight o'clock?
ETHEL:	Up at the Calico Club and <u>what</u> a time!......<u>Remember, Judge-ey</u>?
JACK:	Ha, ha! Did you get that, jury?
BOYS IN ORCHESTRA:	<u>We get it</u>.
JACK:	Now Minnie, were you acquainted <u>with Mr. X</u>?
ETHEL:	Was I? .... We danced together until two minutes of eight and <u>what</u> a struggle.
JACK:	Wait a minute - show the jury how he held you while dancing.
ETHEL:	Like this - now put your left arm up there and your right arm here....
JACK:	Put your head on my shoulder.... Play, George!

(ORCHESTRA PLAYS EIGHT BARS OF "PARADISE" –

JACK HUMS "DUM DEE-DA-DA DA"

ETHEL (HUMS):	Then you'll understand....
JACK(SINGS):	Dum-da-dee-<u>CANADA DRY</u>. Sold at the fountain – Nickel back on the large bottle-
HICKS:	Stop! .... And between dances, you will find Canada Dry Ginger Ale a nice, cool, and refreshing drink.
JACK:	Arrest Hicks for contempt of Court! .... (TO ETHEL) Sorry, Minnie tell us what happened after that?
OLSEN:	Dismiss this witness for lack of evidence.
JACK:	No answer one more question, Minnie - do you know who committed this crime?
ETHEL:	Yes- the <u>Judge</u>! (CROWD MURMURS AND BUZZES WITH EXCITEMENT)
JACK:	Dugan, bring the Judge up to the witness stand.
OLSEN:	Wait a minute you can't do that.... <u>I'm the Judge</u>!
JACK:	Yeah! Well, get in that chair.... Now where were you on the night of October 23d at eight o'clock?
OLSEN:	(VERY SLOWLY AND DELIBERATELY) Bryant nine-eight-six-four.
JACK:	That was changed to Circle eight- three-four-two.... Now Judge Olsen, did you or <u>did you not</u> commit this crime?

OLSEN: Yes, I did it. He was dancing with Minnie <u>and I killed him</u>.... But attorney, I had a good reason. Please oh please don't send me away...

JACK: Oh, you can't take it eh? .... Gentlemen of the jury, you've all heard the evidence. Adjourn to the next room place the guilt where it belongs and bring in an honest verdict.... Go! ... (ASIDE) Here are the cards. Deal me in. (SUFFLING OF FEET AND MURMURING OF VOICES)

<u>What</u> a mystery! First, we were looking for the guy who committed this crime, and now, we're looking for the guy who didn't....

MARY: Attorney oh, Mr. Attorney.

JACK (VERY DIGNIFIED): What is it, Miss Livingston?

MARY: I shot a man last night at eight o'clock and nobody is paying <u>any</u> attention to me.

JACK: Oh yeah? Well, where were you on the night of October 23rd at eight o'clock?

BOTH (TOGETHER): With Hotcha Gardner.

JACK: Was Hotcha the man you killed?

MARY: No, but I aimed at him.

JACK: Well, you ought to get twenty years for missing.

(SHUFFLING OF FEET AND MUMBLING OF VOICES)

HICKS: The jury is ready to give their verdict, Your Honor.

JACK: And what is your verdict?

HICKS (SLOWLY): <u>We all agree that</u>—

ETHEL: (gives another terrific scream)

FRAN: (DOES ANOTHER GOOFY LAUGH)

JACK: And now, ladies and gentlemen, on Wednesday night we will continue this thrilling mystery drama, <u>Who killed Cock Robin</u>? …. <u>What was the motive</u> behind this unspeakable crime? …. Now be sure to tune in on Wednesday night. Meanwhile if <u>you</u> find out anything, let <u>us</u> know …. Who do you think <u>did not</u> do it...? Time alone will tell!

SEGUE INTO NUMBER-

5. SOAT SONG   ORCHESTRA & GARDNER

(OLSEN MAKES HIS OWN ANNOUNCEMENT)

JACK: That was the last number on the fifty-first program on the 24th of October. And don't forget, folks, that on –

FRAN: (GIVES ANOTHER GOOFTY LAUGH)

JACK(WEIRDLY): <u>Mr. X</u>... <u>who is he?</u> …. <u>What is he</u>? …. Who cares? …. Are you waiting for me, Mary?

MARY: Yes, I'm kinda scared tonight, Jack.

JACK: Well, that's something. Come on, Mary…Good-night, folks.

ANNOUNCER: The next time you stop at a soda fountain for a refreshing drink, ask for a glass of Canada Dry, the champagne of ginger ales- it will be made-to-order for you and costs only five cents for a regular glass or ten cents for an extra-large glass. Remember too, that with the exception of a few localities where freight charges do not permit, you can take back your Canada Dry bottles to the dealer and get a cash refund. So that now when you Buy Canada Dry you pay for the contents only. Next Wednesday night at this same time, Jack Benny, Ethel Shutta and George Olsen will again entertain you. This is the National Broadcasting Company.

October 26, 1932

Jack reads news headlines and celebrity gossip. A mid-show commercial mentions cannibals drinking Canada Dry. Jack and Ethel sing a duet called "Meanest Man in Town" rather than doing a second comic dialogue. They perform a parody of 19th century melodramas with a skit titled "Why Girls Leave Home," or "Bertha the Sewing Machine Girl," in which Mary for the first time plays the leading role. She portrays the girl who must journey to New York to work to get the mortgage money to save her elderly father from eviction. She returns wealthy but they agree it doesn't matter if she was a "good girl" or not. Jack and Mary say their farewells to George, Ethel and the orchestra members. They can only inform their radio listeners to "please refer to your local newspaper" to find the show's future episodes on new stations, new evenings and new times.

PROGRAM WJZ   PROGRAM CANADA DRY GINGER ALE, INC.

        AND   DATE WEDNESDAY, OCTOBER 26, 1932.

BLUE NETWORK   TIME 9:30 10:00 P.M.

SIGNATURE JOLLY GOOD COMPANY   ORCHESTRA, ETHEL SHUTTA &
                                                                                               FRAN FREY

1. MISS LIZA JANE   FRAN FREY & GARDNER

2. GERMAN BAND   ETHEL SHUTTA

3. THAT'S HOW WE MAKE MUSIC   ORCHESTRA

4. WHO   TRIO

5. HOW DEEP IS THE OCEAN   ETHEL SHUTTA

SIGNATURE ROCKABYE MOON   ORCHESTRA

CANADA DRY GINGER ALE, INC. WEDNESDAY, OCTOBER 26, 1932.

SIGNATURE JOLLY GOOD COMPANY

ANNOUNCER: Ladies and gentleman, another half hour of entertainment about Canada Dry the champagne of Ginger-ales now available by the glass at soda fountains, as well as in bottles for the home. You'll find the new, large size bottle very economical and particularly convenient for home use. Once more, we present George Olsen, Ethel Shutta and Jack Benny, the Canada Dry Humorist, who will again perform for your enjoyment. George Olsen opens the program with "Miss Liza Jane." Fran Frey and Hotcha Gardner singing.

1. MISS LIZA JANE   FRAN FREY, HOTCHA GARDNER & ORCHESTRA

HICKS: And now – Jack Benny

JACK: Hello, folks, this is Jack O.O. McIntyre Benny......the Earth Galloper, coming to you again thru the courtesy of the Morning Chronic in-Di-gest.... the paper with all the news that's fit to cartoon.......Today we bring you all the late dispatches from around the world brought to us by the Tailors Press...airmail...cable...and Just squealers.... Here they are: - First, prosperity notes.

Workhouse......Pa... A hundred and ten men back to work...some for 30 days...some for 60 days...and one guy for six months....

Bronx, New York...Several men given labor in Hungarian Restaurant...gehochkta labor...Oh well, that's local.

Scranton, Pa....Fifty crooners go back to work....in coal mine...

(SINGS) When the black of the coal
Moots the blue of their eye ---

(WHISTLES)

Twin Beds, New Jersey....Girl triplets born here this morning. They cry in perfect harmony...and are given radio contract.

Nowork, New Jersey....Arthur Barry - collector of rare jewels...is presented with a pair of bracelets....and will return to his country estate in Auburn...He tank he go home now....

	Now Haven, Conn....Famous orchestra leader asks Yale captain for forward pass....thinking it is a complimentary ticket, and is kicked out...How about it, George?
OLSEN:	I bought my tickets.
JACK:	Well, it sounded like you, George...... Washington, D.C... It is said that if Roosevelt is elected, he will be the fifth President with the letter "V" in his name.... Roosevelt......Hoover ... Cleveland....Vilson....and Vashington....it's a good thing Veeler and Voolsey aren't running.... New York City....Ethel Shutta, pretty radio star, receives pearl necklace FROM ADMIRER....Sixth Avenue, New York....Swedish maestro seen in five-and-ten cents store. Borneo - October 24th. Presidential candidate promises cannibals a missionary in every pot. Borneo - October 25th....Natives get impatient and eat President......
HICKS:	Even in Borneo - the cannibals are wild...about Canada Dry Ginger Ale, made--to--order by the glass.
JACK:	And now for our late sporting events...Football news--- Ann Arbor, Michigan....Man, eighty--three, kicks off...leaving wife and three children... Moscow, Russia...Football season gets under way here. Moscow Techk beats the U. of You--chk by four touchk-downs...... Late stock market bulletin.... There seems to be a steady rise in the Goldbergs. Fifth Avenue, New York...George Olsen and his orchestra will play, "German Band", sung by Ethel Shutta.

2. GERMAN BAND   ORCHESTRA & ETHEL

(SECOND ROUTINE)

(JACK AND ETHEL AD LIB INTRODUCTION TO THEIR NUMBER, "MEANEST MAN IN TOWN".

At conclusion of number –

HICKS:	They laughed when Jack Benny started to sing....little did they know they were right.... And if you have a voice as bad or worse than Mr. Benny's, take a glass of Canada Dry Ginger Ale, made-to-order at the fountain. And now George Olsen will make amends by playing, "That's How We Make Music".
	Okay, George.

3. THAT'S HOW WE MAKE MUSIC   ORCHESTRA & ETHEL

(THIRD ROUTINE)

JACK:	Ah you lucky listeners - just wait till you hear this. Tonight, we have procured a real Broadway play for you. We happened to be looking over some old papers while cleaning out the closet and found the manuscript of this masterpiece which is enti-

tled - " Why Girls Leave Home" - that famous old play with a tear - a laugh - a heart throb....and a few hisses.... It was a great success in its day - having had such runs as: one consecutive night in Perth Amboy....another night in Asbury Park...and then direct to the storehouse.... where it ran over a year. It could have run another year – but the storage charges were terrific....

Now the members of the original company have been dead for over thirty-five years, so we have our own all-star cast this evening - which is as good as the cast in "Grand Hotel".... we think.... Of course, what you think - is entirely up to you. And there will be no money refunded after the performance.

We have rehearsed faithfully for five minutes, and will present it to you immediately - without the customary break-in out of town. Here are some of the original criticisms when the play had its premiere in 1890 at the Old Roxy-feller Theatre....

WALTER WIMCHELL - "Why Girls Leave Home" is as fine a play as I have ever looked over the transom at.... Ankle over and see it.

ED SULLIVAN - if you are unable to sleep at night, see "Why Girls Leave Home" - and you will have no further trouble.

LOUIS SOBOL - "Why Girls Leave Home" should never have left home

MAYOR MCKEE - I saw the show and am convinced that I closed the wrong theatres.......

And now, ladies and gentlemen, we are reviving this play tonight for your pleasure.... Remember the title - "Why Girls Leave Home"....and if any of you girls are packing your grips to leave the old homestead tonight, kindly wait until our little offering is over - and you may change your minds....

Meanwhile, George Olsen - who is one of the reasons - will play. "WHO", sung by the trio. Immediately after the number, the play goes on.

SEGUE INTO NUMBER –

JACK(CONTINUES): Get your popcorn - candy - and chewing gum here...Get your ice-cold Canada Dry Ginger Ale, made-to-order by the glass....

FRAN: Right this way, madame, Seats one and three on the aisle....

4. "WHO"   ORCHESTRA & TRIO

(FOURTH ROUTINE)

HICKS: And now for our dramatic offering, "Why Girls Leave Home".... Curtain, music, please.

(ORCHESTRA PLAYS OPENING BARS OF "HOME. SWEET HOME")

(SOUND EFFECT: SEWING MACHINE HUM)

JACK:	(WHISPERS) That was a sewing machine, folks.
	(SOUND EFFECT: SEWING MACHINE AGAIN)
MARY:	Oh, I'm getting sick and tired of this hard work - All I do is work and toil and slave.... This sewing machine is driving me mad!
	(SOUND EFFECT: SEWING MACHINE) (LOUD KNOCK AT DOOR)
MARY:	Who is it?
OLSEN:	(FROM OUTSIDE) It's the landlord.
MARY:	(SIGHS) Come in!
	(SOUND EFFECT: WIND - DOOR SLAM)
OLSEN:	I'm sorry, Miss Pickens - but I came to tell you that I must foreclose the mortgage!
MARY:	Oh, can't you wait a while longer? Surely, you're not going to drive us out into the cold, cold night...What a night!
	(SOUND EFFECT: WIND)
OLSEN:	I've waited long enough. I must have the money in ten minutes or else, I foreclose.
JACK:	(WHISPERS) It looks like we close at four.
OLSEN:	Remember! –ten minutes…good-bye.
	(SOUND EFFECT: WIND AND DOOR SLAM)
MARY:	Oh, what shall I do? what shall I do.... Poor old father. He will soon be homeless... Oh....
	(SOUND EFFECT: SEWING MACHING

KNOCK AT DOOR

WIND WHISTLES DOOR SLAM)

MARY:	Hello, Daddy.
JACK:	Hello, Babe....Pardon me, I'm the father...What are you crying about, my child?
MARY:	Oh, I'm so tired of it all. I work hard all day - cooking and scrubbing and washing... and so on... and so on...
JACK:	So on what?
MARY:	Sew on buttons...
JACK:	Mary, don't button in... with those kinds of jokes.
MARY:	I suppose you know that the real estate man was here today.
JACK:	Did you tell him we don't want any?

MARY:	He said he'd give us ten minutes to pay up or get out.
JACK:	That means we'll lose the old homestead...with the babbling brook...the old elm tree...and the old gray mare...Of course you know the old dump should have been burned down years age...
MARY:	Yes, father.
JACK:	Ah, Bertha! what are we to do?
MARY:	Nellie's the name.
JACK:	That's right Nellie....I must have been thinking of last night...Nellie, we must do something about raising the money. Not that I care about the old homestead, but it's a good excuse to dig up the dough.
MARY:	Father, why can't I leave home? Let me go to the city and make good.
JACK (DIALECT):	To the city...with all those vile temptations!
MARY:	Yes, father. After all, I'm twenty-one. You know that.
JACK:	I've known that for ten years...No, daughter, I can't let you go alone to the city.... What time are you leaving?
MARY:	Right away, Dad. I'll run upstairs and pack now.
JACK:	All right - meanwhile, I'll tune in some lively music on the radio- and forget my troubles.

(SOUND EFFECT: A LITTLE RADIO STATIC—

WHEN PICK UP LIVELY ORCHESTRA AS IF COMING THRU RADIO.

MUSIC CONTINUES VERY PIANISSIMO UNDER FOLLOWING DIALOGUE:-)

MARY:	Oh Dad, I forgot. I can't go away. I 've only ninety-five cents, and the fare to New York is a dollar.... Oh, where can I get a nickel?

HICKS (VOICE COMING FROM RADIO): You get a nickel back on each large Canada Dry bottle.

JACK (DRAMATICALLY): Good! I'm glad we saved the bottle.

(ROUND OF APPLAUSE)

MARY (QUICKLY):	Father, I must hurry now. I'll work hard and write you from New York— Hollywood London and Paris.
JACK:	Send me some postcards from Paris....good-bye, dear...don't drop the carfare.
MARY:	Good-bye, father dear.

(SOUND EFFECT: WIND AND DOOR SLAM)

JACK (WITH FEELING): Heaven keep her away from saxophone players!

(SOUND EFFORT: LOUD KNOCK AT DOOR)

JACK: Come in! (SOUND EFFECT: WIND AND DOOR SLAM)

OLSEN: Well, how about the money?

JACK: What money?

OLSEN: The money for the mortgage...Are you ready to pay it off?

JACK: How much is it?

OLSEN: Fifteen hundred dollars.

JACK: I'm a little bit short.

OLSEN: How Much?

JACK: Fifteen hundred dollars.

OLSEN: Oh, you won't pay it, eh?... All right, sheriff take the furniture out of here!

SHERIFF (BOB RICE): Come on, boys, Grab the piano.

JACK: Wait a minute, Sheriff you dropped your moustache...If you boys will wait a little while, the finance Company will help you......

OLSEN: Nothing is going to help you...Come on, men take that Morris chair.

JACK: Stop!

(ORCHESTRA PICKS UP "HEARTS AND FLOWERS" VERY PIANISSIMO)

Now wait a minute, Blake., Listen to me---

(SOUTHERN DIALECT)

You kin take mah shoes-
You kin take mah clo's—
You Kin take mah dese and dem and dose—
But if you harm one hair of that old Morris Chair—
As, sure as mah name's Ebenezer Pickens, I'm a-goin' tuh kill you

(MUSIC STOPS - TERRIFID APPLAUSE AND CHEERS)

(SOUND EFFECT: HORSE'S HOOVES START HERE IN DISTANCE

ORCHESTRA GOES INTO "HURRY" MUSIC)

OLSEN: Don't listen to him, men, Sheriff, do your duty! Take possession of this house and throw him out!

JACK: Ah, Mistah Blake...please have mercy on me. I'm an old man and only have a few more years to live...Let me die in this old home of mine where I've spent so many happy hours....

OLSEN: You've been telling me that for four years.

JACK: Well, I'm trying the Five-Year Plan don't Russia me away from here

(SOUND EFFECTS MAN STOP HORSE'S HOOFS HERE –

MUSIC CONTINUES TO PLAY "HURRY" THEME)

OLSEN: Put him out, Sheriff...and use force if necessary...All right, come on, fellers. Hurry up.

(SOUND EFFECT: DOOR OPENS AND SLAMS)

MARY: Stop!

(HURRY MUSIC STOPS)

Put these things back where they belong. What's the meaning of this?

JACK: Nellie! my daughter....

MARY: Oh, Father!

OLSEN: We're foreclosing the mortgage. The money is due today.

MARY: How much do you want?

OLSEN: Fifteen hundred dollars.

MARY: Here it is - now get out!

(HEAVY APPLAUSE)

OLSEN (VERY DRAMATICALLY): Foiled Again....Curses!... (HISSES)

(SOUND EFFECT: HEAVY DOOR SLAM)

JACK: Ah Nellie, my child! You saved our little home. But tell me - where did you get all the money?

MARY: In New York, Dad...I worked hard and saved every cent. Wasn't I a good girl?

JACK: What's the difference, Nellie? The home is ours! And next week, folks-- East Lynne.

(AUDIENCE APPLAUDS AS THE ORCHESTRA PLAYS STRAINS OF " HOME, SWEET HOME".

HICKS: The next number, ladies and gentleman, is entitled, "How Deep is the Ocean," played by George Olsen and his orchestra, and sung by Ethel Shutta.

5. HOW DEEP IS THE OCEAN   ETHEL SHUTTA

(CLOSING ROUTINE)

JACK:	That was the last number of the 52nd program, on the 26th of October which concludes the second series of our Canada Dry broadcasts...Well, Ethel- and George I want to tell you both how much I've enjoyed these pat twenty six weeks and having been associated with you and all of the boys.
ETHEL:	That's very sweet of you, Jack and I Just want you to know that George the boys and I....feel the same way.
OLSEN:	Well, Jack I hope you have a nice trip to New Orleans, and I wish you a lot of success on your third series of the Canada Dry Program. I'm sorry that I'm not going with you.
JACK:	Thanks, George and I'll be listening in to you on Sundays and Thursday night programs.
OLSEN:	And I'll be listening in to you on Sundays and Thursdays.
MARY:	Good-bye, Ethel....Good-bye, George....
ETHEL & GEORGE:	Good-bye, Mary...don't get lost.
JACK:	Good-bye, Ethel...
HICKS:	These good-byes come to you thru the courtesy of Canada Dry Ginger Ale---

SIGNATURE MUSIC   "ROCK ABYE MOON"   ORCHESTRA & ETHEL

ANNOUNCER: Remember, you can enjoy Canada Dry the champagne of ginger ales anywhere, anytime, for it is now available two ways - either made-to-order by the glass at soda fountains or in bottles, as always, for your home. The new big bottle is particularly economical and convenient.

Remember, too, that with the exception of a few localities, where freight rates do not permit, you pay for the contents only, that is, twenty cents for the big five-glass bottle, or twenty-five cents for two regular twelve-ounce bottles. In addition, you make a small deposit on each bottle, but this deposit is refunded when the bottle is returned.

This program concludes the present series over these stations. A new series of Canada Dry Broadcasts featuring Jack Benny will begin next Sunday, October 30th. Please refer to your local newspaper for the time and stations. This is the National Broadcasting Company.